cut here

# Internet Survival Cheat Sheet

## UNIX Commands

| | |
|---|---|
| Backspace | **Backspace**, **Ctrl-h**, **#** |
| Cancel an operation | **Ctrl-C**, **q** |
| Change directory | **cd /***directoryname* |
| Change directory back one level | **cd ..** (leave a space after the d) |
| Change directory back to home directory | **cd** |
| Clear the command line | **Ctrl-U** or **@** |
| Copy a file | **cp** *oldname newname* |
| Copy a file to another directory | **cp** *oldname directoryname* |
| Copy several files to another directory | **cp** *firstpartofname* directoryname* |
| Current directory: show path | **pwd** |
| Delete a file | **rm** *filename* |
| List directory contents: full info and hidden files | **ls -al** |
| List directory contents: full information | **ls -l** |
| List directory contents: names only | **ls** |
| List directory contents: names only, several columns | **ls -x** |
| Logout | **Ctrl-d**, logout, exit |
| Move a file | **mv** *filename directoryname* |
| Password (change) | **passwd** |
| Read a text file | **cat** *filename* |
| Read a text file: page by page | **more** *filename* |
| Read the instruction manual | **man** *commandname* **??** |
| Rename a file | **mv** *originalname newname* |
| Repeat command | **!!** or **r** |
| Search for text in a file | **grep** *"this text" filename* |

## Telenet to Archie

| | |
|---|---|
| Search type, selecting | **set search** *type* (*type* may be **regex**, **exact**, **sub**, or **subcase**) |
| Search type, finding | **show search** |
| Searching | **prog** *filename* |
| Paging, turn on | **set pager** |
| Paging, turn off | **unset pager** |
| E-mail a list | **mail** *emailaddress* |
| E-mail, set e-mail address | **set mailto** *emailaddress* |
| Descriptive search | **whatis** *keyword* |
| View a list of FTP sites | **list** |
| View a list of Archie servers | **servers** |
| Maxhits, modify the number | **maxhits** *number* |

## Telnet Sessions

| | |
|---|---|
| Connect to a Telnet site | **open** *hostaddress* or **telnet** *hostaddress* |
| Connect to an IBM mainframe | **tn3270** *hostaddress* |
| Close Telnet connection from Telnet site | **quit**, **exit**, **Ctrl-d**, or **done**. Or try **Ctrl-]** followed by **close** |
| Close Telnet connection from telnet> prompt | **close** |
| Close a Telnet session | **quit**, **q**, or **Ctrl-d** |
| Select an escape character | **set escape** *character* |
| Turn echo on and off | **set echo** |
| Suspend the session | **z** |
| Restart session | **fg** (in most cases) |
| View help | **?** |

alpha books

## Using FTP to Transfer Files

| | |
|---|---|
| Account information | **account** |
| ASCII: prepare to transfer an ASCII file | **ascii** |
| Binary: prepare to transfer a binary file | **binary** |
| Change directory | **cd** |
| Change directory on *your* system | **lcd** (use like the UNIX cd command) |
| Change directory to previous | **cdup** or **cd ..** |
| Close the connection | **close** or **disconnect** |
| Close the connection and exit FTP | **bye** or **quit** or **Ctrl-d** |
| Confirm transfer type | **type** |
| Connect to an FTP site | **open** ***hostaddress*** or **ftp** ***hostaddress*** |
| Current directory: show path | **pwd** |
| Directory listing: full | **dir** |
| Directory listing: names only | **ls** |
| Directory listing: names only, several columns | **ls -x** |
| Directory listing: include subdirectories and put in a text file | **ls -lR** ***filename*** |
| Exit FTP | **quit** or **bye** or press **Ctrl-d** |
| Hash marks indicate transfer progress | **hash** |
| Help: a list of FTP commands | **help** or **?** |
| Help: describe a command | **help** ***commandname*** or **?** ***commandname*** |
| Read a text file | **get** ***filename -*** |
| Read a text file using "more" | **get** ***filename -*** **" \| more"** |
| Transfer a file from the FTP site | **get** ***sourcefile destinationname*** |
| Transfer a file to your computer with Xmodem | **xmodem st** ***filename*** (text file)<br>**xmodem sa** ***filename*** (Apple text file)<br>**xmodem sb** ***filename*** (binary file) |
| Transfer a file *from* your computer with Xmodem | **xmodem rb** ***filename*** |
| Transfer a file to your computer with Zmodem | **sz** ***filename filename etc*** (text file) |
| Transfer multiple files *from* the FTP site | **mget** ***filename filename etc*** or **mget** ***partialname**** |
| Transfer multiple files *to* the FTP site | **mput** ***filename filename*** |
| Uncompress UNIX compress files | **uncompress** ***filename*** |

## Using WAIS (the swais version)

| | |
|---|---|
| Start WAIS | telnet to a WAIS site or run from service provider's menu |
| Deselect all selections | = |
| E-mail a document | **m** |
| Enter keywords on which to search | **w** and then press **Enter**. (Press **Ctrl-C** to cancel) |
| Move the cursor down one entry | **j** or **down arrow** or **Ctrl-n** |
| Move the cursor down one screen | **J** or **Ctrl-v** or **Ctrl-d** |
| Move the cursor up one entry | **k** or **up arrow** or **Ctrl-p** |
| Move the cursor up one screen | **K** or **Ctrl-u** |
| Move to a particular line | type the **number** and press **Enter** |
| Quit | **q** |
| Read about the highlighted database | **v** or **,** (comma) |
| Read a jumbled up document | Press \| type **more**, and press **Enter** |
| Return to the listing | **s** |
| Search for a listing | Press **/** then type the **word** you are looking for and press **Enter** |
| Search selected entries with keywords | **Enter** |
| Select an entry (or deselect a selected entry) | **Spacebar** or **.** (period) |
| Select an entry and move to keywords field | **Ctrl-j** |
| View the Help screen | **h** or **?** |

*by Peter Kent*

alpha
books

A Division of Prentice Hall Computer Publishing
201 West 103rd Street, Indianapolis, IN 46290

*To Nick & Chris, who may, one day, learn to keep the volume down.*

 For information, address Alpha Books, 201 West 103rd Street, Indianapolis, Indiana, 46290.

International Standard Book Number: 1-56761-414-0
Library of Congress Catalog Card Number: 93-73520

97 96 95 94    8 7 6 5 4

Interpretation of the printing code: the rightmost number of the first series of numbers is the year of the book's printing; the rightmost number of the second series of numbers is the number of the book's printing. For example, a printing code of 94-1 shows that the first printing of the book occurred in 1994.

Screen reproductions in this book were created by means of the program Collage Plus from Inner Media, Inc., Hollis, NH.

*Printed in the United States of America*

**Publisher**
*Marie Butler-Knight*

**Managing Editor**
*Elizabeth Keaffaber*

**Product Development Manager**
*Faithe Wempen*

**Copy Editor**
*Barry Childs-Helton*

**Cover Designer**
*Scott Cook*

**Designer**
*Barbara Webster*

**Illustrator**
*Steve Vanderbosch*

**Indexer**
*Rebecca Mayfield*

**Production Team**
*Gary Adair, Katy Bodenmiller, Brad Chinn, Kim Cofer, Meshell Dinn, Mark Enochs, Stephanie Gregory, Jenny Kucera, Beth Rago, Marc Shecter, Greg Simsic, Carol Stamile*

*Special thanks to Art Smoot, Brendan Kehoe, Leo Doyle and Thomas Powell for ensuring the technical accuracy of this book.*

# Contents at a Glance


**1 The Least You Need to Know**
Read this if you're in a hurry to get started. 3

**2 What Is This Thing Called the Internet?**
An overview of what the Internet is—and isn't. 7

**3 So You Wanna Get Wired? For Free?**
The pros and cons of each type of connection, and some hints on finding free (or almost free) connections. 17

**4 If You Have to Pay: Picking a Provider**
Value-shopping for Internet service providers. 29

**5 Let's Get Physical—What You Need to Get Started**
Picking your computer, modem, software, and account name/password. 39

**6 Special Stuff for Dial-In Direct Folks**
Skip this if you're connecting any other way. 51

**7 Your First Trip to the Internet**
Making that first connection, and living to tell. 57

**8 Menus and Shells, Oh My!**
Dealing with the UNIX shell, your service provider's menu system, and various prompts you might see. 73

**9 A UNIX Survival Guide**
The bare minimum UNIX commands you need to know. 81

**10 Please Mr. Postman: An Intro to E-mail**
A basic primer for sending basic messages. 95

**11 UNIX Mail: Down to the Nitty Gritty**
If you're stuck using UNIX mail, here's how to survive. 109

**12 Still More on Mail**
A look at mail aliases, signature files, and other hot topics. 123

**13 Return to Sender, Address Unknown**
Why e-mail gets returned, and what to do about it. 139

**14 Finding Folks with fred and Whois**
Two ways to find someone's address so your mail to them doesn't get returned. 153

# Contents at a Glance


**15 Newsgroups: The Source of All Wisdom**
Newsgroups introduced and briefly explained. 161

**16 More on Newsgroups—and LISTSERV**
Diving into a newsgroup and checking out LISTSERV groups. 177

**17 TELNET: Inviting Yourself onto Other Systems**
The basic telnet skills, from a prompt or menu. 187

**18 Grabbing the Goodies—Downloading Files with FTP**
Finding files and snagging them. 201

**19 More Neato FTP Stuff**
Transfer protocols, FTP hosts, FTP by mail, and more. 219

**20 Archie the File Searcher**
Finding files with Archie (the file searcher, not the cartoon character). 235

**21 Digging Through the Internet with Gopher**
Another way to find files on the Internet. 249

**22 Finding Your WAIS Around**
Dealing with the Wide Area Information Server. 267

**23 Think Global: World Wide Web**
Poking around WWW, browsing, and searching for info. 277

**A Things to Do, Places to Visit**
A list of neato things to explore on the Internet. 289

**B Service Providers and Free-Nets**
A list of some of the most popular service providers. 305

**C Whois Servers**
A list that was too long to put in chapter 14. 329

**D About the Software**
What's on the disk that comes with the book, and how to use it. 339

**Speak Like a Geek: The Complete Archive**
Otherwise known as a glossary. 347

# Contents


**Part I: Untangling the Wires and Getting It Running** 1

**1 The Least You Need to Know** 3

**2 What Is This Thing Called the Internet?** 7

Let's Start With the Basics ........ 8
But That's Not the Internet! ........ 9
It's Like the Phone System . . . ........ 10
Who Owns the Internet? ........ 12
What's in It for YOU? ........ 14

**3 So You Wanna Get Wired? For Free?** 17

The Types of Connections ........ 18
The Bottom-Line Pros and Cons ........ 22
Let Someone Else Pay ........ 24
Find a Free-Net ........ 25
An Almost-Free Account in Washington ........ 26

**4 If You Have to Pay: Picking a Provider** 29

How Do I Know What's Out There? ........ 29
Use an Online Service ........ 31
Comparison Shopping ........ 32
Explaining What You Want ........ 33

**5 Let's Get Physical—What You Need to Get Started** 39

Get Your Account! ........ 40
A Screen to Read, a Keyboard to Type On ........ 40
Getting Connected ........ 41
Picking the Software You Need ........ 43
I've Got a Name ........ 45
The Password Is . . . ........ 46
Do You Need Mail Software? ........ 48

**6 Special Stuff for Dial-In Direct Folks** 51

You Need TCP/IP Software! ........ 51
A Stately Address: Host Number and Domain Name ........ 52

**7 Your First Trip to the Internet 57**

Easy Street: Logging On with a Permanent Connection ..... 58
A Real Challenge: The Dial-in Direct Connection ..... 58
Do-It-Yourself with Dial-in Terminal Accounts ..... 59
Before Going Online ..... 66
Let's Go! ..... 66
Problems? ..... 69
What Now? ..... 70
Logging Out ..... 71

**8 Menus and Shells, Oh My! 73**

Using a Menu (If You're Lucky) ..... 74
Playing with Shells ..... 77
Is That All? ..... 78

**9 A UNIX Survival Guide 81**

A Quick Directory Primer ..... 81
Directory Management, UNIX Style ..... 85
Messing with Files ..... 88

**Part II: An E-Mail Extravaganza 93**

**10 Please Mr. Postman: An Intro to E-mail 95**

Why Use E-mail? ..... 96
Two E-Mail Caveats ..... 97
Now, Where's That Address? ..... 101
Addressing E-mail to Your Compuserve Friends ..... 102
Yet More E-mail Links ..... 103
E-Mail Helpers: Just Add Addresses ..... 106
Internet Etiquette ..... 106

**11 UNIX Mail: Down to the Nitty Gritty 109**

Getting Your Mail ..... 110
Replying (Politely) to Messages ..... 114
Starting from Scratch: Composing Your Own Messages ..... 116
Adding a Text File to a Message ..... 117
Using vi—An Exercise in Futility? ..... 118
Closing the Mail System ..... 121

**12 Still More On Mail 123**

Psst! Use an Alias! ........ 123
Reflective Mail? Using Mail Reflectors ........ 124
Automatic Mail Responses ........ 125
Sending Computer Files by Internet Mail ........ 127
Requesting Files with E-mail ........ 129
Back to the Real World—Using a Mail Program ........ 130
Yes, There's More ........ 137

**13 Return to Sender, Address Unknown 139**

What's Up? ........ 140
Who Didn't Get It? ........ 140
So What's the Problem? ........ 141
Who Ya Gonna Call? ........ 142
The Internet Directory? There Isn't One ........ 142

**14 Finding Folks with Fred and Whois 153**

Using Whois ........ 153

**Part III: Boldly Going Around the Internet 159**

**15 Newsgroups: The Source of All Wisdom 161**

So What's Out There . . . ........ 162
Where's It All Coming From? ........ 164
What's in a Name? ........ 165
Use a Newsreader! ........ 167
Using rn ........ 168

**16 More on Newsgroups—and LISTSERV 177**

Save That Message! ........ 178
Starting a Discussion ........ 180
But Wait! There's More! ........ 181
A Word of Warning ........ 181
Using a LISTSERV Group ........ 182
So Where's the List? ........ 183
Let's Do It—Subscribing ........ 183
Enough Already!—Unsubscribing ........ 184
Getting Fancy With LISTSERV ........ 185

**17 TELNET: Inviting Yourself Onto Other Systems 187**

Let's Go Telneting! ........ 188
Commanding Telnet to Do Your Bidding ........ 191
IBM Mainframe Telnet Sites ........ 193
The HYTELNET Directory—Finding What's Out There ........ 194
Easy Street: Telneting From a Menu ........ 195

**Part IV: Finding People, Finding Files 199**

**18 Grabbing the Goodies—Downloading Files with FTP 201**

Menus, If You're Lucky ........ 202
Hitting the FTP Trail ........ 205
Finding That Pot o' Gold ........ 206
Look For Clues ........ 208
Moving Around ........ 210
Grabbing Files—What Format? ........ 211
You Might Be Able to Do This . . . ........ 215
Compressed (Squeezed) Files ........ 216
So Long, Farewell ........ 218

**19 More Neato FTP Stuff 219**

Grabbing Files From Project Gutenberg ........ 219
File Transfers ........ 225
Speedy Logins—Using the .netrc File ........ 228
But Mine Doesn't Work That Way . . . ........ 229
FTP by Mail? ........ 230
It's Alive! Viruses and Other Nasties ........ 232

**20 Archie the File Searcher 235**

More Client/Server Stuff ........ 236
Getting to Archie ........ 236
Telneting to Archie's Place ........ 237
Working with Clients ........ 243
Mail-Order Archie ........ 245

**21 Digging Through the Internet With Gopher 249**

Which Gopher Do You Want to Use? ........ 250
Using Your Service Provider's Gopher ........ 251

Using Someone Else's Gopher—Through Telnet .............. 252
Here We Go—Let's Gopher It! .............. 253
Saving Stuff .............. 257
Searching for Entries .............. 260
Create Your Own Menu—Placing Bookmarks .............. 260
Using Veronica .............. 262
Finding Gopher Software .............. 264

**22 Finding Your WAIS Around 267**

Getting Started .............. 268
Let's Try It! .............. 268
A Good Server Is Hard to Find .............. 271
Reading and Saving the Info .............. 274
Be Your Own Client .............. 275

**23 Think Global: World Wide Web 277**

Getting to the Web .............. 278
Off to the Alps—Using WWW .............. 279
Save the Info You Find .............. 284
Using Gopher et al .............. 285
Loading Your Own WWW Browser .............. 285

**Part V Wonderfully Useful Stuff 287**

**Things to Do, Places to Visit 289**

**Service Providers and Free-Nets 305**

**Whois Servers 329**

**About the Software 339**

**Speak Like a Geek: The Complete Archive 349**

# Introduction

What have you gotten yourself into? Or what are you about to get yourself into? The Internet is a fantastic service. It provides an e-mail link to almost 30 million people, and the number is rising. It lets you connect to government computers, and find information about the most recent research or legislation. It lets you connect to university computers, and search thousands of different databases. It lets you "meet" people who can help you with just about anything—from planning a trip to Papua, New Guinea, to designing a scanning tunneling microscope. The Internet is the electronic highway at work. Forget the popular magazines' projections for the future—the Internet is here today.

*But.* (And it's a big But.) Using the Internet is like eating soup with chopsticks. If you wanted to create a system that would make its users think they were complete idiots, you couldn't do much better than create the Internet. It's a mess of different ways to connect, strange acronyms like PPP, SLIP, CSLIP, UUCP, and POP, many different ways to find and get data; to the average user, it's a tangle of confusion. Which is why the average user only uses a small percentage of what is available, and why many companies that provide the Internet service also provide training courses. The Internet is not something "you'll just pick up."

# Welcome to *The Complete Idiot's Guide to the Internet*

*The Complete Idiot's Guide to the Internet* assumes that you're no idiot on your own territory. You know how to do your job well, you know how to do everything you need to do to get by—even thrive—in modern life. But there's one thing you don't know: how to use the Internet.

I'm going to assume that you want to get onto the Internet and get some work done. Perhaps you just want to send e-mail, or do a little research on that book you've been planning for years. Perhaps you'd like to find a few "pen pals" on the other side of the world, or find people who share your passion for orchids. And I'm going to assume that you don't really want to know how to use the Internet for its own sake—you want to "get the job done," not become an Internet expert. You don't care about how the Internet Protocol works, for instance, as long as it gets your messages where they are supposed to go.

Sure, you could learn all there is to know about the Internet, given the time and interest. But do you have enough time? Are you really interested? I'm going to assume that the answer to at least one of those questions is No. You don't want to know every UNIX command and how the Internet might use it, but you *do* need to know practical stuff like:

- How to address an e-mail message.
- How to find e-mail addresses.
- How to transfer files from a computer on the Internet back to your computer.
- How to copy and delete the files created during your Internet sessions.
- How to connect to "news groups," and join in discussions on just about any subject you can imagine.
- How to do research in government and university computers.

I have assumed a *little* bit, however. I've assumed you know at least a little about computers—you know what a keyboard is, what a monitor is, that sort of thing. And you have access to a computer or a computer *terminal* (a "dumb" system hooked up to a big computer), and know how to use it. If you want really basic beginner's information about using a PC, check out *The Complete Idiot's Guide to PCs* (Joe Kraynak, Alpha Books). If you are using another type of computer—a Mac, a UNIX machine, or whatever—the techniques described in this book will be similar for you.

## How Do You Use This Book?

You don't have to read this book from cover to cover. If you want to find out about e-mail, go to the e-mail chapter; if you want to know how to use *gopher* to search the Internet for you, go to the gopher chapter. Each chapter is a self-contained unit that contains the information you need to use one aspect of the Internet.

I have used a couple of conventions in this book to make it easier to use. For example, when you need to type something, it will appear like this:

**`Type this`**

Just type what it says. It's as simple as that. If I don't know exactly what you'll have to type—because you have to supply some of the information—I'll put the unknown information in italics. For instance:

**`Type this`** ***`filename`***

I don't know the filename, so you'll have to supply it. Also, I've used the term "Enter" throughout the book. (Your keyboard may have a "Return" key instead.)

A word about UNIX. Most users will be working on a UNIX system. Even if your computer is an IBM-compatible PC or a Macintosh, usually the computer to which you are connected (and through which you work) will be a UNIX machine. Most users will be working with dial-in terminal accounts, which turn their computers into terminals of the computer to which they are attached. So I talk a lot about the various UNIX commands you can use. Although some users won't be on a UNIX machine, much of what you find in this book will be relevant. In a few areas, a particular command won't work on your system; ask your service provider what command to use instead.

Sometimes I'll need to show you longer examples of what you'll see on the Internet. They will appear in a special typeface, arranged to mimic what appears on your screen:

```
Some of the lines will be in actual English.
Some of the lines will seem to be in a mutant dialect of English.
```

Again, don't panic.

If you want to understand more about the subject you are learning, you'll find some background information in boxes. Because this information is in boxes, you can quickly skip over the information if you want to avoid the gory details. Here are the special icons and boxes used in this book that help you learn just what you need:

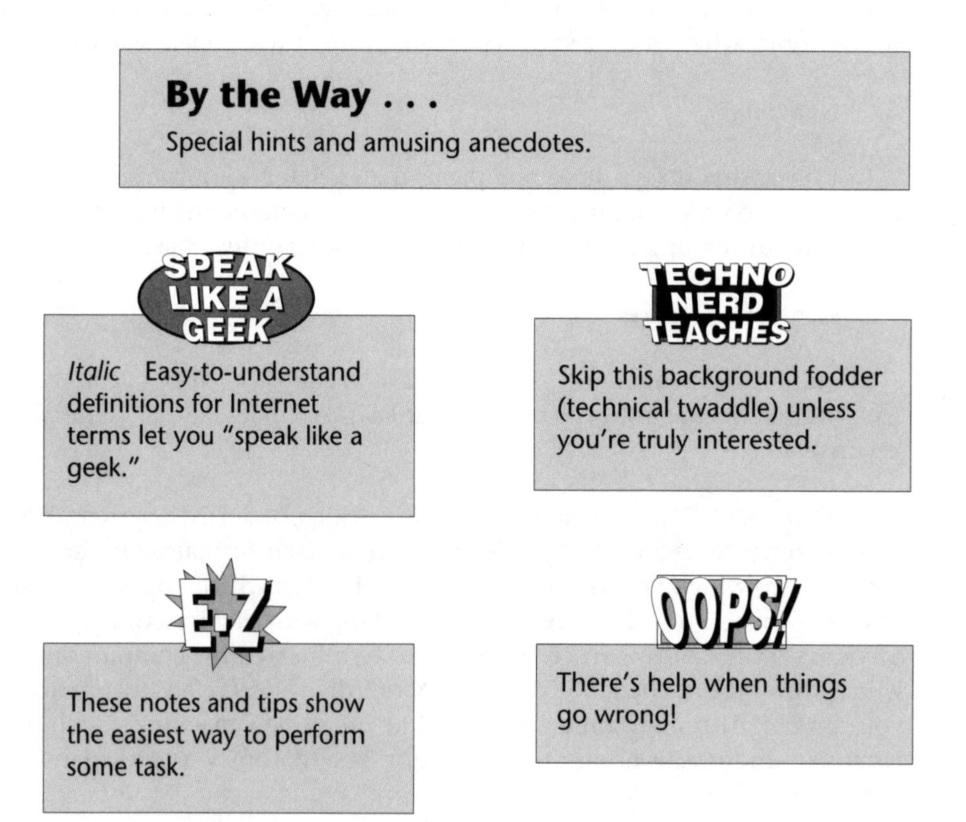

# Acknowledgements

I would like to thank a number of people for helping me with this book.

First, I'd like to thank Art Smoot, an Internet consultant in Boulder, CO, for providing advice and technical editing. And I'd like to thank Alpha Books' editorial staff for their help, in particular Faithe Wempen.

I'd also like to thank the following people for providing the files on the disk that's bundled with this book:

Richard Marks, for UUENCODE.

Scott Yanoff, for the Internetwork Mail Guide and Special Internet Connections.

David Lawrence, for the newsgroup lists.

Stephanie da Silva, for the list of mailing lists.

Arno Wouters, for "How to Find an Interesting Mailinglist."

Jeremy Smith, for "Bigfun."

Mac Su-Cheong's "List of servers for Computer Science-related resources."

Jim Wright for his description of file formats.

Olivier M.J. Crepin-Leblond for the list of Internet country codes.

Michael Strangelove of Strangelove Internet Enterprises, for his newsletter articles.

Billy Barron and Marie-Christine Mahe for "Accessing On-Line Bibliographic Databases."


# Trademarks

## Part I

# Untangling the Wires and Getting It Running

*Maybe you've already got an Internet account. Or maybe you've heard so much about Internet that you're ready to see what it's all about. Then prepare to be overwhelmed. Most manuals and books you'll encounter will probably not be much help, because they're designed for programmers and experienced PC hackers, not for normal people like you. Fortunately, you've got this book to guide you through the maze.*

*The chapters in this part of the book will explain the basics of Internet. They will help you select the sort of account you need, and get the best price (be warned, prices vary dramatically). We'll tell you what you need to connect to Internet, how to get an account, and how to get up and running. Sure, the Internet's confusing, but it doesn't have to be that way. All you need is someone to explain it all to you.*

# Chapter 1
# The Least You Need to Know

First of all, don't panic! There's nothing difficult in this book. The Internet itself is not difficult per se; it just assumes you know a lot of things that you may not already know (like UNIX commands, for instance). Stick with me, and I promise you'll get out alive.

Don't try to learn everything at once; it'll just give you a headache. For now, just breeze through this list of important things you need to know. You'll learn more about each of them later.

1. Internet is not the most user-friendly system you'll find—it takes some time to learn the right commands to use. (And in some cases, you might find your service provider isn't particularly helpful—unless you want to shell out a couple hundred bucks for a training course). One way or another, you need help to learn the Internet. (Which is why you bought this book, right?)
2. There aren't any fixed prices for services in Internet-land. Providers can charge whatever they want, and supply you with whatever services they decide upon. As you might imagine, this leads to some fairly wide variations (in both quality and price) among providers. Prices to get connected range from absolutely free (rarely) to very expensive, and the prices are not necessarily related to the level of service you receive. Spend some time looking around (see Chapters 3 and 4) before (and after) choosing a service provider.

3. There are four basic types of Internet accounts: permanent, dial-in direct, dial-in terminal, and mail. Most beginning individual users (as opposed to large companies) don't need anything more than a dial-in terminal account. It's relatively cheap and easy to use, and, in most cases, you can access all of Internet's services. If you find yourself becoming an Internet junkie, though, you may want to change to a dial-in direct account, which experienced users often find more convenient. See Chapter 3 for more information about account types.

4. Different Internet service providers have different systems, but most users will probably be working on a UNIX system. This is great news if you're a UNIX hacker. For the rest of us, however, it is a bit daunting, especially at first. Spend a little time in Chapter 9 figuring out how to use UNIX.

5. E-mail is the most-used service on Internet. It's easy and convenient, once you know how to use it. You can send messages to practically anyone who's connected to the Internet. Give it a try! See Chapters 10-12.

6. To find e-mail addresses, try using the postmaster, finger, MIT's newsgroup directory, the Knowbot Information Service, Netfind, Whois, and fred. There's no single directory of Internet users, but these odd-sounding systems will help you find that missing person. Chapters 13 and 14 explain how.

7. The newsgroups let you discuss any subject in the world, with people from all over the world. They're similar to what some online services call "BBSs" or "message boards." One person posts a message, another person posts a reply, and so on—you can read everyone's messages, and even post your own. Check it out in Chapters 15 and 16.

8. The LISTSERV groups are like newsgroups, but use e-mail to share messages. Chapter 16 has all the details.

9. Use Telnet to "get onto" other computer systems to view files and search databases. If you like the idea of reading files and using databases or games on computers on the other side of the world, Telnet's for you. How do you know which telnet site contains what? Use HYTELNET to search through a list of Telnet sites for a subject that interests you. Chapter 17 explains the wonders of telnet.

10. Use FTP to grab files from computers anywhere in the world. Chapter 18 tells how to snag goodies from all over the world. Yes, that includes games.
11. One little detail I forgot to tell you in that last item—most of the time, there *isn't* a friendly-looking list that tells you what files are available for the taking. That's why you need special utilities like Archie to find files. You can search for filenames, or file categories. You'll meet Archie in Chapter 20.
12. Gopher (great name, huh?) can help you bypass much of the confusion of the Internet, and go straight to information and files you can use. Dig around in Chapter 21 for more details.
13. WAIS is a relatively simple system for searching the world's computer databases. (I say "relatively" simple because nothing on the Internet it truly simple.) Try it out in Chapter 22.
14. The World Wide Web makes searching for information easy. It's a remarkably simple way to track things down. Get enmeshed in the web in Chapter 23.
15. To explain *everything* about Internet would take several thousand pages, most of which you would never need to read. Remember that if you run into an unusual situation that you can't handle, you should talk to your service provider.

**This page unintentionally left blank.**

Chapter 2

# What Is This Thing Called the Internet?

## In This Chapter

- What is a BBS?
- Why the Internet *isn't* a BBS
- How the Internet began
- Why the Internet can be so complicated
- The remarkable resources of the Internet

When I first started working with the Internet I felt lost. The "documentation" given to me by the company that provided my Internet account was a joke. It was badly organized, misleading, and omitted lots of important stuff. Technical support wasn't much better—phone calls went unanswered, and the help wasn't always helpful. I'll bet there's a good chance you feel the same about your Internet account (if you have one).

I shouldn't lay all the blame on a single company, though. One of the problems with the Internet is one of responsibility—who is responsible for which part? As you'll see in a moment, the way the Internet was born—and grew has been haphazard, to say the least. It's not like a typical *bulletin board system* (BBS), with which you know who is responsible for the system in its entirety—the owner. With the Internet, it's never clear who, if anyone, owns what—and who, if anyone, has responsibility for getting you going. In other words, you may be "left to your own devices."

It doesn't have to be confusing, though, so this book is going to help you cut through the crud and find the information you need to get to the fantastic resources available on the Internet. This chapter starts you out with an overview of what the Internet *is*, of how it has come together to become the world's largest network of computer users.

## Let's Start With the Basics

The word *modem* is a contraction of "**mod**ulate-**dem**odulate." That's what the modem does with the digital signals from your computer when it converts them to the analog signals used by most telephone networks.

Let's start right at the beginning—what is a *bulletin board system* (BBS), what is a *computer network*? A BBS is a computer running special software that lets other computers connect to it. (Actually a BBS could be several computers connected together, but the principle is the same.) A computer user will install a *modem* in his computer, connect the modem to the phone line, use *communications software* to dial the BBS, and voilà, he's "connected."

What can you do once connected to a BBS? Well, you can read messages left by other BBS users, reply to those messages (or leave your own), and copy files to and from the BBS. There may be other services available—perhaps you can play an "online" game with another BBS user (chess, for instance, or some kind of arcade game); you might be able to "chat" with another user, typing what you want to say and reading the other user's almost-instant response; you may be able to search a database, or view photographs or weather maps stored on the other computer.

There are thousands of BBSs spread around the world—all you need to start a BBS is a computer, a phone line, BBS software (which can be found quite cheaply), a modem, and the money to pay the electricity bill. You've probably heard the names of a number of the larger BBSs. Systems such as CompuServe, Prodigy, Genie, America Online—even Penthouse Online. These services often don't use the term BBS—they might call themselves *online services*, or *information systems*, but the principle is the same. They are computers—or groups of computers—to which computer users can connect to communicate with others, find computer files, play games, do research, and so on.

# But That's *Not* the Internet!

The Internet is not a BBS. The Internet is a *network* of networks. A computer network is a group of computers that have been connected together so they can communicate with each other. They can send messages to each other, and can share information in the form of computer files. The Internet connects more than 18,000 of these networks, with more being added all the time. And on those networks are millions of computers, computer terminals, and users—about two million computers and as many as 30 million users, according to some estimates. And it's growing by around 1,000 computers *a day*. It's no wonder that the president of ISOC (the Internet Society) recently suggested that the Internet could conceivably reach 1 *billion* people in the not-too-distant future.

There's nothing astounding about computer networks. I have a small one in my home, connecting my work computer and my kids' "play" computer (which used to be my work computer until technology raced past). Many small companies have networks, connecting two or three computers, or maybe thousands of them.

But the Internet isn't just a network. It's a network of networks. Lots of different networks have been joined together to produce the world's largest group of connected computers. Some of the networks belong to government bodies, some to universities, some to businesses, some to local-community library systems, and some even belong to schools. Most are in the United States, but many are overseas, from Australia to Zimbabwe.

As remarkable as all this may seem, if that's all the Internet was, I wouldn't be writing this book. Sure, the Internet might let you communicate with all these people on all these computer networks through electronic "mail," but that wouldn't be enough for a book.

What makes the Internet so special is the fact that many of the computers on the network are, in effect, BBSs. (Strictly speaking, most computers on the Internet are not set up as BBSs, but they do allow you to log in and do stuff, such as grab files or use databases.) That means that when you connect to the Internet you have the opportunity of connecting to thousands of different systems. Those computers contain government archives, university databases, local-community computing resources, library catalogs, messages about any subject you can imagine, and millions of computer files—over two million at last count—containing photographs, documents, sound clips, video, and whatever else you can put into digital form.

To *log on* or *log in* to a computer system means you tell it who you are, and it decides if it wants to let you use its services. A log-on (or login) procedure usually entails providing some kind of account name and a secret password.

The Internet is more like a data highway than a BBS. Dial up a system on the Internet, or log on through an institution's terminal, and you're on the road. Then you have to navigate your way through the network, to the city that has the data you need. When you dial up a service such as CompuServe, you are connected to a big room with a lot of computers. When you access the Internet you might find yourself in a government computer in Washington D.C., a university's computer in Seattle, Washington, or a community computer system in Elyria, Ohio. Or, perhaps, the Centre International de Rencontres Mathematiques in Marseilles, France.

# It's Like the Phone System . . .

Perhaps the best analogy that one could use to describe the Internet is that it is like a phone system. A phone system has lots of different "switches," owned by lots of different organizations, all connected together. When someone in Denver tries to call someone in New York, he doesn't need to know how the call gets through—which states and cities the call passes through. The telephone network handles it all for him. These private companies have decided amongst themselves the mechanics—the electronics—of the process, and it doesn't matter one whit to the average caller how it's done. The Internet works in much the same way. Just as there's no single telephone company, there's no single Internet company.

## So What's the Catch?

The Internet's resources dwarf those of other online systems, but there's a catch. The Internet is relatively hard to use. Systems such as CompuServe, Prodigy, and American Online make money each time someone uses their services, so it's a good idea for them to make their services easy to use. If it's too hard, people will log off and won't come back.

Actually some of these services haven't done such a great job at making their *user interfaces* easy to use. (A user interface is what the user sees when he or she sits at the computer and tries to use a program or system.) But still, they are way ahead of the Internet. If you use CompuServe, for instance, you have a number of different programs you can use that make the user interface simpler. Called *navigators*, some of these programs are made by CompuServe's own programmers, some by independent companies.

That's not to say the Internet doesn't have the equivalent of navigators, but they are generally not as sophisticated, and the complexity of the Internet makes producing a good "all-round" Internet navigator pretty difficult. (Systems such as Mosaic and Cello, though, are quite sophisticated. Such programs are also known as *browsers*.)

## "Sorry, It's Not Our Problem"

Unfortunately you may run into a case of "it's not our problem." While most *service providers*—organizations that can connect you to the Internet—claim to provide great technical support, many of them are small non-profit organizations that have trouble keeping up with the demand. And because the Internet is such an amorphous creature these organizations can always claim that your problem lies in another area.

For instance, if you are having trouble getting your Internet connection working, they can always point you in the direction of the manufacturer of your software. The Internet has grown so fast in the last year or two that some service providers are providing lousy service. Complaints that it's hard to get a connection, that calls and messages for technical support go unanswered, are becoming more common.

Why, then, is the Internet so difficult to use? Well, it's because of the way the Internet was born, grew, and is managed.

### By the Way . . .

The Internet was originally intended to be a non-commercial system, so most service providers are non-profit organizations. They are often understaffed and underfunded, and don't have the incentive provided by the "profit motive." In recent years, the Internet has opened up to commercial service providers—perhaps this will lead to better service.

# Who Owns the Internet?

BBSs are owned by someone. A company or individual buys a computer, puts it in a room somewhere, and then sells the general public time on the computers. (Or, in many cases, lets interested parties onto the BBS for free—many computer companies have BBSs for their customers, so they can contact technical support, find the latest program files for their systems, and so on.)

There are literally thousands of such BBSs, from the giants we named earlier down to the small systems owned and run by one person. Take a look at a local computer newspaper and you'll see dozens of BBSs listed, designed for use by everyone from *Star Trek* fans to computer-game nuts to swingers. In each case, though, *someone* owns the BBS, whether it's H & R Block (who owns CompuServe), or Fred down the street (who owns The Wizard's Secret Games BBS).

## Nobody Owns the Internet . . .

The Internet's not like that. Nobody "owns" the Internet. Who owns the nation's—or the world's—telephone network? Nobody. Sure, each component is owned by somebody, but the network as a whole is not owned by anyone, it's a system that hangs together through mutual interest. The world's telephone companies get together and decide the best way the "network" should function. They decide which country gets what country code, how to bill for international calls, who pays for transoceanic cables, and the technical details of how one country's lines connect to another.

The Internet is very similar. It all began in the early '70s, with various government computer networks, and it's grown since, as different organizations realize the advantages of being connected. Its origins can be traced back to ARPANET, a Department of Defense computer system that was intended to test methods of making computer networks survive military attack. By dispersing the network over a wide area, and using a web of connections between the computers, a system could continue functioning even when portions of it were destroyed, by redirecting communications through the surviving portions of the network. (This system works so well that it caused the Department of Defense plenty of frustration—when Iraq used it during the Gulf war to keep its "command and control" computer system in operation.)

The NSF (National Science Foundation) gave the Internet a real boost when it realized that it could save money by creating several supercomputer centers connected to a network, so that researchers all over the place—such as in major universities—could connect to them. In the past decade the Internet has grown tremendously, as all sorts of organizations figured they would get in on the act, each one connecting its own network, with its own particular configuration of hardware and software.

## . . . and That's the Problem.

Therein lies the problem. It's one of planning, and it's an inevitable result of the way the network grew. Compare Dallas with London. London's a mesh of intertwining roads. Dallas is, in general, laid out on a grid system. London wasn't planned, it just grew. Dallas was planned almost right from the start.

The Internet wasn't developed as a single, planned system. It just grew. There is no Internet, Inc., no single company that decides what the network should look like. (Which makes it a little confusing when you decide you'd like to use the Internet.) Rather, the Internet is governed by consensus, by diverse organizations getting together to figure out the best way for it all to work.

**TECHNO NERD TEACHES**

So if nobody owns the Internet, who decides how it all hooks together? ISOC, the Internet Society, is a group of interested people—you can join if you want—who elect a "council of elders." This council, known as the *Internet Architecture Board* (IAB), gets together and agrees on how the network will function. They are advised by the *Internet Engineering Task Force* (IETF), another volunteer organization that studies technical problems.

Going out alone into Internetland is like venturing on foot across London, without a guide or map. It'll be interesting, but you may not find what you're looking for. (So take this book along as your guide.)

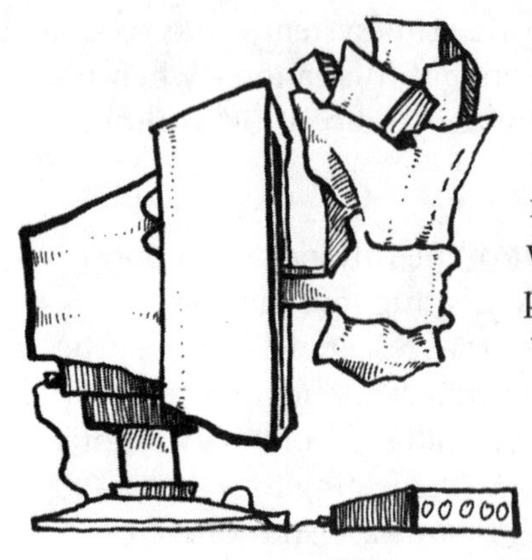

## What's in It for YOU?

Why would you want to use the Internet, anyway? There are about 20 or 30 million reasons. That's how many people already have a way to use the Internet, so that's how many people you could send messages to, if you had the time.

Okay, so there aren't that many *active* users—most people rarely or never use anything but their own organization's computers, and have little idea of what lies out there in Internetland. (When you consider that most Internet users are in the United States, it seems improbable that there are 20-30 million people with even potential access to the Internet—that would be one American in ten. But those numbers are bandied around a lot, though nobody really knows for sure what the numbers are.) But there are plenty of other reasons for using the Internet. Are you going on vacation to Costa Rica and want to check out some good scuba locations? Then take a look at a scuba *newsgroup*, and find out if anyone's been down there recently—leave a public message and see if you get any responses (you probably will).

Would you like to talk with collectors of antiques and vintage "stuff"? How about talking with people who share your interest in high-fidelity audio equipment, interactive multimedia, the importance of romance in love, Star Trek, or tastelessness?

How about checking out Project Gutenberg, an ambitious attempt to convert works of literature to an electronic form? Go online and select from hundreds of works of copyright-free literature. You could check out the Journalism Periodicals Index at the University of Western Ontario, or Project Hermes, which stores decisions of the U.S. Supreme Court. You could research a book or magazine article you are working on using CARL, Denver's online library index—search for books or magazine articles on the subject of interest without ever leaving home. Or use the Reader's Guide to Periodical Literature to search for your subject in virtually every popular U.S. magazine.

It's difficult to give a good idea of what is on the Internet—there's just so *much*. There was once even a Coca-Cola machine—at the Carnegie

Mellon University—connected to the Internet. That wouldn't do *you* much good, but the guys in the Computer Science Department could use the Internet to figure out if the machine had any Cokes left, and if they had been in the machine long enough to cool down. It saved them walking to the basement only to find the machine was empty. (Unfortunately the Carnegie Mellon Cola machine is no longer on the Internet. There are now a number of others, though!)

The Internet is huge. You can find many sources of information listed in this book, but I can only mention a fraction.

- Chapter 15 and 16 discuss *newsgroups*, in which you can leave and read messages from people with similar interests. These chapters name a few of them, and also tell you how to find a list of them. And I've also put lists of thousands in text files on the disk at the back of this book (see Section D after the regular chapters).
- Chapter 18 and 19 discuss how to download files from other computers, and Chapter 17 explains how to connect to another computer so you can use its files and databases. Section A lists computers to which you can connect using these techniques, and you can find more such computers in the text files on the disk.
- Chapters 20 to 23 tell you how to find other sources of information.

## The Least You Need to Know

In this chapter you learned a little background information that will help you understand how the Internet fits together. You don't have to remember the details, but at least remember:

- The Internet is a network of networks.
- Some of those networks contain BBSs—so the Internet is a pathway to thousands of different sources of information.
- Nobody owns the Internet—it's a cooperative venture linking a multitude of companies, government bodies, universities and schools, and community computer networks.

*continues*

*continued*

- Think of any subject. You can find information about it *somewhere* on the Internet.
- Okay, so the Internet can be complicated. That's why you need a good guide. Read on.

# Chapter 3 So You Wanna Get Wired? For Free?

## In This Chapter

- The types of Internet connections
- The advantages and disadvantages
- Finding a free Internet connection
- Finding a Free-Net
- An almost-free connection in D.C.

In this chapter, we're going to look at how to get connected to Internet. Even if you already have an Internet account, you might want to skim through this chapter because it explains the *types* of accounts and the pros and cons of each. And for those who don't have an Internet account yet, we'll look at *how* to get one (it's not as straightforward as you might imagine). For most readers, "money's no object" doesn't hold true, so you want to find the cheapest way to connect to Internet—free if possible.

Unlike systems such as CompuServe and PRODIGY, there's no set charge for connecting to Internet. Most BBSs and online information services have a standard set of fees. You might be able to pick one fee schedule from several, but all customers have the same choices. Not so with the Internet. Because there is no Internet, Inc.—because there is no single organization running the Internet—what you are buying is *access* to the network. You need a connection on a computer through which you can connect your computer or terminal.

Companies and non-profit organizations (more of the latter than the former, right now, but it's changing) called *service providers* buy computers, connect them to Internet, and sell connections to whoever has the money to spare. These service providers set their own rates, and, as you'll see in a moment, those rates vary considerably.

# The Types of Connections

There are four basic ways to connect to Internet, plus a few variations:

- Permanent connections
- Dial-in direct connections
- Dial-in terminal connections
- Mail connections

You won't necessarily hear these terms elsewhere, though. In fact, different service providers use slightly different terms, and the terminology can get blurred. It gets confusing, but the following definitions should clarify things a little.

## Permanent Connections

A *permanent connection* means your computer is connected directly to a TCP/IP network that is part of the Internet. Actually, the usual case is that your organization has a large computer connected to the network, and you have a terminal connected to that computer. (You may even have a computer that is acting as a terminal—that is, all the work is done by the other computer, and your computer is simply passing text to and from your screen.) This sort of connection is often known as a *dedicated connection,* sometimes as a *permanent direct* connection.

Such connections are often used by large organizations—universities, groups of schools, and corporations, for instance. The service provider places a *router* at the organization's office and leases a telephone line that connects the router to the service provider's computer (known as a *host* computer). The details vary—the service provider might provide the router, or might tell the organization which router to buy—but once this is done, the organization can connect its computers and terminals to the router. Because they have a *leased line*, they are always connected to Internet. There's no need to make a telephone call to reach the service provider's computer. Rather, the user will simply *log on* to Internet from his terminal. Once on the Internet, he can transfer files between his organization's computer and other computers on the Internet.

*TCP/IP* means *Transmission Control Protocol/Internet Protocol*. A *protocol* defines how computers should talk to each other. It's like a language—if a group of different people all agree to speak French (or English, or Spanish), they can all understand each other. Communication protocols provide a set of rules that define how different modems, computers, and programs can communicate.

This sort of service is very expensive, of course. Start-up costs might be $6,000 for the hardware and $700 to $1,200 for the leased line. Monthly fees could be $150 to $600 for the leased line, and $10,000 and up for the service provider's annual fees. Getting a dedicated line is, of course, way beyond the scope of this book (which is a computer-writer euphemism for "let's not get into that").

## Dial-in Direct Connections

A *dial-in direct connection* is often referred to as a *SLIP* (Serial Line Internet Protocol), *CSLIP* (Compressed SLIP), or *PPP* (Point-to-Point Protocol) connection. You may also hear the term XRemote, though you probably won't be offered this variation. These are also TCP/IP connections, like the permanent connection, but are designed for use over telephone lines instead of a dedicated network. This type of service is the next best thing to the permanent connection. While a permanent connection is out of the price range of individuals and most small companies, it can be quite cheap to get a SLIP account (as little as $100 to connect, and $15/month, for instance, though most service providers charge more).

There is one important way in which you'll see the difference between dial-in direct and permanent connections: file transfers between your computer and others, as well as "telnet" sessions, will be much *slower* than between your service provider's computer and others on the Internet.

This is a "dial-in" service; you'll need a modem in your computer, and you'll have to dial a telephone number given you by the service provider. Once you have connected to the service provider's computer and logged on, other than speed, you can't tell any difference between a SLIP account and a dedicated account—you can transfer files to and from your computer exactly as if it were a host computer—in fact, it will be identified on the network as a host.

Also, depending on the software you are using, you may be able to run *multiple sessions* at the same time. That is, in the same way that the service provider's computer can let dozens of people work on the Internet at the same time, you will be able to do several different things on the Internet at the same time, in different program windows—you'll be able to transfer files from computer A in one window, search a database on computer B in another window, and work in your own file directories in another window.

Don't confuse this service with a ***dial-up*** connection, though, a service that also requires you to dial a telephone number, but which provides slightly more limited service than SLIP (as we'll see in a moment).

## Dial-In Terminal Connections

With this type of connection you'll have to dial into the service provider's computer. It's confusing that this connection is called a *dial-up,* because you have to dial a call before connecting to a SLIP account as well. (To differentiate, some service providers call this an *interactive* service, which seems only slightly less ambiguous.) I've called it *dial-in terminal connection* because you have to dial the call to your service provider—and once connected, your computer will act as a terminal.

This arrangement is unlike a permanent or dial-in direct connection; your computer won't appear as a host on the network, it'll simply be a terminal of the service provider's computer. All the programs you will run, will run on the service provider's computer. That means that you can transfer files across the Internet to and from your *service provider's* computer, not to and from yours. So you'll have to use a separate procedure to move files between your computer and that of the service provider—normally you'll use a transfer procedure such as zmodem or xmodem. (I explain data transfers in Chapter 18 and after.)

In other ways you won't notice much difference—you can still use all the services that would be available on a permanent connection or dial-in direct connection.

In one way, the permanent connection and dial-in terminal connection are very similar—in both cases your computer is nothing but a terminal of the host computer. (With a dial-in *direct* connection, your computer *becomes*, temporarily, a host computer.)

But there's an important difference. In the case of the dial-in terminal connection, you don't really *want* your data stored on the host computer, and have to mess around to get it back. In the case of a permanent connection, you are either used to having your data stored on your organization's large computer—you are using a terminal and you can probably print directly from the host computer, for instance—or you have the networking tools that let you transfer data readily between the host and the computer sitting on your desk.

## Mail Connections

There are several different mail connections to the Internet. In fact you may already have one. If, for instance, you have a CompuServe or America Online account, you have an Internet mail connection. You can send mail to the Internet, and have friends and colleagues on the Internet send mail to you. On CompuServe you would simply precede the Internet mail address with **INTERNET:**. (I will talk more about sending mail to and from CompuServe in Chapter 10.)

To send a message from the Internet to CompuServe, your associates would replace the comma in your CompuServe ID with a period, and add @compuserve.com at the end (for example: 71234.5678@compuserve.com).

You can even send mail across the Internet to other, non-Internet BBS accounts. And it's possible to use Internet's LISTSERV system to receive Internet discussions on just about any subject through your CompuServe account. (I'll explain LISTSERV in Chapter 16). It's not advisable, though, because CompuServe will charge you 15 cents per message—it'll break the bank. These types of mail connections are also known as *network gateways*, systems by which networks connect to the Internet in a rather limited way.

*UUCP* means *UNIX-to-UNIX Copy Program*. It's a system in which mail may be placed in files and transferred to other computers.

Another form of mail connection is one in which you connect to the Internet in the same way as a dial-in terminal connection—but all you'll be allowed to do is get to the mail system. And finally, you could get a UUCP connection. This is a simple mail connection, using software intended for this purpose (instead of a general purpose communications program). All you can do is send and receive mail and USENET *newsgroup* messages (which we'll look at in Chapter 15).

## The Bottom-Line Pros and Cons

I'm assuming you have (or are going to acquire) one of the first three types of connections—a permanent, dial-in direct, or dial-in terminal connection. I'm going to ignore the mail connections, as they are so limited in capabilities.

You're really not quite ready to decide which of these three types of services you want—there are some other factors to consider, such as cost. But let's at least compare the services, to get an idea of the pros and cons of each.

A **permanent connection** is expensive, but may look like a good deal to a large company. Once connected, you can have as many users as your company's computer and the leased line can manage—there's no charge for individual users. If you have lots of users, it may work out cheaper than giving each one their own account, especially if most of them use Internet infrequently or for just a few minutes a day (to check for messages, for instance). But dedicated service is way out of the price range of most of us. If you are an individual looking for a way to get onto Internet, forget dedicated service.

A **dial-in direct connection** is the next best thing to a permanent connection. It can be quite affordable (if you shop around—more on this in a moment), and provides you all of the benefits of dedicated service once you are logged on. You'll need a modem, of course, but with 14400 bits per second modems running around $150 these days, it's not too steep a cost. You'll need a fast modem, at the very least 9600 bps. Anything less will be too slow.

*Bits per second* is a measurement of how much data a modem can transmit. Computer data is stored in the form of *bits*, each bit being either a one or zero. String enough of these ones and zeros together, and you can describe anything, from a single character to large document (or picture, or sound . . . ). The actual rate at which your modem will transmit will vary, depending on the telephone line condition, what's happening on the computer at the other end, and so on.

You'll also need some software. A dial-in direct connection requires special software, which is not always easy to find—and not cheap. It can cost several hundred dollars, and can be quite complicated to set up. (Some, though by no means all, service providers give you the required software when you sign up.) Some service providers will be very helpful, and lead you through the process step by step. Others will set up your account on their computer and then tell you that you're on your own—it's up to you figure it all out.

These dial-in direct accounts do cost more to set up, but often cost the same as a dial-in terminal connection to run—that is, the same charge per hour. However, if you do a lot of research and copy files from other computers, you're likely to spend less time using the dial-in direct account than the dial-in terminal account. You will also be able to copy files directly from other computers to your computer's hard disk. (If you have a dial-in terminal account, you'll have to copy the files to your service provider's computer, then do a file transfer to copy them from that computer back to yours.)

A **dial-in terminal connection** is a good, low-cost service for the casual user. The set-up fee will be less than for a dial-in direct connection ($20 as compared to $100, for instance), though the charge per hour may be the same, and, of course, you'll still need a modem. You can usually get away with a slower modem, though—perhaps just 2400 bps—because the host computer is doing most of the work, and just sending screens full of text to your monitor which doesn't take much effort. (However, if you plan to copy lots of files from other computer systems, a slow modem means slow transfers between your computer and the host computer—large files can easily take an hour or more.)

You'll be able to do anything on the Internet that you can do with a dial-in direction connection, except that some procedures will take a few more steps. To get a file from a computer in, say, Australia, you'll have to copy it to your service provider's computer, then do a file transfer to get it to yours. (With a dial-in direct connection the file would come straight from Australia to you.)

You may find that the difference in abilities between dial-in terminal and dial-in direct is so slight that you don't want to pay the extra setup money. And another factor that may lead you to dial-in terminal service is the ability to get it for *free*. You probably won't find any community computer networks providing free dial-in direct access to Internet, but, as we'll see, there are a number that provide free dial-in terminal access.

## Let Someone Else Pay

The best way to connect to Internet is to use OPM—Other People's Money. Most Internet users are connected through an organization that has a dedicated connection to Internet. Many large companies have their own computers connected directly to Internet, and allow their employees access to it.

IBM, for instance, is connected to Internet, and claims to have 250,000 employees who could, if they wished, find their way onto the network. These employees don't have to pay anything to use Internet; they just have to get permission from the company. Many government departments have Internet access, and many universities also have connections, and let students get onto the network for free. Most medium-sized and larger colleges have an Internet connection.

Talk with the person in your organization in charge of the Internet connection. You may find that you have to use Internet from a terminal in the organization's building—in the office or from a university department building—though you may be able to dial in from home to your organization's computer, then get onto Internet. This depends on the type of software and hardware that the organization has available.

If you don't know who's in charge of your Internet access—or even if your organization is hooked up—ask around. Ask the head of the computer department, computer center, information services department, or whatever. Ask the people who spend much of their time maintaining, installing, and fixing computers. It may be that only a few people in your organization use Internet, and you won't get on without a bit of searching and diplomacy. Of course most small companies won't have an Internet connection, but if you work for a medium-sized or large business, it may.

> **By the Way . . .**
>
> Even if you are not a student, you may be able to get onto a college's Internet system. Call your local college, see if they have a connection, and find out the requirements for network use. You may find you can use it if you are just a part-time student (though you probably won't be able to dial in from home). Then sign up for Basket Weaving 101.

## Find a Free-Net

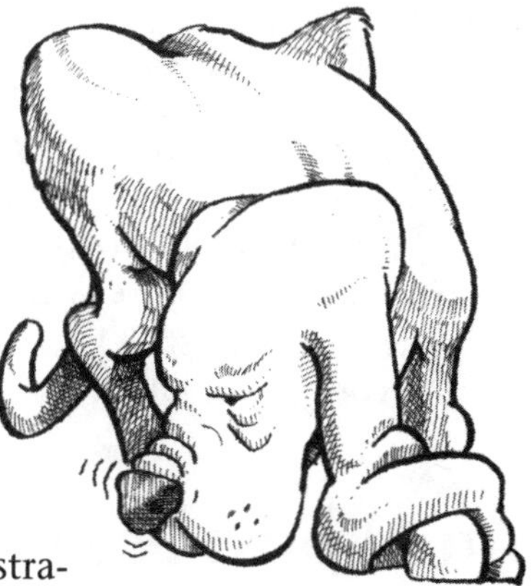

If you can't get an account through your company or college, the next step is to look for a *Free-Net.* These are community computing systems. They may be based at a local library or college. You may be able to use Internet from a terminal at the library, or perhaps even dial into the system from your home computer. And, as the name implies, they don't cost anything. (Well, some may have a small registration fee—$5, perhaps—but if not actually free they are pretty close to it.)

Free-Nets offer a variety of local services, as well as access to Internet. You may be able to find information about jobs in the area, and about local events and recreation. You may be able to search the local library's database, find course schedules for local colleges, or ask someone questions about social security and Medicare.

Free-Nets usually have a "menu" of options based on a simulated "town." There's the Community Center, Teen Center, and Senior Center. There's an Administration Building, where you can go to register your account on the Free-Net; a Social Services and Organizations Center, where you can find support groups and local chapters of national organizations such as the Red Cross; and a Home and Garden Center, where you can find out about pest control and "Family Preparedness Planning." There might even be a Special Interests Center, where you can chat about UFOs, movies, religion, travel, or anything else. And Free-Nets also have a system that lets you send messages to other users.

You'll see the terms Free-Net, freenet, FreeNet, and maybe other variations. All these terms are service marks of NPTN (National Public Telecommuting Network), who prefer to use the term *Free-Net*.

Even without their Internet links, Free-Nets are a great community resource, especially for home-bound people such as the elderly and handicapped. (It's a shame that the very people who could benefit most from a computer system such as this are the least likely to have computers—maybe that will change in the next few years.)

At the time of this writing there were 23 Free-Nets, mostly in the U.S., but also in New Zealand, Canada, and Finland. This number is expected to double in the next year, though, and continue growing apace. We've listed all the Free-Nets working at the time of writing—see Section A at the end of the book—but if we haven't listed one close to you try contacting NPTN (National Public Telecommuting Network). We've placed NPTN's information at the end of the Free-Net list. If you can't find a Free-Net, maybe you should start one in your town. NPTN will tell you how.

## An Almost-Free Account in Washington

While I was writing this book, something interesting occurred in Internetland. The International Internet Association announced that it would provide free Internet access (dial-in terminal accounts) to all and sundry, starting from November 1, 1993. They say they'll have 50 lines open by then, increasing to 200 lines in the near future. These lines will be in Washington D.C., so most people will have to pay for long distance calls, but it's a great offer for those near Washington. There will also be an 800 number that people can use, and the charge will be 20 cents/minute ($12/hour).

The response to this offer was phenomenal, so it became difficult to get more information. It was taking three weeks to respond to messages left on the IIA's message machine. If you want to find out more about this offer, call (202) 387-5445, or fax a request to (202) 387-5446, or write to The International Internet Association, Suite 852, 2020 Pennsylvania Ave., N.W., Washington, D.C. 20006.

At the time of this writing, some Internet users were skeptical about this offer. If this service turns out to be of an acceptable quality, it will be a boon for many. However, much of the country will find it cheaper to go elsewhere. For instance, about the cheapest evening rates I'm likely to get from Denver to Washington D.C. are a little over $5/hour—yet I can get Internet access from a service provider for $2/hour. You might at least call your long distance company and figure out how much it will cost you to dial D.C. at the time of day you are likely to use the Internet, then use that price as a guideline when looking for another service provider.

If you can't figure out where to find a free or almost-free Internet connection, you're on your own—you're going to have to pay. But pay as little as you can. The next chapter explains how.

## The Least You Need to Know

- There are four main types of Internet connections
- A permanent connection is the best type of connection, but it's expensive. You may have one if you are an employee of a large corporation, or a member of an organization such as a university.
- A dial-in direct (SLIP, PPP) connection is the next best thing. It can be complicated to set up, and is more expensive up front, but may be easier and cheaper to use in the long run.
- A Dial-in terminal connection is the most common type of connection for individuals buying their own account. It's cheap and easy to set up—you can use just about any data communications program.

*continues*

*continued*

- If you have an account with a computer "information service" such as CompuServe or America Online, you already have an Internet mail. You could also get a UUCP mail connection from an Internet service provider.
- Ask your employer or local college if you can use their Internet connection.
- Check the list of Free-Nets (Section A at the end of the book) to see if you can get to the Internet through a free community-computer system.
- If you are near Washington D.C., see if you can get a free account from the International Internet Association.

Chapter 4

# If You *Have* to Pay: Picking a Provider

## In This Chapter

- 1-800-number connections and data networks
- Finding a service provider in your area
- Look before you leap
- Comparing costs

If you've looked around and found no way to get a free account, the next stage is to find the service provider with the best rates and the services you need. In this chapter, we'll take a stroll around the block of paid providers, so you can see what's for sale.

## How Do I Know What's Out There?

At the end of the book you'll find a list of service providers. This isn't comprehensive—there are probably some I missed, and their coverage areas may have changed. Still, it's a good start (and I've listed three organizations that can help you track down a service provider); in most cases you'll be able to find several providers you can use.

## Home-Town Operations

Look for all service providers with service in your area, not just the ones which are headquartered near you. Even if a provider is in, say, Maine, they may be able to provide local telephone number support all over the country by buying phone service in lots of different cities. You may find that the service closest to you is *not* the cheapest deal—a service based in another city may have a local phone number in your city, with lower rates.

## One-Eight-Hundreds

Some services provide a 1-800 number you can call, regardless of where in the United States you happen to be. (Others have 800 numbers that work only within their home states.) You won't pay for the phone call connecting you to their computer, but you *will* pay a higher per-minute rate while you are connected than you normally would. For instance, if a service provider normally charges $1/hour for evening use, you may pay $6/hour if you are using their 1-800 number.

Still, a provider with a 1-800 number provides two benefits—it lets people who travel a lot continue using Internet while out of town, and it lets people who are far from a local-number connection get onto the network without paying for long distance calls. The extra $5 or so per hour may still be less than the long distance charges.

## Data Networks

Depending on where you're located, you may be able to use a data network to connect. It's like this: a number of companies have leased telephone lines and numbers all over the country. A service provider can sign up with one of these companies, so the data network is linked to the service provider's computer.

For instance, a service provider named The World has only telephone numbers in the Boston area. But users in, say, Phoenix or Dallas who wanted to use The World's services could sign up with CompuServe Packet Network or PC-Pursuit (Sprint Data Services). These two companies have local numbers spread all over the country, so a user can dial the CompuServe or Sprint number, log onto the network's computer, then log onto The World's computer.

> **By the Way . . .**
>
> You don't need to have a CompuServe Information Service account in order to use CompuServe's Packet Network.

Of course there's a charge, perhaps $5 or $6 per hour. (Some services are as low as $1/hour, during evenings and weekends.) If you find a service provider with low rates but no local number, ask them if they have a data network you can connect through, and then figure out the total cost.

> **By the Way . . .**
>
> The standard of service you'll get can vary widely. Some service providers are very helpful, with responsive technical support, good documentation, and even setup programs that will lead you through installing a dial-in direct connection. Others will set up an account for you on their end, then let you figure out the rest. Also, some services are currently overused—complaints of busy signals when trying to connect, and that the system seems to "hang" when you try to type a command, are common. If you know other Internet users, ask for a recommendation. Otherwise you'll just have to pick one and see what it's like.

## Use an Online Service

You may already have access to the Internet through an online service of which you are a member. (I'm not talking about the capability of sending mail to and from the Internet, as many online services have this ability. I'm talking about being able to log onto your service provider, and then use Internet tools, such as Gopher, FTP, Telnet, and so on.) Delphi, for instance, already provides Internet access. America Online is starting soon; by the time you read this book, they will have some kind of Internet access. CompuServe is in the planning stage. I was told that they may have Internet access by the end of 1994. Even PRODIGY is talking about Internet access.

# Comparison Shopping

Once you've found a few promising service providers—with local numbers, data networks, or 800 numbers—call or write them to get their rates. Before you buy, compare. Making the best deal can save hundreds of dollars in setup fees, and hundreds of dollars a year in *connect fees* (the money you are charged for actually using the service).

## Shopping for Permanent Connections

Shopping for a permanent connection is way beyond the scope of this book. If you are an individual, you don't want a permanent connection (at least, you don't want to pay for one). Permanent connections require routers, leased lines, and all sorts of other expensive items. Startup costs are in the thousands of dollars, and yearly costs in the tens of thousands. Anyone shopping for a permanent connection is probably reading another—much more serious—book. If, by chance, you do need a permanent connection, contact the organizations I name at the end of Section A.

## Shopping for Dial-In Direct

If you want dial-in direct service, you may have to pay a one-time $100 connection fee—or a one-time $250 connection fee. You may have to pay $3/hour during the day, $2/hour in the evenings, and $1/hour between midnight and 8:00 a.m., with a $15/month minimum—or you may have to pay $175/month fee for unlimited use. You'll find a great variety in the way you pay and how much you pay, so compare as many providers as you can.

And remember that the best deal depends on your circumstances. For some users, $175/month for unlimited dial-in direct use is a good deal—that's only about 1.9 hours' worth a day, at $3/hour; if you are going to use more than that, the price per hour will drop. But that's much more than *most* users will use, so a 15-hour/month minimum starts to sound pretty good. And if most of your use will be during the evening, $175 would buy you 2.9 hours each evening at the $2/hour rate. Will you really use that much?

## Shopping for Dial-In Terminal

You can find dial-in terminal accounts for as low as $15 to $25/month for unlimited use, which seems very reasonable. Often, they go for a little more, for example, $3/hour with a $15/month minimum and a $175/month maximum. (That is, once you've used up $175 worth of online time, the rest is free.) And of course, you may have lower hourly rates at certain times, for example, $2 in the evenings and $1 at night.

Remember to check what services are available. Some service providers that sell dial-in terminal accounts may not have all of Internet available to you.

## Shopping for Mail Connections

Simple mail connections are selling well these days, as people become more interested in e-mail connections they can use while on the move. There are a lot of different ways to get an e-mail connection—through CompuServe, GEnie, America Online, and through true Internet service providers. For instance, if you want to send and receive Internet mail with an online service of which you are already a member, it's simply a matter of using an Internet mail address (you'll probably be charged a small fee for each message). If you go with a service provider, you may be charged as little as $10/month with unlimited messages.

# Explaining What You Want

When you first contact a service provider, make sure you are both talking about the same thing. If you don't understand the account types they are talking about (and there are plenty of variations, with many service providers creating their own product names), make sure they clarify what they are offering.

If you want a dial-in terminal account, say:

*"I want an account that I can dial in with a simple telecommunications program, and which allows me full access to the Internet—mail, FTP, USENET, Telnet, and so on."*

(Okay, so you don't know what these terms mean, but you will eventually, and, more importantly, the service provider will.)

If you want a dial-in direct account, say:

*"I want a SLIP, CSLIP, or PPP account."*

If all you are interested in is sending electronic mail, and don't want to use all the other fancy Internet capabilities, say:

*"I want a simple mail account."*

Of course if you are reviewing information sent in the mail, you'll have to dig through it carefully to figure out the different options.

Here are some alternative names you may hear a service provider use for the types of service we've been discussing:

*Permanent* may be called direct, permanent direct, or dedicated service.

*Dial-in terminal* may be called interactive or dial-up service.

*Dial-in direct* may be called SLIP, CSLIP, PPP, or TCP service.

*Mail* may be called UUCP, e-mail, or messaging service.

Once you are both talking about the same thing, you can use the following list of questions to compare the rates of different service providers. This list is intended for use when comparing dial-in direct or dial-in terminal services, *not* permanent connections, as those are far more complicated (I'm assuming you are not looking for permanent service—if you are, you're in the wrong book!), or mail connections (which are quite simple and don't require much comparison).

- **How much is the connect or startup cost for dial-in terminal? For dial-in direct?** To get started you'll usually have to pay a setup charge, a one-time fee for getting onto the system. This might be as little as $20 or as much as $250, depending on the type of account and the particular service provider.

- **Do you provide free software for dial-in direct accounts?** It's possible to get quite cheap dial-in direct accounts (for as little as a $100 setup charge), but you may have to provide your own software. Other service providers charge more, perhaps several hundred dollars, but may give you the software.
- **Is there a fixed fee?** The amount you pay per hour can vary tremendously. Some service providers don't charge by the hour; they charge a single monthly fee, and provide unlimited time on the Internet ($15-a-month unlimited use, for instance). Also, some service providers charge different fees for different modem speeds. Make sure you get the price for the speed of modem you are using.
- **If there's a fixed fee, is it for limited access?** If the service provider is charging a fixed fee, make sure you know what hours you will be allowed onto the system. Some providers may have a low fixed-fee account, but only let you on in the evenings.
- **How much do you charge per hour during weekdays?** Many providers charge an hourly rate. For instance, $3 an hour for online time between say, 8:00 a.m. and 8:00 p.m. during the week. You may have to make a few notes along with the numbers—some providers charge a minimum which gets you a few free hours—$10/month, with four free hours, for instance—and then charge a set fee for subsequent hours—say, $4/hour for the fifth and subsequent hours. And some providers may have two or more payment plans for the same service, so you may need more than one column for each provider. And remember to check rates for your modem speed.
- **How much per hour in the evening?** What hours do you consider "evening"? Rates are usually lower during the evenings—say, 8:00 p.m. to midnight.
- **How much per hour at night?** What hours do you consider "night?" Rates are often lower still between, for instance, midnight and 8:00 a.m., perhaps around $1/hour.
- **How much per hour during weekends?** Check to see if there's a lower rate during weekends. Some service providers use the same schedule for all seven days, the only variation being the *time* of service, not the day.

- **Is there a minimum number of hours I must use each month?** The service provider will probably charge a minimum monthly fee. This may be combined with an hourly rate. For instance, you may have to pay $15/month minimum—which might get you 5 hours at the highest ($3/hour) rate, or 15 hours at the $1/hour rate—then pay an additional amount when you've used up the $15 worth. Or perhaps the minimum buys you a set number of hours at a low rate, with the rate going up once you've used the hours up.
- **Do you have a maximum number of hours I pay for, after which all hours are free?** If a service provider charges by the hour, they may have a maximum—for instance, once you've paid $250 in hourly fees, everything is free for the rest of the month.
- **Do you have a local number?** Ideally you want a service provider with a telephone number in your area code, so you don't have to pay long distance charges.

If a service provider says it has a *POP* (Point of Presence) in your area, it means they have a local telephone number in your area. You won't have to pay for long distance calls to connect to Internet.

- **Is there a surcharge on that local number?** Some service providers charge you extra to use their local number! Perhaps $9 an hour! Ideally you want a *free* local number.
- **Do you have 1-800 access? What is the surcharge? Is it national, or state only?** Some service providers have 1-800 numbers you can use. You'll pay a surcharge—maybe $5–$12/hour—but if you live in the boonies with no Internet number in your area code, you might find it cheaper to use the 1-800 number than pay long distance charges. The 1-800 number is also convenient for people who want to be able to use the Internet while away from home.
- **Do you have data-network access? What is the surcharge?** Some service providers have data networks they work with. The surcharge will vary from $1/hour to about $6/hour, depending on the time of day that you use Internet.

- **What modem speeds do you support?** The faster the modem connection, the better. The slower the connection, the more time everything will take, and the more expensive your online work—in terms of both the money you pay the service provider, and the value of your time. And unlike some BBSs (such as CompuServe), they may not charge you more for using fast modems on Internet—so the faster the modem, the better. (Some providers *will* charge more for fast modems.) If all your service provider can manage is 2400 bps (bits per second), it's probably too slow. They should have at least 9600 bps, preferably 14400 bps. Of course, the data-transmission speed you want to use is limited by the speed of *your* computer's modem. If all you've got is a 300 bps, it doesn't matter if the service provider has 14400 bps modems; *your* connection will be at 300 bps.

- **How much is disk space per megabyte per month?** Your service provider will probably charge you if you store too much stuff—messages and files—on his computer's hard disk. This doesn't have to be a problem, though. A provider may let you use up to 1 MB (megabyte) for free, then charge 50 cents a month for each additional MB. You can store a lot of messages in 1 MB, and you can make sure you always move files from their computer to yours, so you don't go above the limit. (If you have a dial-in direct connection, files will land directly on your computer's hard disk anyway, not on theirs.)

- **How much is domain service?** When you get a dial-in direct account you can establish your own *domain name* or use the service provider's (We'll discuss the pros and cons later, in Chapter 6). You'll have

**SPEAK LIKE A GEEK**

Many people use the term *baud* instead of bps. The two terms are pretty much interchangeable, though not quite exactly the same—and purists will tell you that bps is the more correct of the two. (However, your communications program's documentation may use the term "baud" instead of "bps.") The word "baud" comes from J. M. E. Baudot, who invented the Baudot telegraph code, and it refers to the *modulation* and *demodulation* rate of the modem—the rate at which the modem converts between the computer's digital signal and the phone line's analog signal.

to pay a fee if you want to establish your own domain name, perhaps $20.

- **Do you provide a discount for Complete Idiot's Guide readers?** Some service providers have agreed to give readers of *The Complete Idiot's Guide to the Internet* a special discount. See the coupons at the end of the book.
- **Are there any other charges?** There are as many ways to charge you as there are service providers. Check the fine print.

## The Least You Need to Know

- See the listing at the back of the book for some service providers; there may be others in your area as well.
- Don't look at just the service providers close to you—some non-local ones may have local numbers.
- If you are a long way from a service provider's coverage area, look for one with a 1-800 number or data network-access.
- Remember to check the service provider's modem speed—some still use slow modems.
- Compare costs carefully—rates vary widely.
- Check the coupons in the back of the book to see if a service provider is offering a discount to readers of this book.

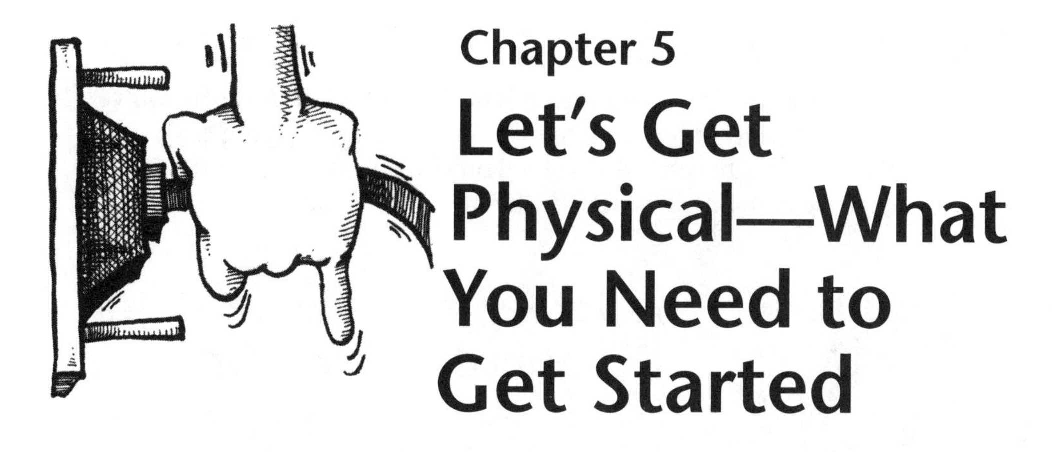

# Chapter 5
# Let's Get Physical—What You Need to Get Started

## In This Chapter

- The type of computer you need
- How to pick a modem
- The type of software you need
- Account names and passwords

If you've decided that Internet's for you, you need to decide if you've got what it takes—if you have the computer hardware and software you'll need. Internet's hardware demands are not extreme, but there are a few things to consider. You are going to need the following:

- An Internet account (of course)
- A computer or terminal
- A modem or connection
- Simple communication software
- Mail software (maybe)
- A login name
- A password

I'm going to use the term *Internet account* (or simply, *account*) throughout this book to mean "access to Internet." You may also hear the term *Internet access, Internet service, or Internet connection.* These all mean the same thing—the ability to "get onto" Internet and use its services.

## Get Your Account!

The first thing you're going to need is an *Internet account*—until you've figured out how to get one, there's not much point in trying to figure out the rest. So if you haven't yet decided on the type of account (and where you're going to get it), go back to Chapters 2 and 3 and do so.

The phrase *dumb terminal* means that your piece of equipment has no actual computing power—all it has is the ability to send and receive text. When you sit and type, the terminal sends the text to the computer, which does whatever it's supposed to do with the text, and then sends some more text back to your terminal, to tell you what it's just done. One of the most common types of terminal is the VT100. Originally a Digital Electronics Corporation terminal, it has become a standard, and many manufacturers' terminals now *emulate* the way the VT100 works. That is, they imitate it by working the same way.

## A Screen to Read, a Keyboard to Type On

You need some electronic way to communicate with Internet, of course. If you are getting your account from an organization with a permanent connection, the system manager will provide you with something or tell you what you need. You might get an actual computer, or simply a *dumb terminal*—a keyboard and a monitor that is hooked up to the organization's computer.

With a direct connection, you are already connected to the service provider's computer; you don't need to establish the connection yourself. If you are dialing into your account, however, (whether it's dial-in direct or dial-in terminal), you'll need an actual computer with a modem and some communication software. That's because the computer must call the service provider's computer and "log on."

What type of computer? You've got a wide choice. You can use any IBM-compatible PC, a Macintosh, an Apple, a UNIX workstation—any computer that can have a modem installed (or to which you can connect a modem), and one that can run communications software. For a dial-in terminal connection, you don't need much of a computer, either. You don't need the latest Pentium PC with a 24-bit color monitor. You can use the earliest 8086 PC if you wish, with a monochrome monitor. (You can pick one of those up for $100 or less if you look hard.)

If you are going to use a dial-in direct connection, the type of computer you require will depend on the type of software you are going to use. Some programs may require more memory than you'll find in an old 8086, or may even require Microsoft Windows. We'll discuss dial-in-direct software in a moment.

# Getting Connected

If you are using a dumb terminal, all you need is a connection to the organization's computer. You don't need to worry about that, though—the system manager will figure out how to connect a wire between the two.

If you are using a dial-in direct or dial-in terminal account (both of which require your computer to "dial in" to the service provider's system), you will need a *modem*. Modems come in two types: internal and external. An *internal modem* is a computer board that plugs into a slot inside the computer, and the phone line plugs into a socket on the edge of the modem. An *external modem* is a box—which contains a board that is much the same as the internal-modem board. You will connect a cable between the computer's *serial port* (one of the plugs on the back) and a similar-looking plug on the modem box. Then you connect a phone line between the phone socket on your wall and a similar socket on the modem box.

The faster your modem, the better. And if you are going to use a dial-in direct connection, you *must* have a fast modem. You'll find anything less than 9600 bps is too slow, and you're better off with 14400 bps. But as I mentioned in the last chapter, some service providers charge more for fast modems, so be a smart shopper.

Internal and external modems are the same thing, just in a different position. They vary slightly in price—external modems are a bit more expensive, because they need a box and an extra socket (for power). They use up your serial port as well, which can be a hassle—many computers have the mouse plugged into the serial port, and may not have a spare one.

Doubling the speed of your modem doesn't halve your costs. The modem speed only affects the transmissions between your computer and the service provider's computer, and much of your online time will be spent waiting for *other* computers to do their work. Still, fast modems will save some money.

## Help! Which Modem Should I Buy?

I can't tell you which modem to buy, because what's available depends on the type of computer you are using. If you already have a modem, use it—it'll probably work fine. If you don't have one yet, you might want to talk to the service provider, and ask for a recommendation. Sometimes modems run into compatibility problems. It's possible (though unlikely) that the modem you buy will have trouble connecting to the service provider's computer. They should be able to give you a list of modems that they know to work well, and perhaps even a list of modems that have problems connecting.

You'll probably find that your service provider is using quite fancy modems, with fancy specifications like V.32*bis*, MNP-5, V.42, V.42*bis*, and so on. These describe the way in which modems communicate and handle problems during a transmission. You may also find that they recommend a top-of-the-line modem costing $300 or $500. Don't do it. Fast (14400 bps) high-quality modems can be bought for $100 to $150 if you look around, and prices are dropping all the time. Try buying from a reputable mail-order company, such as MicroWarehouse (800-367-7080), PC/Mac Zone (800-258-2088), or Direct Micro (800-288-2887). Ask your service provider the modem specifications you must match, then buy a modem that matches.

There are no guarantees, of course. If there's a bug in your modem's *firmware* (the software that makes the modem run), you might *still* have problems, even if your modem matches. Although unlikely, this does happen (as thousands of purchasers of fax/modems from a certain major computer manufacturer—who will remain nameless—can attest). But if you buy from a reputable mail-order company, you can always return the modem and try another.

**By the Way . . .**

One day (soon, perhaps) you won't need a modem. Eventually we'll all have digital phone lines, and you'll just plug your computer into the telephone line and transmit digital signals straight to the other computer—no need to modulate them into analog signals and vice versa.

## Picking the Software You Need

If you have been given a permanent-connection Internet account by your company or college, you probably don't need communication software. Your computer or terminal is already connected directly to a computer that is (in turn) connected directly to Internet. Whatever system is used, it's up to your system administrator, the guy or gal in charge of the organization's Internet accounts.

If you are going to use a dial-in account, though, you'll need a *communication program*. This program tells your modem what to do when it's communicating with the service provider's computer, and displays the *session*—the text that you send and receive while working on Internet—on your computer screen.

If you are using a dial-in terminal account, you probably don't need to buy communication software. Most modems these days come with a program such as Qmodem or Crosstalk. And if your computer uses Microsoft Windows, you have Windows Terminal. If you use an "integrated" package—a program that integrates several mini programs, such as a word processor, spreadsheet, and database—then you may be in luck, because many also include a simple communications program. And a simple program is all you need to get onto the Internet using a dial-in terminal account.

If you *have* to buy a copy, they start at around $50, though you can also find shareware communications programs for much less—call Public Brand Software (800-426-3475) or Software Labs (800-569-7900) for PC-based shareware. Make sure you get a program that can do *xmodem* data transfers (most can these days), or, better still, *zmodem* transfers.

*Shareware* is distributed for free or at a very low cost. To get a shareware communications program from a distributor may cost around $5 or $10. If you like the program, you must register it. Fees vary, but start at around $10 for the simplest communications program, up to around $90 for the most sophisticated.

The more sophisticated communications programs have a lot of advantages, of course—they will allow you to write "scripts" for logging onto Internet, for instance, so the program will automatically enter your login name, password, and so on. Some programs will even "learn" the logon procedure from you—the program watches the first time you log on, and then duplicates the procedure the next time.

When I provide examples of using a communication program, I'll use Windows Terminal, because so many people have it and because it's a fairly basic, straightforward program (though not without its problems). Whatever program you get, though, spend some time playing with it, figuring out how it all works. You need to know how to enter the setup information—modem speed, telephone number, terminal type, and so on. You also need to know how to use the program to connect to a BBS, how to capture text files, and how to do *binary transfers* (xmodem or zmodem transfers, for instance).

**By the Way . . .**

Windows Terminal is actually easier to use than many telecommunications packages, but it's *not* the world's finest piece of programming. And it doesn't have all the "bells and whistles" available with a more advanced program. Eventually you may want to find something better.

If you are using a dial-in direct connection, you will also need TCP/IP software; see Chapter 6.

**By the Way . . .**

If you managed to find a Free-Net connection, then we've pretty much covered what you need to get started—a computer, a modem, and a communications program. Dial the Free-Net and follow instructions. You'll be told about how to register, and how to select a login name and password. And at some point (perhaps not the first day), you should be able to get onto the Internet itself, which we'll get into in later chapters.

# I've Got a Name

To get connected, you will need a *login name*. (You will also see the terms *username* and *account name*.) This is the name of your account, the name you will type each time you access Internet. It tells the service provider who you are, so he or she knows whether to let you on the network—and knows who to bill for the time. It's also going to be part of the "address" that other users will type when they want to send messages to you.

A login name can be up to eight characters, and it's *case-sensitive*. In other words, Pkent is not the same as pkent or pKENT or PKENT. You will always have to type in your login name in exactly the same way (actually you'll probably get your communication software to do it for you).

If you are getting a dial-in direct account, you may be limited to seven characters, because the service provider's computer may need the login name to be preceded by an S. In fact, if you get a dial-in direct account you may be given *two* login names—one for the account itself, and one for a *dial-in terminal account* you may be given to store your mail. Ask your service provider.

Login names are usually made up of the account owner's name—*pete*, *pkent*, *peterk*, or *peterwk*, or whatever—though they can be whatever you want.

If you are using a dial-in direct connection, you will also need to know your host number and domain name. See Chapter 6 for all the details on these.

# The Password Is . . .

You also need a *password*, a secret "code" you will type when the system asks you to do so. Only you are supposed to know your password; the computer assumes that if it receives the correct password, the correct person is trying to log on.

Why do you care if someone else is able to log on as you? Well, first of all, you don't want to pay for someone else's time working or playing on Internet. Nor do you want someone reading your messages, or sending messages under your name, or deleting your files, or communicating in the newsgroups as "you." There *are* people out there who would like your password, and who know a few (computer) tricks to get it. They work on a basic assumption—that your password is easy to figure out because it's a name or a word.

### By the Way . . .

This isn't just theory. There really are people who want to break into your account. Recent stories in the press have reported that many service providers' systems have been "broken into" recently, with at least one organization forced to close down for a while.

In most cases, passwords can be up to eight characters (check with the service provider) And, like the login name, your password is case-sensitive. If you are using **1n=9YT%** as a password, you can't type *1N=9YT%* or *1n=9yt%*. (It should go without saying that this is *only* an example.)

## Passwords: Pick a Good One

So how do you pick a good password? It shouldn't be a recognizable name or word—not the name of one of your kids, or your dog, not a description of your job ("accountant," or "boss" for instance), the name of your house, a character from The Simpsons, or whatever. It also shouldn't be a meaningful number—not your Social Security number, not your date of birth.

Here are a few tips:

- The best password is a random jumble of characters: 1n=9YT%, for instance.
- Random jumbles are difficult to remember, so create what appears to be a random jumble—mix special characters with several short words. I&you%in. You could pick three short words at random from a dictionary.
- Don't give your password to anyone else—but if you do, change it as soon as he or she is finished.
- Don't type your password while someone is watching—but if you do, change it as soon as he leaves.
- Change the password regularly, every month, for instance. (Some systems may force you to do so, stopping you from logging in until you create a new password.)
- Don't write the password down online (in messages, for instance) or anywhere else.
- The longer the password, the better. Five characters is too short. Ask your service provider the maximum password length (probably eight characters).

When you are first given an account, you may be able to tell the service provider what password you want to use, or they may simply assign you one. Log onto the system as soon as possible and *change* the password. Remember, *only one person should know what the password is*, and while your paperwork has been lying around the service provider's offices, several people have been able to see it.

> **By the Way . . .**
>
> If you forget your password, don't worry. Call the service provider. Someone there will be able to assign you a new one. Use it to log on and change the password again.

# Do You Need Mail Software?

If you are getting a mail connection to Internet through a service provider, they may give you (or sell you) some *mail software*. These programs let you read and write your mail messages when you're not connected to the Internet (and therefore not paying online charges). The program will then go online, drop off your messages, and pick up the ones waiting for you. You can tell the program to do it immediately, or schedule it so it does so at regular intervals. (As you'll see in Chapter 10, you'll probably be using a mail program that runs on your service provider's computer.)

If you want to learn more about mail programs and mail readers, see the **comp.bbs.waffle** and **comp.os.msdos.mail-news** newsgroups (you'll learn about newsgroups in Chapter 15.)

You can also find shareware versions—there's UUPC, for instance (K. Derbyshire, Kendra Electronic Wonderworks, P.O. Box 132, Arlington, MA 02174. Internet address: docs@kew.com); and Waffle (Tom Dell, P.O. Box 4436, Mountain View, CA 94040, dell@west.darkside.com).

Then there are *newsgroup/mail readers* (programs that let you read both e-mail and the *newsgroup* message):CMM, a Windows program for use with UUPC (Sylvain Tremblay, Cinétic Systems, 4933 Verreau, Montreal, Quebec, Canada H1M 2C7. Internet address: Sylvain@Speedy.cam.org) and HellDiver, a program for use with Waffle (Rys Weatherly, 5 Horizon Drive, Jamboree Heights, QLD 4074 Australia, rhys@cs.uq.oz.au).

Be warned, however: setting up shareware programs for Internet communications can be complicated. If you are a novice and value your time, you may want to buy what your service provider offers, since it may already be set up correctly to run with their system.

## The Least You Need to Know

- If you're being provided an account by your organization, don't worry about it—they'll tell you what you need.
- If you are getting your own account, you'll need a computer and a fast modem.
- The faster the modem the better—try to get 9600 bps, or (better still) 14400 bps. Only get a slower modem if you're broke.
- Ask your service provider to recommend a modem—buy one that matches the specifications they give you.
- Ask the service provider if they know of any modems that *won't* work with their system.
- For dial-in terminal accounts, just about any simple data communication program should work.
- Pick a sensible password—make it long and seemingly random. Don't select real words, names, or numbers that have a meaning to you.

**A page is a terrible thing to waste.**

# Chapter 6 Special Stuff for Dial-In Direct Folks

If you've decided that dial-in direct is the way to go, you've got some extra things to think about. Are you beginning to think that a dial-in terminal might be a lot less hassle? Well, actually it is. For the casual user, a dial-in terminal is the way to go. The software is easier, the connection is cheaper, the headaches are fewer. But if you're planning to spend a lot of time on the Internet, it may be worth it for you to slog out the details of a Dial-In Direct account. This chapter should help.

## You Need TCP/IP Software!

If you are going to use a dial-in direct account, you need *TCP/IP software* (Transmission Control Protocol/Internet Protocol—now you can forget what it means; most people do).

Remember that a dial-in direct account is supposed to make your computer work as if it had a dedicated account—once connected to the service provider's computer you can transfer files directly to and from your computer to other computers on Internet. (With a dial-in terminal account you have to copy files from the other computers to the service provider's computer, then copy them over to *your* computer.)

So where do you find this TCP/IP software? From your service provider, perhaps? Maybe, but he or she may ask $300 or $400 for it. You can also buy from a software retailer—but it will still be around $300 or $400—maybe less if you can find it discounted.

There are a number of commercially-distributed TCP/IP programs, such as Chameleon (a Microsoft Windows program sold by NetManage—408-973-7171, richard@netmanage.com), PC/TCP (DOS and

Windows program from FTP, Inc.—508-685-4000), and Air Navigator (sold by SPRY; see the coupon in the back of this book). There are also programs available for other computers—ask your service provider what he or she recommends.

### TCP/IP Shareware

There's a multitude of shareware programs for dial-in direct connections, including Windows programs. But as I mentioned before, setting up shareware TCP/IP communications packages on the Internet is no simple matter—it's probably beyond the average novice, unless he wants to invest dozens (hundreds?) of hours in figuring it all out and seeking information. And even many experienced users will find installing the Windows TCP/IP systems quite a challenge.

**By the Way . . .**

There's shareware for not only DOS machines, of course, but for Macs, Sun workstations, other UNIX computers, and so on.

If you've decided that you need a dial-in direct account, you might want to purchase a commercial TCP/IP program—at least then you'll have technical support to help you install it and get it running. Or get a dial-in terminal account, and then search around for shareware programs for dial-in direct (ask your service provider where they are—there's quite likely a directory somewhere on their system with this sort of stuff) and find one you like. But be prepared to spend many interesting hours trying to find something that will work.

## A Stately Address: Host Number and Domain Name

If you are getting a dial-in direct account, you will need a host number. In effect, your computer will be registered as an Internet *node*, with communications passing from your "host" through the service provider's host and vice versa. For instance, your host number will look something like this:

192.94.50.236. Your communication software will need to provide this number to your service provider's computer each time you connect to the Internet. Your service provider will give you this number.

## Host Numbers: A Bit of Techie

When you sit down to work with Internet, your computer (or your computer terminal) is connected to a computer that is connected to the network. For instance, with a dial-in account you use your PC to connect to another computer—which is in turn connected to Internet. The computers that are connected directly to Internet are known as *hosts*, and each one is assigned a unique number. That number is the *address* Internet uses to send the messages to their correct destination. It's made up of numbers identifying the network on which the host may be found—remember, Internet is a conglomeration of networks—and numbers identifying the *routers* used to get the message to the particular host. For instance, the address used by Colorado's Supernet is 128.138.213.21.

The host computers are connected to *routers*. These, too, are computers; they connect various parts of the network, and "route" messages between different areas. The lines between the routers may be telephone lines, or *local area networks* (cable links among multiple computers) in a company or university campus.

## Domain Names: Not Quite So Techie

You also need a domain name—you'll get one even if you don't choose one. The host number is used by the computer equipment itself. In order to make it easier to use for mere mortals, the system also assigns a *domain name* to each host.

> **By the Way . . .**
>
> No matter what kind of Internet connection you have, it wouldn't hurt for you to understand domain names. Consider reading this material and writing it on your heart, even if you're sure you don't want anything fancier than a dial-in terminal account.

The Domain Name System (DNS) uses subsets of *domains* to identify computers and groups of accounts on a computer. For example, one domain is named *gov*. Not surprisingly, that's the domain used by the U.S. Government. But it has domains associated with it. One domain is named *whitehouse*. Actually it's more correctly named *whitehouse.gov*, because a domain is always identified in relation to the domain of which it is a part. And yes, *whitehouse* is the domain at the White House. (Each level in this system is known as a domain, so one domain may have several domains "under" it, each of which may have several more associated with it. Think of these as "subdomains.")

Here's another gov domain— *fdabbs.fda.gov*. This identifies the domain in which you'll find the Food and Drug Administration's bulletin board (*fdabbs*), which is part of the FDA domain (*fda*), which is part of the U.S. Government (*gov*) domain. You can log into this computer and find consumer information, news releases, information about drugs, and so on. And here's the domain I currently use—*csn.org*. That's the computer used by Colorado Supernet (*csn*, the service provider I work through), which is part of a group of "other organizations" (*org*).

As you can see, the lowest-level domain is the left part of the name, the highest-level is the right part. Here are a few more high-level domain names you may see:

- **edu** A national group of educational institutions—most universities and schools are part of this domain
- **com** Commercial organizations (businesses)
- **mil** Military domains
- **ca** Canadian domains

- **cf** Central African Republic domains
- **co** Colorado

As you can see from the last two in this list, there are also country and state domains. Most countries have been assigned codes, though not all are on the network—you probably won't be seeing any **cf** domain messages anytime soon, though there's a domain name waiting for them as soon as they are ready.

Domain names can also be *geographical* names. For instance, *golden.co.us* is a domain in Golden, Colorado, in the United States of America.

When you ask your service provider to give you a particular domain name, the provider has to register the name with the NIC (Network Information Center), which takes about ten days. This group makes sure that domain names are unique, and are correctly associated with the number that identifies the actual computers used by the domain. Domains which are members of the same higher-level domain are not always *directly* and *physically* connected through the same hardware. Domains are simply a method used to help people figure out how the network is organized. What really counts (as far as the computers are concerned) are the host numbers, and the domain name tells you nothing about the actual host computers involved.

## Want Your Own Domain?

When you get an Internet account, you may have no choice about the domain name—if you are getting a company or university access, you will be told what domain name to use. But if you are buying access from a service provider—for yourself, your company, your school, or whatever—you can pick a domain name. Instead of using the host computer's domain name, you can create your own.

For instance, if your company is Acme Potato Peelers, Inc., how about using **apotpeel** as the lowest-level domain? You could then create a name that shows where you are, for instance—**apotpeel.golden.co.us**. Or you could make your company part of the **com** domain (commercial, a domain of businesses). Thus your domain name could be **apotpeel.com.**

The ability to create a domain name is important to an organization, of course. Once you have your **apotpeel.com** domain name, you can then add a few more, one for each department—**sales.apotpeel.com**, **mgt.apotpeel.com**, and so on. But there's another advantage for an Internet account, whether a business or individual—once you have a domain name, it's yours, regardless of the service provider you use. So if the one you are currently using decides to double its prices or reduce service, you can jump ship and take your domain name with you. The new service provider will have to register a change with the Network Information Center, so the host-computer number associated with your domain name will now be the one used by the new service provider's computer.

You'll probably have to pay if you want to create your own domain name—it may only be about $20, but ask before you decide to do so. There are special naming conventions used by libraries, universities, schools, and governmental organizations, but individual companies are able to create domain names in any form they wish.

You don't have to create a domain name, though your service provider may encourage you to do so. You can use the service provider's domain name, if you wish. If you are buying access from Colorado Supernet you can use their domain name—**csn.org**. So if you picked a login name of **joeblow**, your Internet address is now **joeblow@csn.org**.

## The Least You Need to Know

- For dial-in direct accounts, you need TCP/IP software. Expect to pay at least $150.
- The safest way to find TCP/IP software is to buy the program recommended by your service provider. It might not be the best value for your money, but you're assured that it will work.
- *Host numbers* are the addresses that the computers on the Internet use among themselves to identify one another; *Domain names* are the text equivalents preferred by humans because they're easier to remember and decipher.
- Dial-in direct users can have their own host number and domain name. You can select your own domain name, but you'll have to pay for the privilege.

# Chapter 7
# Your First Trip to the Internet

## In This Chapter

- Connecting with different types of accounts
- Setting up your software
- The info you need to know before you start
- The actual logon
- Changing your password
- Getting the heck out of there

Well, it's about time, huh? You're finally ready to get onto the Internet. In this chapter, I'm going to describe how to *log onto* Internet, and a little about what you'll find once you are logged in. You'll also learn how to change your password and how to log off.

The procedure for logging on is different depending on what kind of connection you're using—whether you're using a dedicated link, dialing in with a direct account, or dialing in with a terminal account. (If you are using a Free-Net, just use your communications program to dial the modem number, and then follow instructions.)

The process of identifying yourself before using a computer system—whether a single computer, a small network, or a large network such as Internet—is known as *logging on* or *logging in* to the system.

## Easy Street: Logging On with a Permanent Connection

A permanent-connection account is simplest to log onto. You don't have to worry about setting up communication software—you simply sit at one of your organization's terminals or computers, and enter the commands that have been given to you by the system administrator. I can't say what those commands might be, though they will include entering your login name and password. Your terminal may show your terminal name and a **login:** prompt. You'll type your login name and press **Enter**, and be prompted for your password. To get to the Internet itself, you'll have to enter another command or two. Check with your system administrator for more information.

## A Real Challenge: The Dial-in Direct Connection

Dial-in direct-connection accounts (such as SLIP or PPP) are more complicated. A dial-in direct-connection account allows you to use the Internet as if you were using a permanent-connection account. It will appear as if your computer is an Internet host computer, and you will be able to communicate directly with the Internet—you'll be able to copy files directly to and from your computer's hard drive. And depending on your software, you may be able to run several sessions at once.

To get to this stage, however, you have to install and run special software. Follow the instructions that came with your software. Once the software is up and running, use it to call your service provider's computer and log in. (The service provider should have given you log-in instructions when you signed up.)

# Do-It-Yourself with Dial-in Terminal Accounts

Getting onto Internet using a dial-in terminal account is like calling any BBS and logging in. I'm going to use Windows Terminal as an example, partly because millions of PC users already have it. If you aren't using Terminal, you'll need to read your documentation carefully to figure out how to work with it. If you are using a program other than Terminal, but you are not already familiar with communications software, you might want to read the following description of preparing Terminal. It'll give you an idea of what is involved in preparing for a transmission.

You need to begin by telling the program what sort of modem you have, what port it's connected to, the type of data communications *protocol* you are going to use, and so on. You should be able to get this information from your service provider: at a minimum, they should tell you what to use for the *data bits*, *stop bits*, *parity*, and *flow control* settings. If you are not sure about any other settings, ask them.

Of course, before you can begin, you have to start the program—in the case of Microsoft Terminal, you will double-click on the **Terminal** icon in the **Accessories** program group.

## Who Ya Gonna Call?

First things first: enter the phone number and settings you need. In Terminal, open the **Settings** menu and select **Phone Number** to see the dialog box shown here.

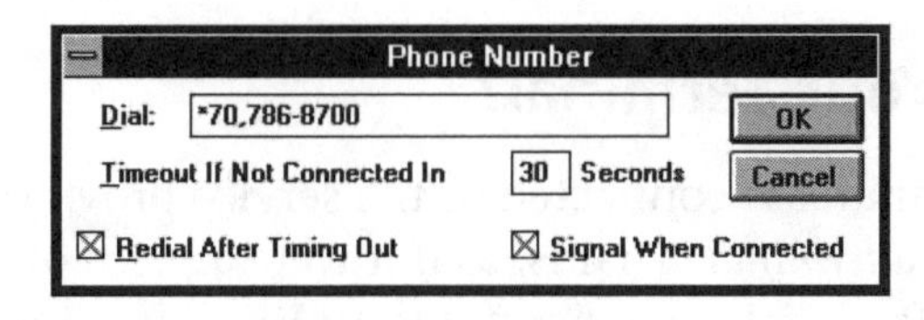


*The Phone Number dialog box lets you enter the service provider's number and a few other details.*

Type the telephone number given to you by your service provider into the **Dial** text box. If it's a long distance number, remember to include 1 plus the area code. You can also precede the number with other numbers and codes. For instance, if you work in an office and need to get an outside line, you may want to put a 9 first (or whatever number you need to dial to get a dial tone).

If the line you are using has call waiting, you will want to turn off that feature before calling Internet—dial the code (probably ***71**) that turns it off. (Call waiting tones can disturb your Internet session, and even cause you to lose data.)

You can separate numbers with commas—for most modems, a comma means "pause for one second." For instance:

```
9,,123-4567
```

will tell your modem to dial 9, wait for two seconds, and then dial the telephone number.

Notice that there are three other items in this dialog box. **Timeout If Not Connected In** is the amount of time you want to wait after dialing the call—if your modem hasn't connected to the service provider's modem within that time, it will stop trying. **Redial After Timing Out** tells the program to try dialing the call again if it was unable to connect within that time—if, for instance, the line was busy. And **Signal When Connected** tells the program to sound the computer's beep when connected.

Some programs have more options, of course—you might be able to define when and how often to redial, what sound should play when the computers connect, and so on.

## What Type Is Your Terminal?

Once your computer is connected to the service provider's computer, it's going to act as a *terminal*. That is, as if it were a piece of equipment designed to interface with that computer. In Windows Terminal you will open the **Settings** menu and select **Terminal Emulation** to see the following figure. Terminal has only three options: TTY, VT100, and VT-52. Unless your service provider has told you otherwise, select **VT100**. Other communications programs will have more options, but again, select VT100 (or **VT102**, if you don't have VT100), unless told otherwise. If you have a preference for a different type, ask your service provider about it—they may be able to work with many different types.

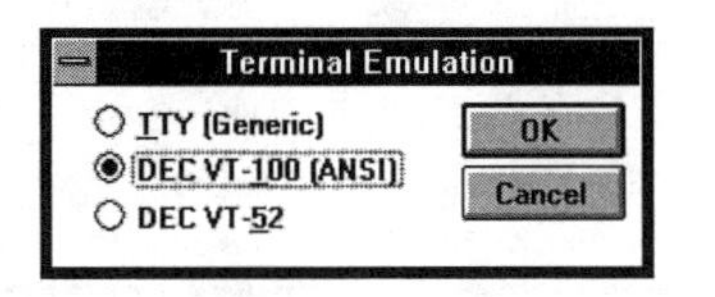


*The Terminal Emulation dialog box lets you tell Terminal how to act once connected to the service provider's computer.*

The next thing to do is configure your terminal preferences. Open the **Settings** menu and select **Terminal Preferences** to see the following figure. In this dialog box you can define various factors related to how your computer will act while it is "emulating" a terminal. Leave **Line Wrap** selected—this tells Terminal to wrap long lines onto two lines if necessary, rather than just throwing away the text at the end of the line.

Leave **Local Echo** unselected, unless you run into problems later. Most systems these days are what is known as "full duplex." When you type a character, it's sent by the modem to the other computer, which instantly "echoes" it back—so it appears on your computer screen. If you are going to be connected to a computer that is "half duplex" (unlikely), you will want to use Local Echo so Terminal itself displays the text you type, without waiting for it to be sent back from the other computer.

The **Sound** option is not important—it lets the other system get to your computer's beeper, which few systems will try to do anyway. You can usually leave the **CR->CR/LF** options turned off, as well—these tell Terminal to add a *linefeed* (that is, move to the next line) each time it gets a *carriage return* instruction from the other computer (that is, an instruction to move back to the left column). Most computers will do this automatically, so you won't have to worry about it.

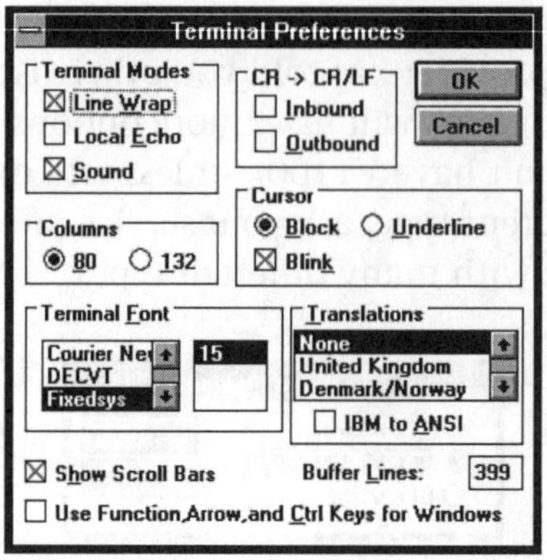

*The Terminal Preferences dialog box lets you define terminal characteristics.*

You can also set up the number of text **Columns** you want—you'll probably want to use 80, though you might use 132 if you have a large screen—and what the text **Cursor** should look like. The **Terminal Font** simply defines what the characters in the window will look like while you are working, and the **Translations** are used if your computer is using a character set different from the one used by the service provider's computer—again, you'll generally leave this alone.

The **Show Scroll Bars** and **Buffer Lines** let you set up how Terminal will handle text as it scrolls out of the top of the window—whether you want to be able to use scroll bars to go back and re-read the text, and how many lines of text should be kept (once you've exceeded the number of buffer lines, the oldest lines are lost as new ones arrive).

Finally, there's the **Use Function, Arrow, and Ctrl Keys for Windows**. You need to *clear* this check box—if it's selected, you won't be able to use the Arrow and Ctrl keys, which your service provider's computer will almost certainly expect you to be able to do. Some other Windows communications programs will automatically turn off these keys—so if you want to select text from the screen during a session, for instance, you'll have to use the menu commands, not the Ctrl-C command.

## Telling Your Modem How to Behave

Select the **Communications** option from the **Settings** menu to see the following figure. The Communications dialog box lets you set up communications parameters, the manner in which your computer and modem will communicate with the service provider's system. Select the maximum speed of your modem at the top of the box, in the **Baud Rate** area. If the box doesn't include your modem's speed (14400, for instance), select the next highest (19200).

Purists would say that modem speed is not really baud rate, it's *bps (bits per second),* but many communications programs use the term *baud rate* instead, and many people regard the two as the same.

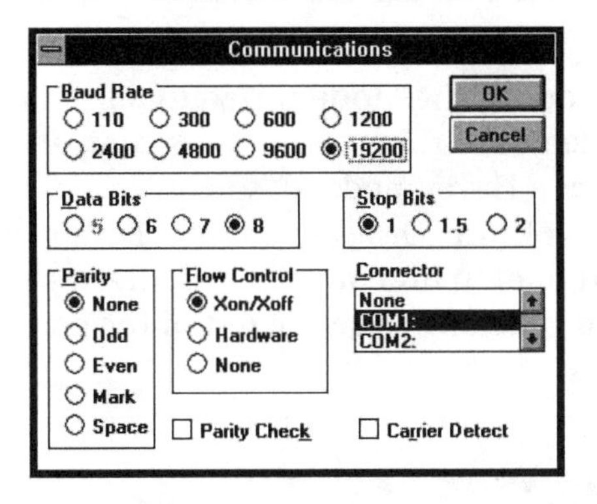


*Here's where you tell your modem how to do its job.*

You should also select the **Data Bits**, **Stop Bits**, **Parity** (most systems use 8 data bits, 1 stop bit, and no parity), and **Flow Control**. This is all information that your service provider should give you, and is related to exactly how the modem should transmit the information. The **Connector** is the computer port that you are using to transmit the data, usually COM1 or COM2 on a DOS computer. The **Parity Check** option tells Terminal to display a question mark when it receives a character that it knows has an error (a character with a "parity error"). If you don't select this option, it simply displays a garbage character, even if it knows that it's wrong. And you probably won't need **Carrier Detect**—use this if your modem is unable to connect to the service provider's computer (assuming you are sure that everything else is set correctly).

## Helping Your PC and Modem Talk

In order for your computer to communicate with another computer, it first has to know how to communicate with its own modem. Open the **Settings** menu and select **Modem Commands** to see the following dialog box.

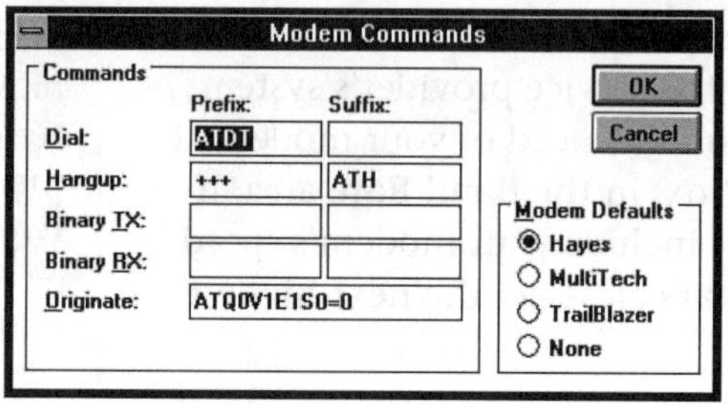

*The Modem commands dialog box is where you tell Terminal how to communicate with the modem.*

You can select one of the **Modem Defaults** from the box on the right. In fact most modems these days are "Hayes compatible" (that is, they work in the same way as a Hayes modem), so you can select the Hayes option button if you are not sure. Or read your modem's manual (or call the technical support line) to find out what should appear in the **Originate** text box. You can generally leave the rest of the dialog box alone.

### By the Way . . .

If your telephone line is a "pulse" line, you should change the **Dial** entry to ATDP. Few lines these days are pulse, though—most let you use either pulse or tone phones.

## Psst! Wanna Know a Shortcut?

Now let's set up a few function keys, to make it easier to work online. You will be able to use the function keys by pressing the key itself, or by clicking on a "key" that will be displayed at the bottom of the Terminal window. Open the **Settings** menu and select **Function Keys**.

Each function key has a line on which you can enter a label and the text that you want to transmit. The bottom of the Terminal window will have two lines of keys—the top line will have F1, F3, F5, F7, while the bottom will have F2, F4, F6, and F8. Take a look at the following figure, for an idea of how this works. Here are the function keys I defined (don't worry too much what they are all about—you'll find out later):

| | | |
|---|---|---|
| F1 | Enter | Pressing F1 or clicking on the button at the bottom of the screen is the same as pressing the Enter or Return key. (The code ^M means Enter.) |
| F2 | Username | This will type my username and press Enter. |
| F3 | Password | This will type my password and press Enter. |
| F4 | Menu | This will type menu and press Enter. On the system I'm about to log onto, this will take me to a menu of options. |
| F5 | xmodem-txt | This will type the command that is used to transmit a text file from the service provider's computer back to mine. |
| F6 | Shell | Instead of typing menu and pressing Enter I can make Terminal type shell and press Enter. This will take me to a UNIX command line. |

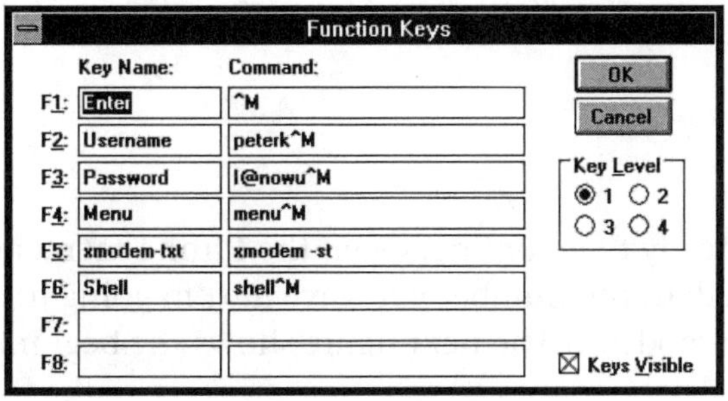

Function Keys

| | Key Name: | Command: |
|---|---|---|
| F1: | Enter | ^M |
| F2: | Username | peterk^M |
| F3: | Password | l@nowu^M |
| F4: | Menu | menu^M |
| F5: | xmodem-txt | xmodem -st |
| F6: | Shell | shell^M |
| F7: | | |
| F8: | | |

OK
Cancel
Key Level
1 2
3 4
Keys Visible

*Use the function keys to help speed up your online session.*

## Other Stuff You Can Change

That's all we need to look at right now. There are other options, however, such as the ability to automatically print the text as it appears on your screen, to "capture" the text in a text file, and to transfer binary files. Spend some time figuring out what your communications program can do for you, and you'll save time in the long run.

### Save It!

Don't forget to save your settings. Open the **File** menu and Select **Save**. Terminal will ask you to provide a filename—type **INTERNET** or something similar, and click on **OK**. Now, the next time you want to use Internet, you can open the existing settings file—you won't have to go through this messing around each time.

## Before Going Online

Before you actually go online, you need to know what you are going to do once you get there. Your service provider should give you a list of options. For instance, the service provider I'm currently using gives me these choices once I've entered my password:

| | |
|---|---|
| *menu* | If I type **menu** and press Enter, I'll see a menu of choices. |
| *shell* | If I type **shell** and press Enter, I'll see a UNIX command line. |

Actually, there are lots of other choices, such as commands that will let members of certain groups get to certain programs. But you really don't need to know all of them, because they are either for system maintenance, or for people other than you. Your system provider or system administrator should tell you what options you have.

## Let's Go!

Now you are ready to go online. Open the **Phone** menu and select **Dial**, and Terminal dials the number you gave it. (I'm going to assume you've installed your modem!) The next figure shows the beginning of our session.

```
Terminal - INTERNET.TRM
File  Edit  Settings  Phone  Transfers  Help
ATQ0V1E1S0=0
OK
ATDT786-8700
CONNECT 14400/ARQ


Annex Command Line Interpreter   *   Copyright 1991 Xylogics, Inc.
C2
Checking authorization, Please wait...
Annex username: peterk
Annex password:

Permission granted

<<<<<<<< Colorado SuperNet, Inc Boulder Annex Terminal Server >>>>>>>

                Type 'help' for available commands

CSN-UCB-annex: menu

Enter | Password | xmodem-txt | | Level: 1
Username | Menu | Shell | | 00:00:17
```

*Getting online is straightforward, once you understand what's going on.*

Let's go through this session piece by piece:

```
ATQ0V1E1S0=0
```

This line tells the modem to get ready, because the modem's about to dial.

```
OK
```

This is from the modem, telling us it got the message.

```
ATDT123-1234
```

This line tells the modem to dial the number.

```
CONNECT 14400/ARQ
```

This tells us that the modem has connected with the service provider's modem.

```
Annex Command Line Interpreter   *   Copyright 1991 Xylogics, Inc.
```

This is a header sent by the service provider's computer. When I saw it I pressed Enter—some systems require that you do so to "get their attention."

```
Checking authorization, Please wait...
```

Another line sent by the service provider's computer. Just wait.

```
Annex username: peterk
```

The service provider's computer sent a line asking for my username. I typed **peterk** and pressed Enter (actually, I clicked on one of the function buttons I set up at the bottom of the Terminal window, but it's the same thing).

UNIX has an irritating habit of not telling you if you entered your login name incorrectly. If you mistype the name, UNIX will ask for your password and *then* tell you that you made a mistake, without letting you know if the mistake was with the password or the login name. That's supposed to confuse bad guys trying to break in to your account. It may confuse you, too.

```
Annex password:
```

The service provider's computer now asks for my password. I type it and press Enter (or click on the password function button). Just in case someone's looking over my shoulder, the service provider's computer doesn't "echo" it back to my computer, so it doesn't appear on my screen.

```
Permission granted
```

The system checks my username and password and tells me it's okay.

```
<<<<<<<< Colorado SuperNet, Inc Boulder Annex Terminal Server >>>>>>>
```

Another "header" line. It just identifies where you are.

```
Type 'help' for available commands
```

This just reminds me that I can type help (and press Enter) at the next line.

```
CSN-UCB-annex:  menu
```

When this line appears, I can type one of the options—I typed menu and pressed Enter, so I can go to the system's Main Menu.

# Problems?

There are a few problems you may run into.

**You see garbage on the screen.** If you see something like __p/÷_´#£ä__, you've probably got something set incorrectly. Check your baud rate, stop bit, parity, and flow control settings.

**You see something like this: ~~xx~xxx~xx.** Your baud rate may be set incorrectly.

**You see something like this at the beginning of lines: ^7M or ^K or ;H2J;H2J24.** You may be using the wrong terminal type.

**Your service provider has a menu system you should see, but you see a jumbled mess.** You're probably using the wrong terminal emulation.

**You can't see the characters you type.** Turn Local Echo on.

**You see every character you type twice.** Turn Local Echo off.

**There's a blank line after each line of incoming text.** Turn off Inbound CR/LF.

**There's a blank line after each line of outgoing text.** Turn off Outbound CR/LF.

**Incoming text is displayed on one line.** Turn on Inbound CR/LF.

## By the Way . . .

Not all problems are at your end—your service provider can also screw up and enter your account information incorrectly. Once you've checked everything at your end, if you are still having problems call your service provider and describe the symptoms. In particular, make sure you are using the correct login name, password, and terminal type. If you are using a dial-in direct account, make sure you have the correct Internet Protocol Host Number.

# What Now?

I'm going to explain how to work on your service provider's computer in the next chapter. But before we move on, let's learn two more things: how to change a password and how to log off.

## Changing Your Password

You'll remember that I told you to change your password when you log on the first time. That way, only you and the system administrator have access to your account, not anyone else who may have seen your password on your account's paperwork.

> **By the Way . . .**
>
> A word about UNIX. Most users will be working on a UNIX system. Even if your computer is an IBM-compatible PC or a Macintosh, the computer to which you are connected and through which you work, will usually be a UNIX machine. So I've talked a lot about the various UNIX commands you can use. But some users won't be on a UNIX machine. Still, much of what you'll find in this book will be relevant. In a few areas, though, a particular command won't work on your system; ask your service provider what command to use instead.

To change your password from the UNIX *shell*, use the **passwd** command. You'll know if you're in the shell if you see something like this on the last line by itself: **teal%**. You probably won't see teal (that's the name of the computer, you'll see something different). And in some cases the % will be replaced by $. Still, what you are seeing is the "prompt," the line that's waiting for you to type something. So, type **passwd** and press Enter. (You'll learn more about the UNIX shell in the next chapter.)

If you are using a menu—some service providers have a list of options from which you can choose—there'll be a menu option for changing the password somewhere. (On the system I'm using, for instance, I select **14. SuperNet Services/** and then *3.* **Change Your Password.**)

Either way, you'll be asked to enter your current password, then you'll have to enter the new one, twice. Because the password won't be "echoed" back to you, you won't see it on your screen when you typed it. Typing it twice makes sure you actually typed what you thought you typed.

> **By the Way . . .**
>
> The system may check the new password before it accepts it—to make sure it's valid and not used elsewhere—and then rewrites the entire password file (containing all users' passwords). So changing your password may take several minutes, depending on what else the computer is doing at the same time. Be patient.

# Logging Out

When you are finished, it's time to log out of your service provider's computer. You don't want to just hang up your modem—that's rude (and anyway, your service provider's computer will continue billing you until it realizes that you've gone).There's a proper way to end a session.

If you are working with a menu system, you'll have to type a particular character. On my system I have to type **q** and the system asks if I want to exit—I type **y**, and my connection is closed. Or I can type **Q** and the connection is closed without the menu system asking me for confirmation first.

If you are at the UNIX shell, there are a few ways of logging out, depending on the type of shell. You may be able to press **Ctrl-D**; type **logout** and press **Enter**; or type **exit** and press **Enter**. Or maybe any of the above. Try them all, and use the one you find easiest. Or add a shortcut to your communication program. For instance, if you are using Terminal you can enter the logout command in a function button, so just clicking on the button logs you out.

Windows Terminal requires that you also hang-up after logging out—select Hangup from the Phone menu. Many, perhaps most, communications programs will hang up your modem for you once they realize the other end has hung up.

## The Least You Need to Know

- Each system's log on procedure will be slightly different—so get the details from your service provider.
- Spend some time learning your communications program. It has lots of useful features.
- As soon as you log on, change your password.
- Use the **passwd** command at the UNIX shell prompt, or find the Change Password option on the menu if you have one.
- Log out using **Ctrl-D**, or by typing **exit** or **logout** and pressing **Enter**. If your service provider's system has a menu, you'll probably type **q** or **Q**.

# Chapter 8
# Menus and Shells, Oh My!

## In This Chapter

- What is a UNIX Shell?
- Using a service provider's menu system
- % and other UNIX prompts you might see

Once you've logged onto to your service provider's computer, what are you going to find? If you are lucky, there'll be a menu system once you get there. If not—and there's a very good chance there won't be one—you'll probably have to use a "command line," the UNIX *shell*. In this chapter, we'll take a quick look at shells and menus; then in chapter 9, you'll get down to some UNIX commands you can practice at the shell. (Most users are connected to the Internet through UNIX machines, though you may find yourself working with a non-UNIX system. If so, check with your service provider for information about working at the "command prompt." And if you have a dial-in direct account, spend some time with your program's documentation.)

If you are used to working with DOS, the term shell may be misleading. In DOS a shell is something that takes you *away* from the command line, that lets you work on the system using menus or a graphical user interface. In UNIX the shell is where you type commands, the equivalent of the DOS command line.

You and UNIX speak different languages. You can't understand UNIX, and UNIX can't understand you. So you use a translator, a *shell*, to communicate. You type commands into the shell, and it translates them into UNIX language. Then, when UNIX wants to tell you something, it tells it to the shell, and the shell translates it into something you've got at least a small chance of understanding.

# Using a Menu (If You're Lucky)

If you are lucky, your system has some kind of menu. This insulates you from the UNIX command line, though not completely—at some point you'll have to get to the command line to do *something* (so you'll want to read the information about the UNIX shell later in this chapter even if you do have a menu to work with.)

But the menu systems used by most service providers are usually not very good. Get a group of Internet users together and you'll hear descriptions such as "pretty primitive" and "horrible." One comment I heard recently, "It's not painless, but it's not awful" might actually be considered a compliment, relatively speaking.

Of course I can't tell you what your system will do. You'll likely have a series of menus that help you select important commands and lead you to different areas of the Internet, and may have a system by which you can use most services by pressing a single keystroke command. Whatever you have, it probably won't be comprehensive—it will probably miss bits and pieces, leaving you to fall back on the shell. Spend some time figuring out what the system can do for you, though. Take a look at your service provider's documentation, as awful as it may be, and spend an hour or two just exploring.

As an example of what a menu may do, let's take a look at the menu in the system I'm using, on Colorado Supernet.

As we've already seen, during the log on procedure I'm presented with a prompt that allows me a choice of what I want to see—a shell or a menu. If I type **menu** and press Enter, this is what I'll see:

```
Terminal - INTERNET.TRM
File  Edit  Settings  Phone  Transfers  Help
 ^*^*^*^  SuperMenu :  Colorado SuperNet's Information Network  ^*^*^*^

                     << SuperMenu Main Menu >>

 --> 1.  About SuperMenu.
     2.  Search SuperMenu Titles <?>
     3.  Commercial Services/
     4.  Communities/
     5.  Databases/
     6.  Education/
     7.  Events & Entertainment/
     8.  File Transfer (FTP)/
     9.  Help/
     10. Libraries/
     11. Mail/
     12. News and Weather/
     13. Phone Books/
     14. SuperNet Services/
     15. Tools for Information Retrieval/


Help ?   Quit q   Main-Menu m   Menu-Up u   BackPg <   NextPg >      Page: 1/1

 Enter      Password      xmodem-txt              Level: 1
 Username   Menu          Shell                   00:08:30
```

*A typical Internet menu from a service provider.*

As you can see, there's an arrow on the left side of the screen, indicating what menu option is selected. I can choose an option in two ways—I can move that arrow up and down the list using the **arrow keys** on my keyboard, and then press **Enter** when it's pointing to the option I want. Or I can type the **number** of the option, and press **Enter**.

Actually, there are a few more ways to get around. Pressing **k** moves the arrow up, **j** moves it down, and **right arrow** selects an option. And once I've selected an option that leads to another menu of choices, **u** (or **left arrow**) brings me back to the previous menu.

Then there's **m**—if I find myself in a menu lower down the "tree" of menus, pressing **m** will bring me right back to the Main Menu. Typing **?** displays help information. Pressing **q** will display a message asking if I want to exit the menu—if I press **y** (as in yes), I'll be logged off the system. Or pressing **Q** logs me off the system without even confirming first.

> **By the Way . . .**
>
> You may notice that the system works very slowly compared to your desktop computer. It's a big computer, but there are lots of people working on it at the same time. When you select a menu option you may have to twiddle your thumbs for 20 or 30 seconds while you wait for something to happen.

What do all these menu options do for me?

**About SuperMenu** Displays information about how the menu system was created. Turns out it's based on Gopher, a public-domain program usually used for digging through Internet to find information. We'll learn more about Gopher in Chapter 21.

**Search SuperMenu Titles** Lets me search for information about my service provider's services by typing a keyword.

**Commercial Services** Takes me to some businesses—I can enter the databases of several booksellers—O'Reilly, UTC, Quantum, and SoftPro—and search for a book or even place an order. And I can contact a company that sells UNIX "add-in and add-on peripherals."

**Communities** This takes me to a list of Free-Nets to which I can connect using *Telnet* (I spoke a little about Free-Nets in Chapter 3, and you'll learn about Telnet in Chapter 17).

**Databases** This lets me "telnet" to other computers, so I can search their databases.

**Education** This also lets me telnet to other computers, but specifically computers at universities or colleges.

**Events & Entertainment** This takes me to a rather limited listing of local events.

**File Transfer (FTP)** Takes me to an automated FTP (File Transfer Protocol) system. FTP is used for finding and transferring files from other computer systems. We'll look at FTP in Chapter 18.

**Help** This takes me to a list of subjects that I might need help with, such as how to change my Backspace key or how to check on how much online time I've used recently.

**Libraries** This lets me search various library and research databases. The menu takes me to many of these resources by telnetting.

**Mail** Takes me to the mail system, so I can send and receive messages over Internet.

**News and Weather** Lets me view news and weather, and, strangely, reach the "newsgroups." Newsgroups on Internet are the equivalent of forums in CompuServe or message areas of BBSs, they are not the same as what we normally think of as the "news." We'll look at newsgroups in Chapter 15.

**Phone Books** Lets me use various directories for tracking down people, such as Whois (see Chapter 14) and directories on other computer systems (using FTP).

**SuperNet Services** Takes me to a menu of options that let me find billing information, change my password, temporarily use the UNIX shell, send a suggestion to the service provider, and so on.

**Tools for Information Retrieval** Lets me use various tools for tracking down information, such as Gopher (Chapter 21), WAIS (Chapter 22), and World Wide Web (Chapter 23).

A menu such as this is a great help. You can get plenty done without ever seeing the UNIX shell and knowing about UNIX commands. But you won't be able to get *everything* done. You may find that you can't use the menu system to FTP or telnet to some systems, you may not be able to transfer files to and from your computer (if you have a dial-in terminal connection), and so on.

If you are lucky enough to have such a system, take some time learning it. Read the documentation and find out what's available. You'll save a lot of time if you know what it can do for you.

# Playing with Shells

Let's take a look at the UNIX shell—even if you have a menu available, you'll eventually want to go to the shell to do *something*, because the menu probably won't have everything you need. You might need to go to the shell to transfer files back to your computer, or to view files stored in your *home* directory on the hard disk (more about the home directory in a moment).

UNIX is an *operating system* used on most large computer systems. An operating system is a program that tells the computer's hardware what each application program wants it to do and vice versa. It "liases" (all right, *makes a liaison*) between the hardware and software. There are lots of different versions of UNIX, but it's unlikely to matter to you which version the service provider's computer is using, as most (but not all) commands will be the same.

There are several UNIX shells you could be using. You probably have the C *shell* (the % prompt) or the *Bourne shell* (the $ prompt). You might also have the *Bourne Again shell*, the *Korn shell*, the *bash shell*, or a modified version of the C shell, such as *tcsh*. And if you're really lucky, you may be able to select *which* type of shell you use when you log on! Ask your service provider what's available if you get a kick out of this sort of stuff.

How do you get to the shell? It may be there immediately when you log in; if not, you can choose it from the menu that appears instead. You'll remember that when we logged in (Chapter 7) we were given a choice of the type of access we wanted. On my service provider's system I can type *shell* or *menu* and press Enter. Shell takes me to the UNIX operating system. If I am at the menu and then decide I want to go to the shell, I can choose a menu command that takes me there. In the case of my service provider I select

```
14. SuperNet Services
```

then I select

```
14. Unix Shell (Suspend Supermenu Temporarily).
```

What do I see when I get to the UNIX shell? Something like this:

```
teal%
```

"Teal" is the name of my service provider's host computer, and % is the UNIX *prompt*, the character that says, "okay, let's go. . . type something."

If you are used to working on a DOS computer, you are used to seeing > as the prompt. The % is the same thing. You may see a **$** prompt instead, depending on the type of UNIX shell you are using. (If you are used to working on a Macintosh, you are used to no prompt at all, but you've probably heard other users griping about them.)

## Is That All?

Hardly. To use the shell, you need a basic understanding of UNIX commands, which is unfortunate since very few DOS users study UNIX in their spare time. Luckily for you, Chapter 9 presents some UNIX basics to help get you up to speed.

## The Least You Need to Know

- Depending on your service provider's setup, you will either be presented with a menu or with a shell interface when you log into the Internet.
- If your service provider has a menu system of some kind, spend some time reading the documentation and figuring it out. Menus can save you a lot of time!
- If your Internet connection consists only of a shell, you'll probably see a UNIX prompt, such as **%** or **$**.
- Don't despair if you don't understand UNIX commands. Just turn to Chapter 9.

**Here's that blank page thing again.**

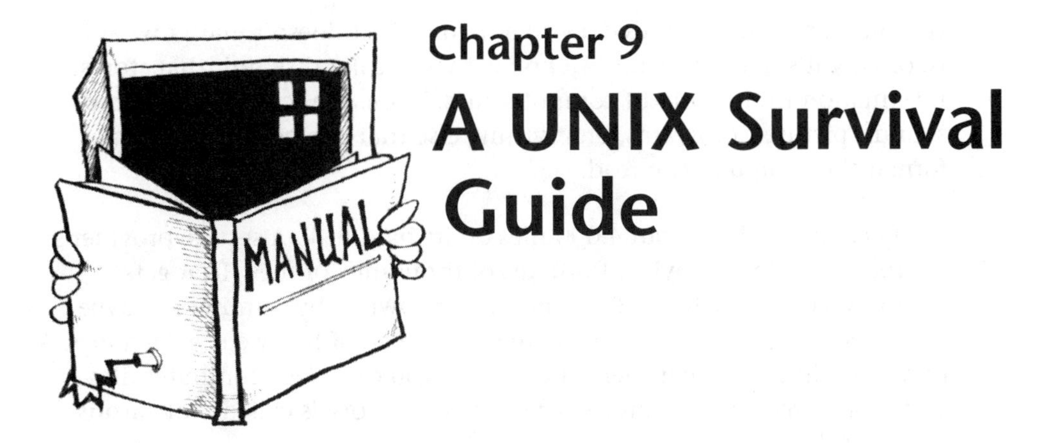


# Chapter 9
# A UNIX Survival Guide

## In This Chapter

- Don't be afraid—it's only UNIX!
- Directories—what's in them, and how to move around
- Files—copying, deleting, moving, etc.
- Reading and finding files

Most Internet users eventually find themselves at a UNIX prompt, wondering what they should type next. (As I mentioned in the last chapter, some systems are not UNIX-based, in which case you are going to have to find more information from your service provider on your dial-in direct program's documentation.)

UNIX can seem intimidating to a new user, but it's actually quite straightforward, once you know what to type. Read this chapter and, while you are working online, refer to the commands on the reference card we've included. You'll soon get into the swing of it.

## A Quick Directory Primer

Most of you probably know a little about directories already, but for those of you who don't, here goes. The service provider's computer (and your computer, probably) stores data on a hard disk. It doesn't matter what this is, or why it's hard. It's simply a box with a circular disk in it that stores information in the form of computer files. These files can contain words, sounds, pictures, programs, or anything else that can be converted to a format the computer can read.

My computer has about 4,000 files on its hard disk. A service provider's computer has tens, maybe hundreds, of thousands of files. That gets complicated, especially when those files are owned by hundreds, maybe thousands, of different people. So to organize all of this we use *directories*. A *directory* is like a compartment into which you can place computer files—and more directories. A directory within a directory is called, not surprisingly, a *subdirectory*.

Subdirectories can also hold computer files—and more subdirectories. It's like a filing cabinet that contains hundreds of file folders, which may contain documents, and many of which contain document folders. And many of those document folders contain not only documents, but smaller folders—which may also contain documents and smaller folders. We call this the *directory tree*, because it's a branching system. It makes finding and using the files on a hard disk much easier.

You will have a *home* directory on the service provider's computer. For instance, this is the *path* of my home directory:

```
/home/clients4/peterk
```

A directory path describes how to travel along the directory tree to a particular directory. In this case, it tells us the hard disk contains a directory named *home*. This directory contains a directory called *clients4* . The *clients4* directory contains a directory called *peterk*, my home directory. The *clients4* directory contains other directories, hundreds of them, one for each of the client accounts. But I don't care about those directories—and even if I did, the computer wouldn't let me get to them, because they don't belong to me.

## Checking Out Your Home Directory Files

Each time you log onto a UNIX system—the service provider's computer—you will be placed "in" your home directory. That is, the computer will assume you are working in the home directory, and that (for instance) new files you create will be placed there. If you transfer files from another computer using FTP (which you'll learn about in Chapter 18), they'll be placed in the directory you were in when you started FTP (though you can select a different directory if you wish).

What, then, can we do with this directory? First, let's take a look at it. Type **ls** and press **Enter**. You'll see a list that looks something like this:

```
my.signature network.guide newlist.txt s-list.txt sig.txt
temp/winq200a.zip winsuper.txt xmodem.log
teal%
```

This list shows the files and directories in your home directory. Notice the *temp/*. The / indicates that this is a directory. The others are files. (On some systems, the / won't appear unless you type **ls -lf**. The f "switch" will also cause the list to include "hidden" files. In UNIX, files beginning with a period are normally hidden.)

Unlike DOS, which uses \ to separate directories in a path, UNIX uses / to separate them.

Let's get some more information. Type **ls -l** and press **Enter**. Here's what you'll see this time:

```
-rw———   1 peterk      258 Oct  8 12:28 my.signature
-rw———   1 peterk    22942 Sep 30 08:05 network.guide
-rw———   1 peterk     5972 Oct  6 13:48 newlist.txt
-rw———   1 peterk    10985 Oct  5 08:13 s-list.txt
-rw———   1 peterk      255 Oct  7 09:15 sig.txt
drwx———  2 peterk      512 Oct  8 12:48 temp/
-rw———   1 peterk   282126 Oct  1 09:18 winq200a.zip
-rw———   1 peterk    15599 Oct  1 09:28 winsuper.txt
-rw———   1 peterk    17911 Oct  8 12:29 xmodem.log
teal%
```

You can see the file or directory name on the right of each line, but there's more. Let's take a look at two lines:

```
drwx———   2 peterk       512 Oct  8 12:48 temp/
-rw———    1 peterk    282126 Oct  1 09:18 winq200a.zip
```

**d** or - The first character indicates whether the entry is a file or directory. A hyphen (-) means it's a file, a **d** means it's a directory.

**r** Means the owner of the object can read it. If he can't, there's a hyphen instead.

**w** Means the owner of the object can modify it (write). If he can't, there's a hyphen instead.

**x** Means the owner of the object can execute it—he can get into the directory, or execute the file (run it) if it's a program file. If he can't, there's a hyphen instead.

The next characters are related to what *other* people can do with the file. Characters 5 to 7 define what members of the user's *group* can do, and the last three characters define what user's who are *not* group members can do. (Each user on a UNIX computer is a member of a group—but we don't really need to get into that.)

**TECHNO NERD TEACHES**

If you really want to know more about this group thing, type **id** and press **Enter** at the UNIX prompt. You'll see your *uid* (user identification number) and your *gid* (group identification) number. Or try typing **who am i** (or maybe **whoami**) and pressing **Enter**. You'll see your login name (and perhaps your terminal ID), along with the date and time.

The first number on the line shows the *link count*, which we don't want to get into. Ignore it.

Next comes the *owner name*. That's you, generally (me in this example). After the owner name, you might see the *group name*—but not in this example. Next you'll see the file size, the number of bytes (characters), followed by the date and time the file or directory was created (or last modified), and finally, the filename or directory name.

# Directory Management, UNIX Style

Oh no, this is *not* going to turn into a book on UNIX. But you need to know a few simple UNIX commands to be able to conquer the shell. (I've also included a quick reference table of UNIX commands on the tear-out sheet at the front of the book.) Here are some UNIX commands you can use to work with directories:

Computer files contain two parts—a listing in a table somewhere, and the actual data, stored on the disk and referenced by the listing. UNIX lets you use different names for the same block of data on the disk (using the **ln** command). The *link* is the information that links the particular table entry to the particular block of data. So if a file has two names, it has two links. The *link number* next to a directory name is the number of subdirectories in the directory, plus two. Why? Because UNIX adds the current directory and the parent directory.

OOPS!

Your Backspace key doesn't seem to work? Try pressing **Ctrl-H** or # instead.

## Viewing the Contents

Use these commands to see what you've got.

| | |
|---|---|
| **ls** | to see a simple list of files and directories. |
| **ls -l** | to show the list with the file sizes and other information. |
| **ls -al** | to list everything, including hidden files. |
| **ls \| more** | to stop the list after every page (press **Enter** to show the next line, or **Spacebar** to show the next page). |
| **ls -l \|more** | for the full-information listing, broken down page by page; you may be able to use the DOS **dir** command to show a full listing (the equivalent of **ls -l**). |

## Moving Around

When you first log on, you are in the *home* directory. This is also the *current* or *working* directory (that is, the directory you are in at the moment). To play around in a different directory, you can change the working directory.

Use the following commands:

| | |
|---|---|
| **cd ..** | to move back to the previous directory level. Important: note that there's a space between the **cd** and the .. (unlike in DOS). |
| **cd *directory name*** | to go directly to a different directory. For instance, type **cd /home/clients4/*othername*** and press **Enter**. |
| **pwd** | to report your current location, in case you're not sure. |

## Creating and Removing Directories

| | |
|---|---|
| **mkdir *directory name*** | to create a new subdirectory in the working directory. |
| **mkdir */existingname/newname*** | to create a subdirectory in a particular directory. |
| **rmdir *name*** | to delete an empty directory. |

## What About Those File Names?

Actually, UNIX is not so far away from the DOS so many of us know and love. But what about those names? These are not your traditional "8.3" DOS names (8 characters in the name itself, 3 in the extension). How about this for a name, for instance:

```
Where-can-I-find-the-source-to-C-news?
```

Yes, this really is a filename. Here are a few rules for naming files in UNIX:

- Names are *case-sensitive*, which is tech-speak meaning that the computer regards uppercase and lowercase letters differently (unlike DOS, for instance). **FILENAME.TXT** is *not* the same as **filename.txt**. This is very important—you can save hours of confusion if you remember this.
- While old versions of UNIX limited you to 14 characters in a name, new versions have no limit.
- Don't use these characters: / | \ ! @ # $ ^ & * ( ) . And some UNIX versions don't like you to use **?** or – (minus sign)
- You may be able to put spaces in filenames, but don't bother, because it may upset some programs.
- You can use periods to separate words, such as *Where.can.I.find.the.source.to.C.news?*. UNIX doesn't have file extensions in the same way DOS does. It simply regards the period as a character like any other.

## UNIX: The Sensitive Operating System

UNIX is case-sensitive in general, not just in its filenames. In other words, you have to type the commands correctly—you can't type RM if you want to delete a file (it's **rm**). This can be confusing at times. Sometimes UNIX will fail to carry out a command, and it'll quickly be obvious why—you typed *text.txt* instead of *Text.txt*, for instance. But sometimes you'll have to put your thinking cap on to figure it out, especially when using long names. For instance, if you type

```
rm Textwin7thOct93.zip
```

and UNIX tells you that file doesn't exist, maybe you mistyped a character. Or maybe you used a zero instead of an uppercase letter O in *Oct*. (On many machines, in fact, you may not be able to tell the difference between a zero and an O. If your communication program allows it, select a font in which the characters are distinct.)

# Messing with Files

If you are using a dial-in terminal connection, you'll be copying files from other computers into your directories on the service provider's computer. What are you going to do with all these files? At some point you may want to do a *file transfer* to get them onto *your* computer. We'll explain that in Chapter 19. But eventually you'll want to delete some, rename some, and even move some. Here's how.

## Deleting Files

Use the **rm** command to delete a file—for instance:

```
rm delete.this.file
```

## Moving Files

Use the **mv** command to move a file. Type

```
mv filename directoryname
```

## Renaming Files

You can also use the **mv** command to rename a file. Type

```
mv oldfilename newfilename
```

## Copying Files

To copy a file, use the **cp** command. For instance:

```
cp originalfilename newfilename
```

To copy the file to another directory, type

```
cp originalfilename directoryname
```

To copy the file to another directory with a new name, use

```
cp originalfilename directoryname/newname
```

## Viewing a Text File

There are a couple of ways to view the contents of a text file. If it's a short file, type

```
cat filename
```

and the file will be displayed on your screen. If it's long, type

```
more filename
```

and it will be displayed page by page—press **Spacebar** to see the next page, or **Enter** to move line by line. And press **q** to stop viewing the file.

## Finding Lost Files

UNIX has some neat little tools for finding files. If you know the name of the file you want, but aren't sure where it is, type

```
find . -name filename -print
```

If the file is in the working directory (the one you are in when you use the command), UNIX will simply repeat the name to you, like this:

```
./filename
```

If it's in another directory, it will show you which, like this:

```
./directoryname/filename
```

The **find** command will only search through the working directory and its subdirectories (and their subdirectories)—it won't go the *other way*, and search the directory of which the working directory is a subdirectory. And remember, make sure you type the name correctly, with each letter in the correct case. You can't type **lost.file** if you are looking for **Lost.File**.

## Using grep

If you don't know the name of the file you need, but you do know some of the text inside it, you can use the **grep** command. Type

```
grep "these words" *
```

For instance, you might type

```
grep "IBM main frames" *
```

and press **Enter**. The asterisk tells grep to search all the files in the current directory. You can enter a filename if you want to specify which file or files; you can omit the quotation marks if you are only looking for one word. For instance,

```
grep IBM work.txt
```

searches for *IBM* in the file called *work.txt*, and

```
grep IBM w*
```

searches for *IBM* in all the files that begin with the letter *w*. When grep finds what it's looking for, it will name the file in which it found the text, and display the line or lines containing the text, like this:

```
winsuper.txt:in IBM main frames, workstations and personal
computers
```

*Grep*? What kind of name is that? It means *global regular expression and print*. Obvious once it's explained, isn't it?

Using this command, you'd better get the case of the specified text correct—if you typed **ibm**, it wouldn't find IBM. But if you are not sure of the case, you could type

```
grep -i "these words" *
```

The command will find matches regardless of the case of the letters. The only problem with this is that you are also telling grep to search for partial matches. If you are searching for *she*, you'll also get *sheet*, *shear*, and *sheaf*.

If you don't want to see the line containing the matching text (you just want the filename), you can use **-l**, for instance:

```
grep -l -i "these words" *
```

There's plenty more you can do with *grep*, and there are even *egrep* and *fgrep* commands. But that is—you guessed it—beyond the scope of this book.

## More Useful UNIX Stuff

Here are a few more useful UNIX commands:

**Repeating the last command** If you want to repeat the command you just carried out, type !! and press **Enter**. This only works in the C shell, though. If you are using the Korn shell, try **r** instead. Tough luck if you are using the Bourne shell.

**Canceling what's happening** If you want to stop what is happening, try pressing **Ctrl** and **C** at the same time (**Ctrl-C**). If that doesn't help, try **Ctrl-X**, or **q**.

**Finding Help** You can see instructions explaining a command using the **man** (as in "manual") command. Type **man *commandname* | more**. For instance, **man grep | more** will display the help information on the **grep** command. (The **| more** part of the command tells UNIX to display the information one page at a time—press **Spacebar** to see the next page, **Enter** to move a line at a time.)

## Did You Leave Something Running?

It's easy in UNIX to make a mistake and leave a program stalled or running in the background. You might try to run a program and get a message like **There are stopped jobs**, or **You seem to have left a rn running, process 13178**. This is not always your mistake, of course—sometimes the system just locks. So you end the session—leaving a program running in the background. Try typing **fg** and pressing **Enter** to run the program in the "foreground." Or "kill" the process. First, find the *PID* (process ID)—type **ps -u** (or, if this doesn't work, try **ps -e** or **ps -a**) and press **Enter**. You'll see something like this:

```
USER    PID   %CPU  %MEM   SZ   RSS  TT  STAT  START TIME  COMMAND
peterk  13178  0.0   0.2   384  112  p2  D     12:03 0:02    rn
```

Then type **kill %PID** and press **Enter**.

## There's Plenty More

No doubt this introduction to UNIX has left you eager for more. There's plenty more you can do in UNIX, but I'm not going to explain it here (except specifics, such as using xmodem and zmodem for transferring files, explained in Chapter 19). I've got enough on my hands with the Internet. If you'd really like to find out more about UNIX and how it can improve your life, get hold of a good book on the subject, and settle in for some good times. (Try *The First Book of UNIX*, published by Alpha Books!)

### The Least You Need to Know

- The UNIX shell prompt (a % or $) tells you that you can enter a command.
- Type **cd** and press **Enter** to return to your home directory. Type **cd *directoryname*** to go directly to a particular directory.
- Type **cd ..** and press **Enter** to go back one directory (but remember to leave a space between cd and ..). If you are not sure where you are, type **pwd** and press **Enter**.
- Type **ls -l | more** to see a full-information listing of a directory, page by page.
- Use **rm *filename*** to delete a file, **mv *filename* *directoryname*** to move a file.
- Use **more *filename*** to view a text file page by page.
- Cancel commands using **Ctrl-C**, **Ctrl-X**, or **q**.

# Part II
# An E-Mail Extravaganza

*Is there anyone out there? Yes indeed, there is. There are millions of people hooked up to the Internet in one way or another, and you can send electronic mail (e-mail) to almost any of them. Pretty staggering, huh? Internet's e-mail system gives you a rapid, cheap link to literally millions of other computer users. In fact, e-mail is the only reason most Internet users ever log on.*

*Like everything else on Internet, though, e-mail is not as straightforward as it could be. Addressing messages is a pain, and so is getting them returned to you because you typed a period in the wrong place. But don't worry—the chapters in this section break it down into bite-sized pieces. You'll learn about addressing messages, using different mail readers and writers available, and even how to send computer files as mail messages. And if you can't find someone's mail address, I'll show you how to track it down.*

# Chapter 10
# Please Mr. Postman: An Intro to E-mail

## In This Chapter

- The e-mail advantage
- Making yourself understood
- Addressing the envelope
- Sending mail to another network
- Easy living with mail programs
- E-mail etiquette

Internet's most popular feature is its *e-mail* system. Few Internet users use even a small fraction of the vast information resources available to them. Rather, they use Internet as a cheap and convenient way to send messages to friends across town, to colleagues across the world.

E-mail (from the term *electronic mail*), simply means sending messages across a computer network. Instead of writing a message, placing it in an envelope, and dropping it in a mailbox, you can send the message across Internet to any user anywhere.

# Why Use E-mail?

The advantages of e-mail are obvious. It's cheap—often cheaper than sending a message by mail—and almost always cheaper than making a phone call. It's fast. Messages can be delivered in seconds. There's no waiting for a week or two while your letter is delivered to France, no waiting on hold while the receptionist finds the person you need to contact.

### By the Way . . .

The last time I e-mailed my buddy Al Gore, he received the message *and responded* within ten seconds. (Well, admittedly not personally, but he's been busy. His and Bill's Internet mailboxes receive around 30,000 messages a month—though some of them are addressed to Socks, Chelsea's cat—so they respond automatically with a polite message, saying "thanks very much, but I've been busy," or something similar. If you have something special to say, you can contact Al at **vicepresident@whitehouse.gov**. If you'd prefer to chat with Bill, try **president@whitehouse.gov**.)

E-mail is also convenient. A friend told me he uses E-mail to contact a colleague in Japan. He doesn't need to worry about time zones, figuring out exactly when his Japanese colleague gets up, or finding the overlap between an American day and a Japanese day. Nor does he need to worry about explaining to a Japanese receptionist what he wants. He just sends a message over Internet, and reads the reply the next day. (Nothing's 100%, however—sometimes messages will take hours to get through; sometimes—not often—they'll get lost.)

You can also use e-mail to send the same message to several people at a time. You can create *mailing groups*—write one message, then tell your e-mail program to ship it out to everyone in a particular group. Or simply write a message addressed to one person, then "CC" ("carbon copy") it to other e-mail users.

# Two E-Mail Caveats

Of course, e-mail is not the solution to all the world's ills, and it can't replace a nicely-formatted report or a face-to-face meeting. By its very nature, e-mail has some limitations; you should be aware of them.

## None of That Fancy Stuff . . .

E-mail can get your message across, but it's no substitute for a word-processing program's output. When you're sending text messages with Internet e-mail, they're just that: text. No special formatting is allowed. You can't use bold or italic text, for instance. You can enter carriage returns, to format paragraphs and lines, but that's about all.

E-mail of the near future, however, will probably overcome this limitation. Already messages can be sent over CompuServe using bold and italic text, and a variety of different fonts (if the user has a special *navigator* program, that is). No doubt that feature will eventually reach Internet as well.

## . . . and They Can't See Your Face

Many people regard e-mail messages as a form of conversation—sure, we're using written messages, but somehow it's less formal than if it were written on paper. So people often write as if they were chatting to the recipient, in a very informal manner. The problem with this is that the recipient can't see your face, and can't hear the inflection in your voice. Consequently, what you regard as a flippant or sarcastic remark may be regarded as deadly serious when the person to whom you sent the message reads it.

This is both an individual and cultural problem. Some people (and some cultures) are simply more serious than others. What you feel is "obviously" a joke may not be so obvious to the other person. My compatriots, the British, have a very dry sense of humor, so you can probably get away with using sarcasm in messages to British friends and colleagues without worry. But you may want to be more careful with messages to others.

Many people simply call these character faces "smiley faces," but if you'd like to impress your friends with a bit of technobabble, you can call them *emoticons*. And if you really want to impress your colleagues, get hold of *The Smiley Dictionary* (Seth Godin). It contains hundreds of these things. You wouldn't have thought there were that many possible combinations that made sense, eh?

## Face-Time Substitutes

Over the last few years, e-mail users have developed a number of ways to clarify the meaning of messages. You might see <g> at the end of the line, for example. This means "grin," and is shorthand for saying, "you know, of course, that what I just said was a joke, right?" You may also see :-) in the message. Turn this book sideways, so that the left column of this page is up and the right column is down, and you'll see that this is a small smiley face. It means the same as <g>, of course—"that was a joke, okay?"

## Emoticons Galore

The smiley face is just one of many available symbols, though by far the most common. You *might* see some of the following, and may want to use them yourself. Perhaps you can create a few of your own.

| | |
|---|---|
| `:-(` | Sadness, disappointment. |
| `8-)` | Kinda goofy-looking smile. Or wearing glasses. |
| `:->` | A smile. |
| `;-)` | A wink. |
| `*<¦:-)` | Santa Claus. |
| `:-&` | Tongue-tied. |
| `:-o` | A look of shock. |
| `:-p` | Tongue stuck out |
| `,:-) or 7:^]` | Ronald Reagan |

You might even try really weird stuff, like this smiley cow I found in the alt.ascii newsgroup (more about newsgroups in Chapter 15):

```
]:o_
 ¦O =
 ¦_o=
```

Or you can get really artistic with something like this (don't turn your head sideways for this one):

```
   ;~; ,     .~.
  ._#_.)  [ _#_ ]
 ( @ @     '^. .^'
 ' ).(       \./
  ( v )      /q\
   \¦/       \¦/
   (¦)       (¦)
   ~ ~       ~ ~
```

And lots of people put smiley art in their *signature* files, so it goes out with every message they send (there's more about signature files in Chapter 11). Like this:

```
              - - - - - - - - - - - - - - - - -   ,,        .

     _  .
   /# /_\_    ¦  Speed limit????  69 Dude!!!  ¦    ¦\_¦/__/¦
  ¦  ¦/o\o\   ¦                               ¦    / / \/ \  \
  ¦  \\_/_/   ¦      'Kacagolan of XYZ'       ¦   /__¦O¦¦O¦__ \
 / ¦_   ¦     ¦                               ¦   ¦/_ \_/\_/ _\ ¦
¦  ¦¦\_ ~¦    ¦    Mt. Ararat,  /\   Armenia  ¦   ¦ ¦ (____) ¦ ¦¦
¦  ¦¦¦ \/     ¦                /    \         ¦    \/\___/\__/
¦  ¦¦¦_       ¦        /\    ////\ /\/\\      ¦   (_/          ¦¦
 \//  ¦       ¦      ///\\\////////\\\\\\     ¦    ¦           ¦¦
  ¦¦  ¦       ¦___/////\\\\//////\\\\\\\\\____¦    ¦           ¦¦\
  ¦¦_  \      ¦ RAFFI RAZMIG KOJIAN ¦  HAPPY  ¦    \          //_/
  \_¦  o¦     ¦ raffi@watserv.ucr.edu¦ HAPPY  ¦     \______//
  /\___/      ¦ raffik@aol.com      ¦ JOY JOY¦      __ ¦¦ __¦¦
 /  ¦¦¦¦__    ¦- - - - - - - - - - - - - - - ¦     (____(____)
    (___)_)   ¦   -Picture by Norman Sippel-  ¦     /***********\
```

## Message Shorthand

There are a couple of other ways people try to liven up their messages. One is to use obscure abbreviations, such as:

BTW By the way.

FWIW For what it's worth

FYI For your information.

IMHO In my humble opinion.

IMO In my opinion.

LOL Laughing out loud (used as an aside to show your disbelief).

OTF On the floor (laughing). (Used as an aside.)

PMFBI Pardon me for butting in.

PMFJI Pardon me for jumping in.

RTFM Read the &*^%# manual.

ROTFL or ROFL Rolling on the floor laughing (used as an aside)

ROTFLMAO Same as above, except with "laughing my a** off" added on the end. (You didn't expect me to say it, did you? This is a family book.)

TIA Thanks in advance.

YMMV Your mileage may vary.

The real benefit of these is that they confuse the average neophyte. They certainly don't save any real money—e-mail is so cheap that cutting a message by 15 or 20 characters won't have much affect on the "bottom line."

You'll also see different ways to stress particular words—you can't use bold and italic, remember. A word may be stressed by using underscores (_**now!**_), or, perhaps less frequently, with asterisks (***now!***).

# Now, Where's That Address?

You might imagine that addressing a message would be simple. But Internet is such a conglomeration of different networks, and provides access to so many different e-mail systems, that addressing a message may not be straightforward. Let's take a quick look at a few rules.

Remember that your Internet "address" is made up of two parts: your login name, and your "domain" name. These two parts are separated by an @ sign—the text to the left of the sign is your login name, to the right is your domain name. Take, for instance, *peterk@csn.org*. The first part, *peterk*, is the login name, *csn.org* the domain name. The domain name is used to describe *where* you can be found on the network—you will be given this name when you first open an account. (We looked at this in detail in Chapter 6, so if you skipped that chapter you might want to backtrack for a moment.) Internet looks up your domain name, finds the associated number—the address of the computer that is handling your mail—and uses the number to direct your message to the correct place.

Internet uses the *Domain Name System* (DNS) to look up names. The *local server* (computer) starts by contacting a *root server*, a computer that knows the number associated with the highest-level domain in your domain name. For instance, if you are sending a message to *joeblow@apotpeel.com* the root server tells your local server which computer is responsible for the *.com* domain. The local server then contacts the *.com* computer and asks where *apotpeel* is. Then, with the complete domain number it needs, the local server addresses the message and sends it off.

When you send a message through Internet, all the system initially cares about is the name of the computer (the domain) that collects mail for the person you are trying to reach. It's kind of like the mail-sorting machines at the Post Office that only look at the ZIP codes. So, for instance, if you are sending a message to *joeblow@thiscompany.com*, Internet looks only at *thiscompany.com*. Even if the first part of the address is wrong—if the login name is really *joblow*, not *joeblow*—the message will still get to the correct domain. But when the domain checks the login and finds it doesn't match any login in that domain, the message will be sent back.

## Addressing E-mail to Your Compuserve Friends

After Internet, one of the most popular public e-mail system is that run by CompuServe. Eventually you'll probably want to send an e-mail message to a CompuServe user, or have a CompuServe user send you something. CompuServe is linked to Internet, so you can, indeed, send and receive CompuServe messages.

All you need is the CompuServe ID (identification number) of the person to whom you want to send a message. CompuServe IDs are generally five-digit numbers, followed by a comma, followed by two or more numbers, such as 71601,1266. You can't put a comma in an Internet address, though—you have to replace the comma with a period. So, to send a message to this person you would enter an address in this format:

**71601.1266@compuserve.com**

To send a message from CompuServe to your Internet account a user would precede your Internet address with INTERNET:.

For instance, to send a message from CompuServe to *joeblow@thiscompany.com*, a CompuServe user would enter the following as the address:

**INTERNET:joeblow@thiscompany.com**

Messages are sent between CompuServe and Internet very frequently, and it works quite well.

There are other rare CompuServe address formats. For instance, some organizations have private CompuServe mail areas, in which case you would use this format: ***user@department.organization*.compuserve.com**. We've put a document on the accompanying disk that explains how to address messages to just about any network connected to the Internet. See Section C at the end of the book for more information (it also tells you where to find the MAILGUID.TXT file on the Internet, in case you don't have a DOS computer and can't use the copy that came with this book).

# Yet More E-mail Links

There are a number of other e-mail systems that you can send messages to through Internet, such as Bitnet, Fidonet, Sprintmail, MCImail, and UUCP. But the system is not perfect, and what may work in one area may not work in another—you may have to try a couple of different forms of the address to get a message through. (Once you've found the form that works for that network, you'll be able to use that format for future messages.)

## PRODIGY

To send a message to a Prodigy Information Service user, you will add **@prodigy.com** to the end of the user's PRODIGY address.

## America Online

To send a message to an America Online information service user, you will add **@aol.com** to the end of the America Online user's normal address. To go the other way, the America Online user simply uses a normal Internet address without modification.

## GEnie

To send a message to the GEnie information service, you will format the address like this: **recipient@genie.geis.com**. To send a message the other way, a GEnie user would tag **@INET#** onto the end of the normal Internet address (for instance **peterk@csn.org@INET#**).

## Bitnet

Bitnet addresses look very similar to Internet addresses—they are in the form *name@host*. You will then add **bitnet** to the end, so the highest-level domain is called **bitnet**. For instance, the address might be something like

**jblow@golden**. Try **jblow@golden.bitnet**. If that doesn't work, ask your system administrator or service provider for an Internet-Bitnet *gateway* name (a gateway, in this context, is a a computer that links one network to another). Then replace the @ with % and throw away the .bitnet (**jblow%golden**). Then place an @ followed by the name of the Internet-Bitnet gateway. The Bitnet address will end up looking like this: **jblow%golden@cunyvm.cuny.edu.**

## Fidonet

Fidonet addresses look something like this: **Joe Blow 1:6/1.2**. Replace the space between the names with a period, and replace the space between the last name and first number with an @ (**Joe.Blow@1:6/1.2**). Then add the letters p, f, n and z in front of the numbers (**Joe.Blow@p1:f6/n1.z2**). Replace the colon and backslash with periods, and add .fidonet.org (**Joe.Blow@p1.f6.n1.z2.fidonet.org**). *Is this fun, or what?*

Still, the message might not go through. If not, replace the @ with % and add @zeus.ieee.org at the end (**Joe.Blow%p1.f6.n1.z2.fidonet.org@zeus.ieee.org**).

## MCImail

This works in a similar way to messages sent to CompuServe. Simply add **@mcimail.com** to the end of an MCImail address. MCImail addresses can be numbers (**1111111@mcimail.com**), or names (**joe_blow@mcimail.com**).

## Sprintmail

If you are given a Sprintmail address you will probably only get two parts, a name and an organization—such as **Joe Blow/APOTPEEL**. You will have to drop these items into the following address, with a period between the first and last name. For instance:

**/PN=Joe.Blow/O=APOTPEEL/ADMD=TELEMAIL/C=US/@sprint.com**

## UUNET

UUNET addresses look like Internet addresses—**joeblow@golden.uucp**. Remove the .uucp and replace the @ with %, and put an @ at the end (**joeblow%golden@**). Ask your system administrator or service provider for a UUNET-Internet gateway, and add that to the end. For instance, **joeblow%golden@uu.psi.com**.

You may be given a UUNET "path" that looks like this:

. . .**!uunet!*host*!*name***

This isn't really an address. It shows the route taken to get to its destination—once you get the message to **uunet**, it will send it on to **host**, which will send it on to the person. You have to reverse this: ***name%host@gateway***.

No, it's not just you—all these different mailing-label schemes really *are* a royal pain in the derriere.

## And More!

The networks we have mentioned aren't the only ones, they're just the most common. Here are a few more you may run into:

- GEONET (GeoNet Mailbox Systems)
- NASAMAIL
- ENVOY (Telecom Canada)
- BIX (Byte Information eXchange; Byte magazine)
- ATT (AT&T)
- MFNET (Magnetic Fusion Energy Network)
- and a couple of dozen more

There's no way I'm going to describe all of these, so if you'd like to see a detailed description of how to work with all these networks, take a look at the MAILGUID.TXT document on the accompanying disk. See Section C for information on how to use this file, or how to find the file in a non-DOS format.

### Don't Lose Those Addresses!

If someone gives you an e-mail address, don't lose it! Add e-mail addresses to your address book from business cards, letters, e-mail you receive, other people's address books. Losing an Internet e-mail address is not like losing a telephone number. Lose a phone number and you can look in the phone book or call information. But getting an e-mail address can be a *lot* more difficult. We'll discuss some of the options in Chapter 13, but none are perfect. So if you ever come across an address you think you might need, save it!

## E-Mail Helpers: Just Add Addresses

You'll probably have a choice of different e-mail programs you can use. These are simply "interfaces" or "front ends," programs that sit between you and Internet.

Your service provider will probably provide you with a couple of different programs from which to choose. They vary from the arcane and irritating to the reasonably good. This *is* Internet, though—don't expect anything wonderful. Take a look at what's available, and pick the one you find easiest to use. If you've got the time and inclination you can search for other mail programs on the Internet and experiment with them.

There are a couple of dozen programs available, several for each type of computer system you are using, so it's not possible for this book to show you exactly how your system will work. However, in the next chapter we'll take a look at a couple of different programs. And all programs have a variety of common features, so if you understand the feature in one program you'll be able to use it in the others.

## Internet Etiquette

There's an etiquette to Internet (sometimes called *Internetiquette*). Follow these rules to avoid upsetting people and embarrassing yourself. These rules apply to e-mail and the newsgroups, which you'll learn about in Chapter 15.

**Don't write something you will regret later** Lawsuits have been based on the contents of electronic messages, so consider what you are writing and whether you would want it to be read by someone other than the recipient. A message can always be forwarded, read over the recipient's shoulder, printed out and passed around. . . You don't *have* to use Internet—there's always the telephone. (Oliver North has already learned *his* lesson!)

**Consider the tone of your message** It's easy to try to be flippant and come out as arrogant, or try to be funny and come out as sarcastic. When you write, think about how your words will appear to the recipient.

**Give the sender the benefit of the doubt** If a sender's message sounds arrogant or sarcastic, they may be trying to be flippant or funny! If you are not sure what they are saying, ask them to explain.

**TURN YOUR CAPS LOCK KEY OFF** MESSAGES THAT ARE ALL CAPS ARE DIFFICULT TO READ. YOU ARE NOT USING A TELEX MACHINE, SO WRITE LIKE A NORMAL HUMAN BEING.

**Don't use lines over 60 characters long** Some mail systems will let you enter lines as long as you wish. Keep them to about 60 characters, so that the lines can be indented a few characters and still be short enough to fit on a screen. (When you forward or reply to a message, the existing text is usually indented a little way).

**Read before you send** It will give you a chance to fix embarrassing spelling and grammatical errors, and to reconsider what you've just said.

**Be nice** Hey, there's no need for vulgarity or rudeness. (Except in certain newsgroups, where it seems to be a requirement for entrance.) However, you can get away with a lot more in the Internet than you can on CompuServe, America Online, PRODIGY, or any other commercial service.

## The Least You Need to Know

- E-mail can be a quick and inexpensive way to keep in touch with friends and colleagues.
- <g> means "grin." So does :-).
- You can use dozens of different smileys, or *emoticons*—but don't expect anyone to understand them all.
- Addressing most e-mail messages is no problem. You may run into problems now and again. You can find detailed information about addresses in the MAILGUID.TXT file. See Section C at the end of the book.
- Experiment with the mail readers available to you and find the easiest to use.

# Chapter 11
# UNIX Mail: Down to the Nitty Gritty

## In This Chapter

- Starting UNIX Mail
- Viewing, reading, saving, and deleting
- Replying to a message
- Sending your own messages
- Inserting text files into messages
- Using vi, a UNIX text editor

If you are lucky, your service provider will have some kind of improved e-mail system that you can use, such as Pine or Elm. If you are unlucky, you'll only have a standard UNIX mail interface.

In this chapter, I'm going to explain how to use the UNIX mail system—because almost all service providers supply it. In the next chapter I'll describe Pine as an example of what a mail program does, and get into some more advanced mail stuff, such as sending computer files as mail and using a mail signature. Whatever system you have, you'll be able to do many or most of the same things you'll see in these chapters, though perhaps in a slightly different manner.

Even if you are using a Mac or PC, once you've dialed into your service provider's computer, you are probably working in UNIX. Your computer is simply working as a *terminal* connected to the UNIX computer. (Not all Internet host computers are UNIX machines, though the majority are.) Thus, most users will be able to use the UNIX mail system.

# Getting Your Mail

If you don't have a mail system such as Pine available, you'll have to use the basic UNIX mail system. It's not the best system available, but it's usable. We'll assume you are at the UNIX shell's prompt. To get to the mail system, type **mail** and press **Enter**. You'll see another prompt, probably &. For instance:

```
teal% mail
&
```

Mail's commands let you view a list of messages, read messages, and reply to and compose messages.

## By the Way . . .

When you first enter mail, the first message in the list—the oldest one—is the *current message*. As you'll see, certain commands work on the current message. For instance, if you press **Enter** at the **&** prompt, Mail will display the current message. But the current message changes, depending on various actions you take. Once you've read message number 1, for instance, the message number 2 becomes the current message. (Sounds confusing, but you'll catch on quickly.)

## Looking A-head(er)

When you look at a list of mail messages, you're actually looking at the message *headers*, brief descriptions of the message size, date, recipient, sender, and so on. You can view a list of your mail messages using these commands:

**h** Displays the first 20 message headers.

z Displays a screenful of message headers. Each time you use the command you see the next screenful. Or use z- for the *previous* screenful.

(These won't do anything if you have less than one screenful of message headers!)

**top *numbers*** Shows the top few lines of the messages, showing where the message comes from, and when it was sent (plus some information you won't want, such as what route it took to get to you). For instance, **top 1-5** shows the top information for messages 1 to 5; **top 5-$** shows the information for messages 5 to the end of the list.

**f** Displays the header for the current message.

**f *numbers*** Displays the headers for the specified messages; **f 5-$** shows the headers for message 5 to the end of the list.
Here's what a header list looks like:

```
>    1 aesmoot@aescon.com Thu Oct  7 18:06   36/1350  Re: More on SLIP
     2 Markus.Sadeniemi@osteri.funet.fi Fri Oct 8 05:45 45/1709 Re:Internet Book
     3 pgold@copper.Denver.Colorado.EDU Fri Oct 8 12:50 19/614 Re: Do a favor?
U    4 root             Sun Oct 10 01:43  157/5019  teal:/homeclients4 is ful
P    5 aesmoot@aescon.com Sun Oct 10 03:54   46/1905  Re: More on SLIP
     6 tpowell@cerf.net   Sun Oct 10 23:18   62/2372  Internet Book (fwd)
     7 Melisa_Parker@qm1.psi.com Mon Oct 11 15:13   35/1198  Internet Book
     8 root             Tue Oct 12 01:41  144/4630  teal:/homeclients4 is ful
     9 hfunk@CNRI.Reston.VA.US Tue Oct 12 12:49   27/935   INET-Connect
N    10 tpowell@cerf.net  Thu Oct 14 09:46  50/1741  Re: Internet Book (fwd)
N    11 aesmoot@aescon.com Thu Oct 14 09:54   34/1182  Re: More on SLIP
```

(Okay, this is a mess, but it's UNIX.) What does this information tell us? Some of the messages have a letter in the left column: a **U** means the message hasn't been read, a **P** means you've just used the **pre** command to "preserve" the message in the mailbox instead of moving it out of the box (more on this later), and **N** means it's a new message, one that has arrived since the last time you checked your mail. The rest of the header contains the following information: a message number, the address it was received from, the date and time it was received, the size of the message (the number of lines and characters), and the message subject. One of the messages is also preceded by >. This is the *current* message, the one on which commands will operate unless you select another message as the current one. (You'll see how to do that in a moment.)

## Read It and Smile

To actually read a message, you may prefer to read it in a text editor, or save it in a text file and read it later, as we'll see in a moment. But you can use one of these commands (you probably won't very often, but you *could*):

**p** Displays the current message.

**p $** or simply **$** Displays the most recent message.

***number*** Displays the message assigned that number. For instance, press **5** and press Enter to view message 5.

**p *numbers*** or simply ***numbers*** Displays a particular message. For instance, **p 9** displays message 9; **p 9-15** displays messages 9 to 15; **p 9-$** displays messages 9 to the most recent. Or use any of these commands *without* the p, that is, just type the numbers you want.

**t** The **t** command works in the same way as the **p** command.

**Enter** or **n** If you've just entered mail, it displays the first message in the list. Otherwise it displays the message following the current message.

**-** Displays the message immediately before the current message.

**Ctrl-C** If you want to stop a message from scrolling across your screen, use **Ctrl-C**, or maybe **Ctrl-X**.

The problem with all these commands is that unless a message is short, it's going to scroll by so fast you won't be able to read it. And **Ctrl-C** will stop the message completely, not stop and start it.

There are several things you can try. You can use an editor to view the message, you can let the mail save the message in **mbox**, the saved-message file, or you can save the message in a file that you create. You'll learn to do all these things in the following sections.

## Viewing Mail with an Editor

Every UNIX shell has an *editor* available, in which you can view, create, and edit text files. In fact you may have several editors available to you. Find out from your system administrator or service provider which editors are available, and try them out.

To put a mail message into an editor, use **e *number*** or **v *number***. For instance, typing **e 5** and pressing **Enter** places message 5 in the editor. Then you can scroll through the message at leisure, probably by pressing the arrow keys. (The **e** command puts the message in the editor chosen with the **setenv** command. The **v** command puts it in the **vi** text editor.)

To change your default editor, go to the UNIX shell prompt (not the mail prompt), then type **setenv EDITOR *editorname*** and press **Enter**. For instance, **setenv EDITOR vi** tells your system that whenever you call the editor, you want to use **vi**.

Later in this chapter, we'll look at vi, a text editor that almost everyone has access to. If the editor you're using is vi, to exit it press **Esc** three times, then type **:q!** and press **Enter**. (To exit another text editor, check your documentation to find out how.)

## Stick It in a File

You can copy your messages into a text file if you wish, and then read them at your leisure later. Use one of these commands:

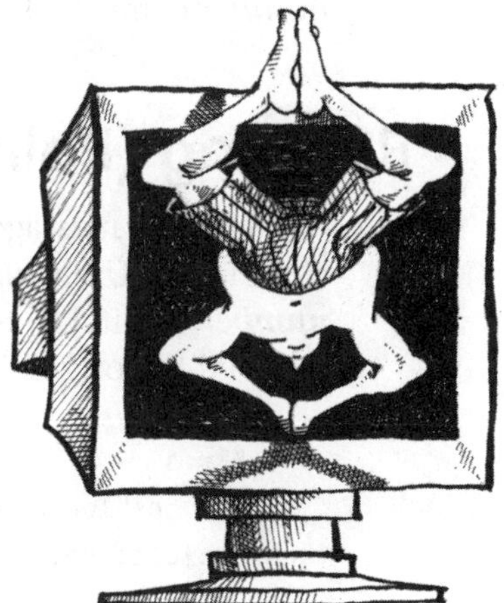

**s *numbers filename*** This will save the entire message (or messages) in the named text file. For instance, **s 4-$ msg.txt** will save all of the messages, from number four to the last, in a file called msg.txt.

**w *numbers filename*** This works in the same way as the **s** command, except that it won't include the "From" line. You still get all the other header rubbish, so you might as well forget this command.

Once you've got the messages into a text file, you'll have to leave the mail system to read them—you'll be able to use the UNIX **more** or **cat** commands to read them (see Chapter 9), or even copy them back to your computer (if you have a dial-in terminal connection) and read them in a word processor there.

Use this file-saving method to organize your messages into "folders." You could create a file called *personal*, one called *hobbies*, one called *business*, and so on, and copy messages into the appropriate file.

When you use the **q** or **quit** commands to close the mail system, the mail you have just read is removed from the mailbox and saved in a file called **mbox**. You can use the same (**more** or **cat**) methods to read this file. If you don't want a message to be removed and placed in the mbox file, use the **pre *number*** command before you exit. ("Pre" stands for "preserve" and that's exactly what it does to the message you specify.)

### ZAP! Deleting Messages

Tired of that dull old message? Delete it. This not only removes it from the mailbox, but makes sure it is not copied into the **mbox** file. Use the **d *number*** command. For instance, **d 3-7** deletes messages 3 to 7. Actually the message is still there (for the moment at least), though you won't see it in any lists. Still, if you want to retrieve *(undelete)* the message, use the **u *number*** command. For example, **u 3-7** would bring those messages back.

## Replying (Politely) to Messages

If you find a message that makes you want to reply, use one of the **r** commands. Use **r *number*** to reply to the sender of the message; use **R *number*** (capital R) to reply to the sender *and* send a copy to everyone who received the original message. You'll see something like this:

```
& r 1
To: joebloe@apotpeel.com
Subject: Re: New model
```

The mail system entered the new message's **To:** line and **Subject:** line for you automatically, so you can now write a message. (If you want to cancel a reply, press **Ctrl-C** twice.) But let's step back a bit, and look at how to send a message from scratch.

**By the Way . . .**

Sometimes your mail program may not be able to figure out the **From** address, and will be unable to create the **To** address. If this happens, the message will be returned to you, and you'll have to re-enter the correct address manually.

## Quoting or Forwarding the Original

You'll soon notice that it's common among the e-mail crowd to include the original message in the reply. That's simply a way to remind the recipient (the author of the original message), of what he or she said. Most mail programs have some simple way to do this. In UNIX Mail, you use the **~f *number*** command. For instance:

```
& r 1
To: joebloe@apotpeel.com
Subject: Re: New model
~f 1
```

You used the **r 1** command to reply to message 1, then used the **~f 1** command to include the original message in the reply. Then you can use a text editor (use the **~v** or **~e** command) and insert your message within the body of the original message—this way, you can answer the original author's points one by one, by following the original text with yours.

Of course, this is also a simple way to forward a message, to send it on to someone else. Simply start writing a message, then use the **~f *number*** command to include another message.

There's a variation of this command, the **~m *number*** command. It includes the file in the same way that ~f *number* does, but it also places a tab before each line, so the recipient can quickly identify which lines he wrote. (More advanced mail programs use a character such as > instead of the tab, or in conjunction with it, to make it even clearer.)

# Starting from Scratch: Composing Your Own Messages

You don't even have to start the mail system to begin sending a mail message. Whether you are inside the mail system or still at the UNIX-shell prompt, use this command (if you *are* inside the mail system, you can abbreviate this **mail** command to simply **m**.):

**mail** ***address***

(Remember, we discussed addresses in Chapter 10.) An example might be **mail joebloe@apotpeel.com**. You can send the message to several people, by separating addresses with a comma and a space. (As you'll see later, you can also use an *alias* or *mailing list* here in place of a single address.)

When you press **Enter**, the mail system prompts you for a subject. Type the message subject—something that succinctly describes what is in the message—and press **Enter** again. Now you'll see a blank line. Just start typing. You'll have to press the **Enter** key at the end of each line—don't make the lines too long (don't go over about 60 characters).

When you've finished the message, press **Enter**, type a period (.) on the last line, and press **Enter** again. The mail system will ask you for a **Cc:** (the address of the person you want to send a copy of the message to). You'll enter the Cc addresses, if any, in the same way you entered the original address. Then press **Enter** to send the message. Here's what it all looks like:

```
& mail joebloe@apotpeel.com
Subject: Your new potato peeler
Mr. Bloe.
I've just seen an ad about your new super duper
potato peeler. I wonder if you could send me information
about this, with details on how to order 10,000.
Thanks v. much.
.
Cc: fred@ourplace.org
&
```

If you were in the mail system when you started to send the message, you will still be at the & prompt. If you were at the UNIX-shell prompt (probably the % prompt) when you started, you'll find yourself back there, so you can write messages from the UNIX shell without really going into the mail system.

You can also send a Cc: by using the **~c *address*** command anywhere in the message. And you can send a "blind" carbon copy with the **~b *address*** command. A copy will go to the people sent "blind" copies, but the original message won't show any indication of these other copies.

## Adding a Text File to a Message

Sticking a text file into a message is useful in three cases. The most common one is when sending a long message. You can type it in a word processor and save it as a text file, begin your mail message, and plop down the saved file into the message at the right spot. *Much* easier than trying to write the whole long thing in a clunky UNIX editor.

To cancel the message at any time while writing it, press **Ctrl-C** twice.

Another use is for transmitting non-text files—as text. For instance, let's say you want to send a database or spreadsheet file, a picture or a sound, or whatever kind of non-text file you wish. Well, Internet's mail programs don't generally handle such files. They usually permit only text messages to be transmitted. But don't fear; there is a way around the problem. Convert the file into text first, transmit it, and then convert it back to its original format at the other end. (We'll look at this procedure in the next chapter.)

The third common use is to add a *signature* to a message. This is usually four or five lines of text telling the recipient something about the sender—it's usually the sender's name and address, something like this:

```
=====================================================
¦ Joe Bloe              ¦Internet: Joeblo@this.here¦
¦ 2291 N. Coors Drive   ¦   CompuServe: 11601,12666¦
¦ Podunk, CO, 80000     ¦      Phone:  303-555-4321¦
=====================================================
```

The signature is often something else, perhaps something weird. I recently received a message with the signature, "Barney eats children!" (My two-year-old vehemently disagrees, claiming that Barney only eats "food.") You might also see quotes from famous people, pieces of poetry, or pictures created with the text characters. Some users go to such an extent that various *newsgroups* (which you'll learn about in Chapter 15) have taken to rejecting messages with long signatures.

If you want to use a signature file, create the file and place it in your home directory. Give it a simple name, such as **s**.

Now, when you want to insert your signature file in your message—or any other kind of text file—type **~r *filename*** on a new line (make sure the ~ is the first character on the line) and press **Enter**. (That's why you want a nice simple filename, like **s**, so it's easy to type each time.) You can then continue with the message if you wish. When you send the message, the text file will be inserted at the ~r point. Other mail programs let you add signature files to messages automatically—you tell the program where the file is, and it will add it for you each time you write a message. With UNIX Mail, though, you must use the ~r command.

**By the Way . . .**

In the next section, you'll learn about a text editor you can use for writing mail messages. But you can only use this **~r** command while in mail itself, not in an editor. Many editors have their own (usually superior) methods of including text files—check your system's documentation.

# Using vi—An Exercise in Futility?

Most UNIX systems come with an amazing text editor called **vi**. This editor is to most modern word processors what a horse and cart are to a Chevy truck—it'll get the job done (with a little effort), but you won't use it if you've got the Chevy available. Still, in case you *don't* have a Chevy, let's take a look.

When you've started your mail message, place the cursor on a new line (you can start on the first line if you want, or type some of the message and then start vi), type ~**v**, and press **Enter**. You'll see something like this:

Once you've used vi a few times, you might even get to *like* it. To be fair to UNIX freaks, if you know what you are doing, it can be quite quick and easy to use, somewhat like EDLIN is to old-time DOS users. Just don't admit it to your friends.

```
~
~
~
~
~
~
~
~
~
"/tmp/Re26352" 0 lines, 0 characters
```

This, believe it or not, is vi's *text editor screen*, the equivalent of being inside a word processor's screen or window.

Vi has two modes: a *command mode* (in which you enter commands such as moving the cursor), and an *input mode* (in which you type). When you first start vi you are in command mode, so press **a** to change to input mode (we'll come back to that in a moment). Now you can type. You are going to have to enter *carriage returns*—that is, press **Enter**—at the end of each line (vi won't do it for you). Don't make the lines too long; limit them to about 60 characters.

In some versions of vi, you may be able to use the cursor keys to move the cursor around. Other versions don't like it, and do strange things (like adding a line). In such a version, you'll have to use the command mode to move the cursor. You may find you can use Backspace in vi, to move the cursor back a few spaces so you can type over something.

## Jumping into Command Mode

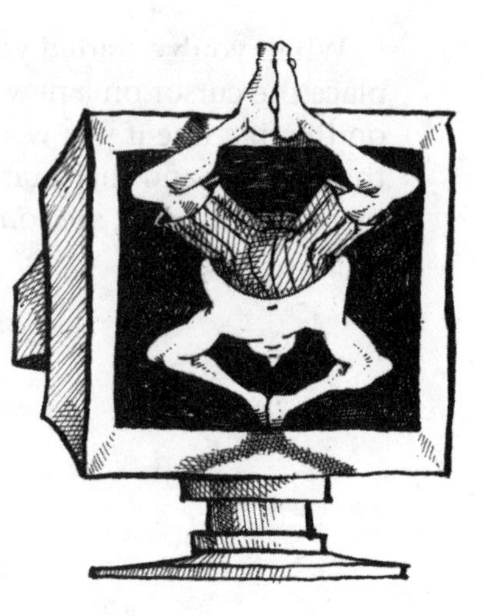

Now, when you are ready to move the cursor back to fix something, you'll need to enter command mode. Press **Esc** once. Then use one of these wonderful commands (remember, they're case-sensitive!):

**To move the cursor** Use the **arrow** keys. If they don't work, try **h**, **i**, **j**, and **k**. You can also press + to move to the beginning of the next line, - to move to the beginning of the preceding line (use the hyphen and + sign on the keyboard, not the numeric keypad), **G** to move to the end of the file, and **1G** to move to the beginning of the file (isn't this great?). And **Ctrl-f** will move you down one screen at a time, **Ctrl-b** back one screen at a time.

**Adding text** When you've got the cursor in position and are ready to add new text, you have a few options, each of which returns you to input mode. Press **R** to replace text, **i** to insert text before the cursor position, **a** to insert text after the cursor position, **A** to add text at the end of the current line, or **O** (the capital letter O, not zero) to add text on a new line in front of the cursor position.

**Deleting text** To delete text, press **dd** to remove an entire line, **D** to delete from the cursor to the end of the line, or **x** to delete a single character. Just press and hold the **d** key to delete line after line.

**Undo** To undo changes, press **u** to undo the last change, or **U** to undo changes to the current line.

**Save** To save your changes, but continue working in vi, type **:w** and press **Enter**.

## Closing vi

To close vi, press **Esc** three times. Your computer will beep. Now type **ZZ** (remember, uppercase), and press **Enter**. This will save the work you have done. Or type **:q!** and press **Enter**. This abandons all the work you have done and closes vi. Either way you will see **(continue)**. You can now continue working in your e-mail message. You can add more text, though you won't be able to go back and make changes to the previous stuff (unless you reopen vi, of course). Finish the message in the usual way—type a period (.) on a blank line, and press **Enter**; enter a Cc name (if needed) and press **Enter** again.

You opened vi using the **~v** command. If you use **~e** instead of ~v, you'll probably see another text editor, perhaps *emacs* or *pico*. It's the text editor that is set using the **setenv EDITOR** command at the UNIX prompt. For instance, **setenv EDITOR pico** or **setenv EDITOR emacs**. You may find it easier to use than vi. Try pico, if your system has it—I think it's easier to use than vi or emacs.

# Closing the Mail System

How do you get out of the mail system? There are a couple of ways. Type **x** and press **Enter** to leave all the read mail in your mailbox. Or type **quit** (or simply **q**) and press **Enter** to leave the system and move the messages you have just read into a text file called **mbox**, which you will be able to read later. Deleted messages are removed, and unread messages remain. But messages you *send* are not placed anywhere—you've got no record. One of the advantages of the more advanced Internet mail systems is that they save a copy of your sent mail.

## The Least You Need to Know

- Start UNIX mail by typing **mail** and pressing **Enter**.
- View a list of messages by typing **h** or **z** or **z-** and pressing **Enter**.
- Read a message by typing its message number and pressing **Enter**.
- Reply to a message by typing **r** and the message number and pressing **Enter**.
- Use the **~f** or **~m** commands followed by the message number to include the original message in the reply or in a new message.
- Start a mail message (from the UNIX prompt or the Mail prompt) by typing **mail address** and pressing **Enter**.
- To use a text editor while writing a message, type **~v** or **~e** on the beginning of a line and press **Enter**.
- Cancel a message by pressing **Ctrl-C** twice.
- Close Mail with the **q** or **x** command. The **x** command tells Mail not to remove messages you've read.

# Chapter 12
# Still More On Mail

## In This Chapter

- Mailing with aliases
- Mail reflectors—public mailing lists
- Getting an automatic response
- Sending files by converting them to ASCII
- Reading and writing messages in Pine
- Signature files revisited

In the last chapter you saw how to send mail if you're a poor unfortunate soul using the UNIX mail program. Though you might not realize it from gazing at the UNIX prompt, there are many cool things you can do with mail, and I'll tell you about a few of them in this chapter. We'll also take a look at Pine, a popular mail program that you might have available.

## Psst! Use an Alias!

Some Internet addresses, you have no doubt noticed, are rather long and confusing. You'll save yourself a lot of time if you create a nickname or *alias* list that speeds up sending messages to people you mail to frequently.

Files with a period before the name are *hidden files*. They won't appear when you use the **ls** command at the UNIX prompt to list your files. If you want to see all the hidden files, use the **ls -a** command.

This information is stored in the *.mailrc* text file, a file that stores information about your mail system; it may be in your home directory.

If you are using UNIX mail, you'll have to edit this .mailrc file. Use a text editor to open that file. For instance, if you want to use vi to edit the file, type **vi .mailrc** and press **Enter**. Now, add the aliases you want to use in this format:

**alias *nickname address***

For instance:

**alias joeb joebloe@apotpeel.com**

Now, instead of writing the entire address each time you want to send a message to this person, you can just type **joeb**.

You can create mailing lists in the same way. For instance, let's say you want to create a mailing list containing members of your sales staff. We'll call the list **staff**. Enter each address in this format:

**alias staff *address***

You can put several addresses on one line, by separating them with a comma and space:

Some mail programs let you create aliases and mailing lists without messing with the .mailrc file. See your program's documentation.

**alias staff *address*, *address*, *address***

Now, when you are ready to send a message to everyone on the list, you'll just type **staff** in the address field, and the mail system will pick out all the individual addresses for you.

## Reflective Mail? Using Mail Reflectors

There's another kind of mailing list, a *mail reflector*. This is a kind of public mailing list—when a message is sent to a reflector's address, it's sent out automatically to all the people in the reflector's mailing list. This is a convenient way to control a mailing list used by a group of people—everyone in the sales department, the history department, or whatever—centrally.

You won't be able to create your own mail reflector—that's done by a system administrator. You can, however, request that you be added to the mail reflector—usually by sending a message to an address like this:

***username*-request@*hostname***

For instance, if you want to join the **history@wecu.edu** you would send a message to

**history-request@wecu.edu**.

Mail reflectors are often used to create "discussion groups." People send messages to the reflector, and everyone on the list gets to read the message and respond if they wish. There's a different way to join these "LISTSERV" groups—we'll look at this in more detail in Chapter 16.

# Automatic Mail Responses

You may have noticed how some e-mail addresses send a response back to you automatically. For instance, you might send a message to info@*hostname*, and whatever you write in the message is ignored—the system simply sends a "form letter" back to you, describing its services. Lots of people and organizations use this automatic-response system, even the President of the United States.

It's pretty simple to set up your own automatic response. You're most likely to want to do this when you go on vacation, so (not surprisingly) there's a UNIX command called **vacation**. At the UNIX prompt type **vacation** and press **Enter**:

```
teal% vacation
```

Then you'll see a text editor, something like this:

```
This program can be used to answer your mail automatically
when you go away on vacation.
```

```
You need to create a message file in /home/clients4/peterk/.vacation.msg
first.

PICO 1.7      File: /home/clients4/peterk/.vacation.msg          Modified
```

Type your message. Notice that you can type $SUBJECT to make the vacation program grab the incoming message's subject line and drop it into the message.

```
From: peterk (via the vacation program)
Subject: away from my mail

I will not be reading my mail for a while. I'm going to Disneyland!
(Well, okay, I'm going on a sales trip.) Your mail regarding "$SUBJECT"
will be read when I return.

^G Get Help ^O WriteOut ^R Read File^Y Prev Pg  ^K Del Line ^C Cur Pos
^X Exit     ^J Justify  ^W Where is ^V Next Pg  ^U UnDel Lin^T To Spell
```

When you are finished, close the text editor (in this case, by pressing **Ctrl-x**). The program will ask you some simple questions (such as "Would you like to see the message now?") and then send you on your way.

That's it. Now, each time a message comes in, your message goes out automatically. When you come back and want to stop this, use the vacation command again:

```
teal% vacation
```

The vacation program will show your messages to you, and let you discontinue the auto-response or continue it.

**By the Way . . .**

Many UNIX systems will have this vacation program. But if you find that it isn't on the system you're using, ask your service provider if something similar is available.

# Sending Computer Files by Internet Mail

Internet's mail system transmits *text*. That is, the only thing being transmitted is text characters—Internet isn't even transmitting a *file*, really, it's just sending characters, which are then placed in a file at the other end. That means you can't send computer files containing programs, sounds, desktop-publishing or word-processing pages, spreadsheets, graphics, smells, or whatever else programmers have figured out they can store in a computer.

There is, though, a way around this problem. You can convert a file to text, send the *text file*—which could be huge—across Internet, and then have the recipient convert it back to its original format. There are various programs for doing this: **uuencode** and **btoa** are UNIX programs for doing this, and **BinHex** is a Macintosh program. There's also a UUENCODE program for DOS computers (included on the disk with this book!). There are others available, as it's a relatively simple programming task.

Okay, I lied. You **CAN** send computer files by Internet. It's just not easy. You can use a system called MIME (Multipurpose Internet Mail Extensions) to do so. But you're going to have to do so without *my* help, because MIME is in its infancy, not widely used, and difficult to work with. Believe me, it's *way* beyond the scope of this book. The Pine mail program has MIME, though, so you might want to play with it—to quote the authors, its "an early implementation of MIME so we undoubtedly have made some made mistakes."

For instance, let's say you want to use Internet to send a colleague a small program you have written, or maybe a photograph. The file is called YOURDATA.TIF. You can encode it on your computer, or on your service provider's computer. We'll look at the latter case first.

## Converting the File in UNIX

Let's assume the YOURDATA.TIF file is on the service provider's computer, ready to be sent with mail. First, let's convert it to ASCII:

```
uuencode ourdata.tif <yourdata.tif> 1.uue
```

This will use the YOURDATA.TIF file to create an ASCII file called **1.uue**. It also puts the name "ourdata.tif" inside the ASCII file; when decoding the file, the recipient has the option of using the name you specify, or of giving it a new name. You don't have to do this—if you omitted **ourdata.tif**, the actual filename would be inserted instead—**yourdata.tif**.

Now, you include this encoded file in your mail message. You'll start a message, write a line or two if you wish—explaining to your colleague what the file is, and perhaps even providing instructions on how to decode it. Then you'll send the message.

When the file gets to the other end, your colleague will see the beginning of the message and realize it's an encoded file. The next step at that end is to save the message in a file, using whatever command the recipient's mail program uses to do so (UNIX mail, for example, uses the **s *filename*** command).

Then your friend will decode it. Let's take a look:

```
uudecode savefilename
```

This will decode the saved file (***savefilename***). It will then save the converted file in a file that bears the name you included in the original (in this case, **ourdata.tif**). If your colleague prefers a different name, that too is possible:

```
uudecode savefilename decodefilename
```

Once the file is decoded, your colleague can use it, or do a *file transfer* to get it back to his or her computer—which we'll look at in Chapter 19.

Your colleague shouldn't even have to worry about removing the actual message text and header from the file before converting. The uudecode program can figure out where the encoded text begins and ends.

## Encoding and Decoding on Your Computer

You can also encode and decode files on your own computer, transferring them to and from the service provider's computer as needed. In fact UUENCODE and UUDECODE—which converts back to the original format—are so useful and simple to use that we've included DOS versions on the bundled disk. (See Section C for more information.) The program works in the same way as the UNIX version. See the included documentation file for more detail.

There's a significant problem with the uuencode program you are likely to have on your service provider's computer. If you convert a file to ASCII, then send it in e-mail to *another network*—to CompuServe, for instance—the recipient will probably be unable to decode the file because some of the characters have been corrupted. In some cases it will be decodeable, but generally it won't.

The latest version of Richard Marks' DOS version of UUENCODE and UUDECODE (written to coincide with this book), gets around this problem. And if you are sending files to systems such as CompuServe or America Online, the recipients won't have the uuencode and uudecode programs available "online" as Internet users have—they will have to download their mail files and then convert them on their own computers. They can find UUENCODE and UUDECODE somewhere in the information service's libraries, but you may want to send the programs to them by U.S. Postal Service mail if you plan to send files by e-mail regularly.

## Requesting Files with E-mail

In Chapter 18 you'll learn about using FTP, a method by which you can "travel" to computers all over the world and grab files of all kinds: programs, graphics, sounds, text and word processing documents, and so on. There are also a few methods for using Internet's mail system to grab files automatically. As this isn't, strictly speaking, e-mail—but simply a way to *use* e-mail to automate file transfers—I'm not going to cover it here, but I'll explain how it works in Chapter 19.

# Back to the Real World—Using a Mail Program

If you are lucky, you have a mail program other than UNIX mail. The service provider I'm working with uses Pine, a mail interface that is relatively easy to use. (No, it's probably not as good as the e-mail system you use on your company's network, or as good as the one that comes with the CompuServe navigator you use—but it sure beats the plain ole' UNIX mail interface.) Let's take a look at how Pine works. (Even if you don't have Pine, you may want to scan the list of commands, to get an idea of what your program should be able to do.)

## Using Pine

To get to Pine, I have to select the **11. Mail** option from my service provider's Main Menu, then select **1. Read or Send Mail**. You can also run it directly from the UNIX shell, by typing **pine** and pressing **Enter**.

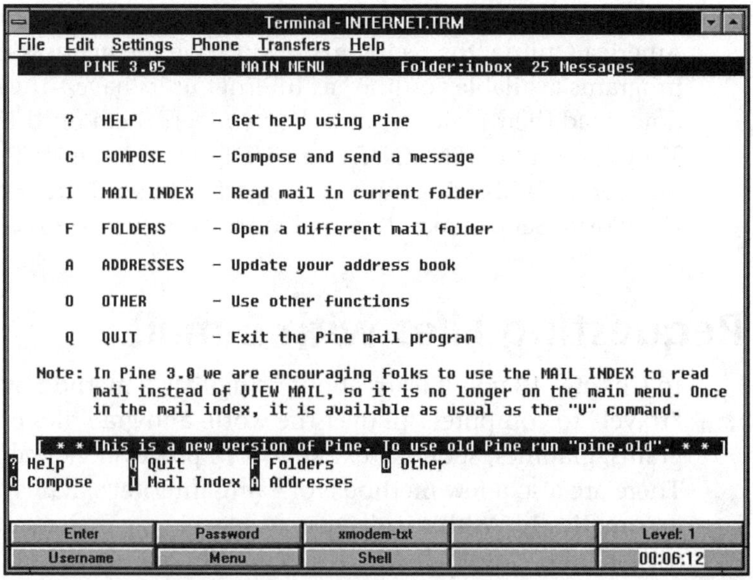

```
Terminal - INTERNET.TRM
File  Edit  Settings  Phone  Transfers  Help
      PINE 3.05           MAIN MENU         Folder:inbox  25 Messages

          ?   HELP          - Get help using Pine

          C   COMPOSE       - Compose and send a message

          I   MAIL INDEX    - Read mail in current folder

          F   FOLDERS       - Open a different mail folder

          A   ADDRESSES     - Update your address book

          O   OTHER         - Use other functions

          Q   QUIT          - Exit the Pine mail program

   Note: In Pine 3.0 we are encouraging folks to use the MAIL INDEX to read
         mail instead of VIEW MAIL, so it is no longer on the main menu. Once
         in the mail index, it is available as usual as the "V" command.

  [ * * This is a new version of Pine. To use old Pine run "pine.old". * * ]
? Help         Q Quit         F Folders      O Other
C Compose      I Mail Index   A Addresses

Enter      Password      xmodem-txt            Level: 1
Username   Menu          Shell                 00:06:12
```

*The Pine Main Menu is your starting point for the mail system.*

I then see another menu with several options, as you can see in the next illustration. I can select the option I want by typing the letter that precedes it.

**?—HELP** View the Pine user's manual.

**C—COMPOSE** Write a message.

**I—MAIL INDEX** Read the mail in the current folder. I can select the folder I want to use with the F command, but by default the current folder is the "inbox," the folder that holds incoming mail.

**F—FOLDERS** If I select this, I see a list of mail "folders." (Each folder is actually a text file that holds the messages.) There's my *inbox, sent-mail, saved-messages* (a file that holds messages to me that I've read), *sent-mail-oct-93, sent-mail-sept-93,* and so on. I can use the arrow keys to select the one I want.

**A—ADDRESSES** Pine has an "address book," a file in which I can save the addresses of people I send messages to. When I'm writing a message, I can quickly view the address book and "drop" the correct address into place. The address book also lets me set up mailing lists and aliases (though Pine calls them "nicknames").

**O—OTHER** This lets me get to a few commands I don't use often. I can read a "news" file about Pine (a sort of README file that contains information about the current release). If I need to leave my terminal for a while, I can lock my keyboard (I'll have to type my login password to get working again). I can enter a new login password, or select a printer (if you're lucky, your communications program will let Pine print a document on your computer's printer). One more command lets me view the amount of space used by my mail folders—a useful little utility, because if I use too much disk space, I have to pay an extra fee.

**Q—QUIT** Exits the program and takes me back to the menu system or to the UNIX shell.

## Using the Mail List

To read my mail, I type **I**, which displays a list as in the following illustration. To read a message, I use the **arrow** keys to select it, then press **Enter**. To see the next page of the index, I press **Spacebar**.

```
Terminal - INTERNET.TRM
File  Edit  Settings  Phone  Transfers  Help
     PINE 3.05        MAIL INDEX        Folder:inbox  Message 25 of 25

   20  Oct  6 InterNIC Reference  (2,906) How to Order Books
   21  Oct  6 InterNIC Reference  (6,379) North American Internet Access Provi
   22  Oct  6 InterNIC Reference (47,595) PDIAL: Public Dialup Internet Access
   23  Oct  6 InterNIC Reference  (2,165) Re: Connecting to Internet
   24  Oct  6 Eddy Mullet        (23,689) Re: Internet Book
   25  Oct  7 Ed Krol               (630) Re: Internet Book

? Help       M Main Menu P Prev Msg   - Prev Page F Forward    D Delete
O OTHER CMDS V View Mail N Next Msg SPACE Next Page R Reply    S Save
Stop  Pause  Bytes: 59392  Receiving: SESSION4.TXT
Enter     Password     xmodem-txt          Level: 1
Username  Menu         Shell               00:18:33
```

*Pine's mail index is a lot easier to use than UNIX mail is!*

As you can see from the two lines at the bottom, there are a number of other commands.

**?—Help** Displays more help information.

**M—Main Menu** Takes you back to Pine's Main Menu.

**P—Prev Msg** Moves the highlight up the list of messages.

**-—Prev Page** Displays the previous page in the list.

**F—Forward** Lets you create a new message, and puts the selected text in the message so you can forward it.

**D—Delete** Marks the message as *deleted* (puts a **D** in the left column). When you quit Pine, you'll be asked if you want to get rid of the deleted message, or you can use the X command to remove it immediately.

**V—View Mail** Displays the selected message. This is the same as pressing Enter.

**N—Next Msg** Moves the highlight down the list of messages.

**SPACE—Next Page** Press **Spacebar** to see the next page in the list.

**R—Reply** Lets you send a reply to the selected message. You'll be asked if you want to include the original message in the reply; if you say yes, Pine will indicate each line of the original with a > so the person you are replying to can see the original text easily. And if the original message went to other recipients, you'll be asked if you want to "reply to all recipients."

These commands are *not* case-sensitive, by the way. Pressing **D** is the same as **d**.

**S—Save** Lets you save a message in a particular folder. You can also create a new folder with this command. This is similar to UNIX mail's **s** command (though UNIX mail doesn't think of the file as a "folder").

If you type **O**, you'll see a few more commands:

**E—Export Msg** Lets you save the selected message. The same as UNIX mail's s command.

**C—Compose** Lets you begin writing a new message.

**U—Undelete** If you deleted a message, you can use this to undelete it.

**T—Take Addr** Grabs the address from the selected message, and drops it into the address book.

**G—Go to Fldr** Lets you go directly to one of the other mail folders, such as sent-mail.

**O—OTHER CMDS** Displays more commands (we'll look at them in a moment).

**Z—Sort Folder** The folder is initially sorted by the order in which the messages were received. But you can use this command to change the order, sorting them by the subject, the From name, the date sent, the size, or in reverse arrival order (with the most recent at the top of the list).

**L—Print** This may print the message on your printer if your communications software allows it.

**X—eXpunge** If you use the D command to delete a message, the message is marked with a **D** in the left column. The X command will actually remove it from the list.

**J—Jump** Lets you jump to a particular message number—quite useful if you have a huge list of messages.

**W—Where is** Searches the message Number, Date, From, and Subject for text you can specify.

**Q—Quit** Closes Pine.

## Reading Mail

If you select a message and press **v** or **Enter** you can read the message. You'll see most of the commands that we've just looked at, with a few variations. The - and **Spacebar** commands now move you through the message itself (- is up, **Spacebar** is down).

There's an **I** (Mail Index) command to take you back to the message list. And there's an **A** (Attachments) command. This is intended for use with the MIME (Multipurpose Internet Mail Extensions) system we mentioned earlier. **A** lets you extract the non-ASCII attachments, or, if the attachment is a GIF file, view the picture (maybe—it depends on your terminal). However, even if you are not using MIME (you probably won't be), you can still use the **A** command to strip out all the header garbage, extracting the body of the message and dropping it into a file.

## Writing Messages with Pine

As you've seen, you can begin writing a message several ways with Pine. The **C** command starts a brand new message; **R** replies to the selected message—and, if you wish, includes the original message in the new one; **F** lets you forward a message, putting the original into a new one. In the following illustration, we've got a brand new message.

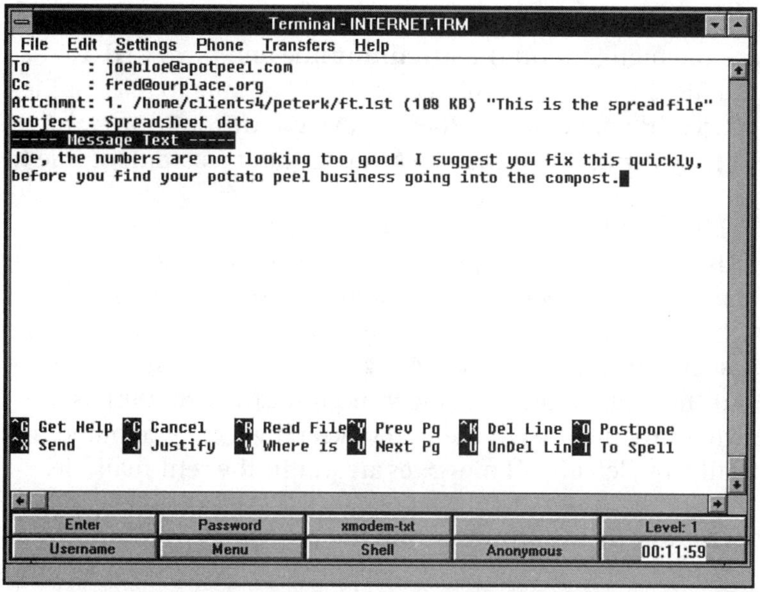

*Entering a mail message into Pine. Notice that this one has an attachment.*

Let's take a look at what you can do here.

```
To       : joebloe@apotpeel.com
Cc       : fred@ourplace.org
Attchmnt: 1. /home/clients4/peterk/ftpsites.lst (108 KB) "This is
the spread file"
Subject : Spreadsheet data
```

The commands that are available vary, depending on which line contains the highlight. While on the first line, **To:**, you can use the **Ctrl-T** command to go to the address book; you'll select an address and then press **M** to copy it into the To: line.

You can use a similar method with the **Attchmnt** line. Again, this is for MIME attachments, non-text files that you want to send with the file. MIME is in its infancy, and even the authors of Pine say it may not work correctly. You can experiment with it if you want, but remember that the recipient will also need "MIME-enabled" software to be able to read the file. If you place the highlight on the **Attchmnt** line and press **Ctrl-T**, you'll see all the files in your home directory. You'll be able to select a file, and even move to other directories. When you've got the one you want, you can press **S** to select it. You'll then be asked to enter a comment line to go with it.

There's also the **Ctrl-R** command, which is available as long as the highlight is in any of the header lines. This adds two new header lines: **Bcc** (Blind carbon copy) and **Fcc** (File carbon copy). We discussed blind carbon copies in the last chapter—it's when a message is sent to the blind-carbon-copy people, but the original message shows no indication that it has been done. And the file-carbon-copy is a method of keeping a copy of outgoing mail automatically; by default, all messages are put in the sent-mail file.

Here's what else you can do while writing the message:

**Ctrl-G—Get Help** Displays help information about composing messages.

**Ctrl-C—Cancel** Cancels the message, without saving or sending.

**Ctrl-R—Read File** Inserts a text file. This is the same as UNIX mail's ~r command. You'll be able to select from a list of files in your home directory, and move around into other directories.

**Ctrl-Y—Prev Pg** Moves up the message to see what you've already written.

**Ctrl-K—Del Line** Deletes the current line.

**Ctrl-O—Postpone** Lets you save the message without sending it. The next time you try to compose a message, you'll be asked if you want to continue with the postponed message.

**Ctrl-X—Send** Sends the message.

**Ctrl-J—Justify** This reformats the paragraph the cursor is in—Pine assumes that a paragraph is ended with a blank line. Any contiguous lines not separated by a blank will be reformatted to clean up ragged edges (useful if you've been editing the text).

**Ctrl-W—Where is** Searches your message for what you've written, or for text from other sources (inserted using the Ctrl-R command, or from a message you are replying to or forwarding).

**Ctrl-V—Next Pg** Moves down the message.

**Ctrl-U UnDel Lin** Deletes the last lines you deleted. You can combine this with Ctrl-K to move blocks of text around in a message.

**Ctrl-T—To Spell** Checks your spelling. Not as sophisticated as most word processors' spell checkers, but useful nonetheless.

### Signature Files

In the last chapter, we looked at how you can insert a signature file into an e-mail message using UNIX mail's **~r** command. With Pine—and many other mail programs—you can get the program to remember to place the signature file for you. All you need is a text file called **.signature** in your home directory. (The period before the name means it's a hidden file—don't worry about that, though—simply create the file and give it the name. Hidden files in UNIX don't have the same significance that they do in DOS.)

## Yes, There's *More*

Okay, so I haven't described everything that Pine can do. Pine's help system is actually quite good, so if you've got this program, spend a little time looking around. That goes for whatever program you happen to be using. Find out how the program can help you deal with your mail, and you'll save lots of time and hassle in the long run.

Some mail programs have other useful features, but you may not be able to use them! For instance, you may be able to request a *notification of receipt* (when the message arrives a message is sent back to you, so you know for sure it got where it was supposed to go). You may also be able to get a *notification of reading*—this tells you the user actually read the message.

*Message cancel* lets you retrieve a message you've sent—assuming it's retrievable, which it may not be (it depends on where it's reached when you decide to cancel it). There are also systems such as MIME (Multipurpose Internet Mail Extensions), a little-used system that lets you send computer files as e-mail. And there's *multi-media mail*, a system that includes voice and graphics along with the mail message.

But these features are all seldom-used, and depend on both sides—the sender and recipient—using software that matches. These features will become more common on Internet in the future, but for now, you probably won't be using them.

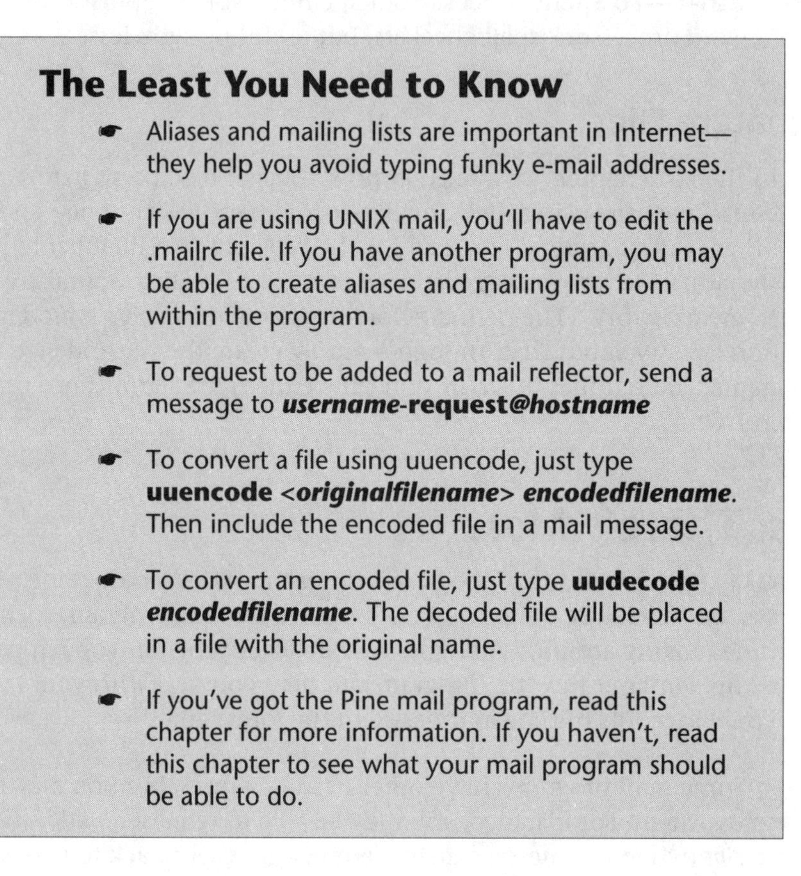

## The Least You Need to Know

- Aliases and mailing lists are important in Internet—they help you avoid typing funky e-mail addresses.
- If you are using UNIX mail, you'll have to edit the .mailrc file. If you have another program, you may be able to create aliases and mailing lists from within the program.
- To request to be added to a mail reflector, send a message to ***username*-request@*hostname***
- To convert a file using uuencode, just type **uuencode <*originalfilename*> *encodedfilename***. Then include the encoded file in a mail message.
- To convert an encoded file, just type **uudecode** ***encodedfilename***. The decoded file will be placed in a file with the original name.
- If you've got the Pine mail program, read this chapter for more information. If you haven't, read this chapter to see what your mail program should be able to do.

# Chapter 13
# Return to Sender, Address Unknown

## In This Chapter

- Why e-mail gets returned, and what to do about it
- Where to look for e-mail addresses
- Using finger to find login information
- Searching for newsgroup users
- Use a Knowbot to automate searches
- Using Netfind

Nothing's simple on the Internet. You might be sure that you've entered the correct e-mail address—you might even have used your mail program to "grab" an address from a message you received—but just when you think you've finished with an e-mail message, it comes back. You look in your inbox and find something like this:

```
22  Nov  8 Mail Delivery Subs  (1,274) Returned mail: Host unknown
```

You view the message, and find a horrendous mess of header lines with comments like **Host unknown (Authoritative answer from nameserver)**.

Your message has gone out onto Internet, and nobody knows what to do with it. There may even be occasions when you *have* used a *correct* address—and still Internet can't deliver it.

## What's Up?

There are four reasons that your mail may not be delivered, with some variations:

**Host unknown** Internet can't find the host that you put in the e-mail address. Remember that e-mail addresses are in the format *user@host*. For some reason Internet can't get through to the host.

**User unknown** Internet can get your mail to the host—but the host claims it doesn't recognize the user, so sends it back.

**Service unavailable** The address is fine—but the host computer is not accepting mail at the moment. The mail system may be shut down due to hardware or virus problems. Or maybe the message was sent at a time when the host simply doesn't accept mail—some systems refuse mail during certain times.

**Can't send** The host is known, and the host might be inclined to accept the mail, but Internet can't get through to the host—maybe the network is damaged, maybe the host itself is out of business due to hardware problems, or maybe it's changed its mail configuration and the information hasn't been passed on to the right people.

Look carefully at your returned mail and you'll see one of these reasons, or something like it, somewhere in the header—usually, but not always, on the Subject line near the top.

## Who Didn't Get It?

If you sent a message to several people, you should check carefully to see who didn't receive it. For instance, you may have used a mailing list or sent "carbon copies" to other people. The message could have been delivered to all but one person. So look at the header carefully to see who didn't get it. You'll look in the "Transcript of session follows" section. For instance:

```
—— Transcript of session follows ——
550 apotpeel.com (TCP)... 550 Host unknown
554 <joebloe@apotpeel.com>... 550 Host unknown (Authoritative
answer from name
server)
550 ourplace.org (TCP)... 550 Host unknown
554 <fred@ourplace.org>... 550 Host unknown (Authoritative
answer from name server)
```

You can see that this message was sent back from two addresses, because in both cases Internet couldn't find the host. The message may have gone through to other recipients.

# So What's the Problem?

Why is your mail coming back? There are a variety of reasons:

**You typed the address incorrectly** You could have made a mistake while typing the address. Take a look at the address in the returned message to confirm that you got it right. See if you typed a zero instead of an **o**, or a one instead of an **l**, for instance.

**A mailer incorrectly modified the domain** A mail server somewhere saw the address, misunderstood it, and added its own domain. If the returned message shows the address you entered, and some higher-level domain stuff that you *didn't* put in the address, this is what's happened.

**You've been given an incomplete address** Some people assume too much when they hand out their addresses—they give you part of it, assuming you know where they are and understand how to complete the highest level of their domain. Also, in many cases a complete address is only needed if the mail is *leaving* your host and going elsewhere. If your host sees an incomplete address, without the higher-level domain, it may assume the address is to someone in the same domain. So if someone is used to giving their address to other local users, they may forget about the higher-level-domain part of the address.

**You used a correct address, but the mailer doesn't know it's correct** There's not much you can do about this, except complain. Some mail servers may not have the latest domain information.

**The mail program that sent you a message didn't fill out the From name correctly** Not all mail programs fill out the From name correctly. They abbreviate it, stripping out the higher levels of the domain name. The From name is for reference only—it's not used to actually deliver the mail. However, if you use your mail program to "grab" the From name and put it into your address book (or to reply directly to this message), you're going to have an incorrectly-addressed message. If you know the From address is wrong, you should correct it before you use it, of course. Check the body of the message to see if the sender included a "signature" with his full mail address.

## Who Ya Gonna Call?

So, what to do about these problems? If it's a system problem, with a mail server not recognizing a message or modifying it incorrectly, there's not much you can do except talk to your service provider. If you can see what the problem is, then correct the address, strip out all the header garbage you don't need, and resend the message—you could use your mail program's Forward command to do all this.

You might also have to try contacting the person some other way (the telephone, remember?) and get the correct address. Sometimes, though, you may be stuck with a bad address and no other way to find the person. That's when things might get tough.

## The Internet Directory? There Isn't One

There is no single directory in which you can look up an Internet user's mail address. Finding an address takes a little more work than that. One problem is that the Internet is an amorphous blob that seems unrelated to geography. Although there's no single directory of Internet users, there *are* many different directories—the problem is, if you've no idea where the person is, which directory do you use?

While researching this book, for instance, I came across the names of two people I wanted to talk to about a particular program. I'd seen their names in a couple of documents, but no addresses were included. Where were these people? It turned out that one was in England, the other in California. There are a number of different techniques you can employ for finding people.

## Talk to the Postmaster

If you are sure a user is at a particular host, you could ask the host's "postmaster." Write an e-mail message to **postmaster@*hostname***. Provide as much information about the person as you can, and maybe the postmaster will be able to send you the correct mail address.

## Ask Someone Else

Think about who else the person might know. Other people the person has worked with or you know has communicated with. Then e-mail them and ask if they know where he is.

## finger Them

UNIX has a command called **finger** that lets you ask a host about someone with a name that you know. You enter the command in this format: **finger *name@host***. For instance, you are looking for someone named **Smith** at the host named **apotpeel.com**:

```
teal% finger smith@apotpeel.com
[apotpeel.com]
Login name: bsmith                        In real life: Bert Smith
Directory: /ftp/./                        Shell: /bin/true
Never logged in.
No unread mail
No Plan.

Login name: gsmith                        In real life: George Smith
Directory: /ftp/./                        Shell: /bin/true
Mail last read Tue Nov  9 10:18:03 1993
No Plan.
```

You've found two Smiths, a Bert and a George. Bert has never used his account, though (see the "Never logged in" line). Sometimes you'll see a "Last login" line with a date, also—this gives you an idea of how often the account is used. Or maybe you'll see a "Mail last read" line.

What name are you going to enter? You can enter a complete first name, complete last name, or complete login name. (If you enter a login name, you'd better get the capitalization correct—for first and last names it doesn't matter.) You can even enter **finger @*host*** with no name, to see a list of all the people currently logged onto that domain, or simply **finger** by itself—you'll see a list of all the people currently logged on *your* domain.

Notice the **No Plan** line in the earlier example. This refers to the user's plan file, a hidden file in their home directory. It's simply a text file with whatever the user wants to tell people when they "finger" him. Take a look at this example:

```
teal% finger bloe
Login name: joeb                        In real life: Joe Bloe
Directory: /home/clients4/joeb          Shell: /bin/csh
On since Nov  9 09:32:01 on ttyra from ucb-annex.csn.or
Mail last read Tue Nov  9 10:18:03 1993
Plan:
 ====================================================
 ¦  Joe Bloe           ¦Internet:joeb@apotpeel.com ¦
 ¦  2291 S. Coors St.  ¦     CompuServe: 79999,9999 ¦
 ¦  Podunk, CO  80228  ¦       Phone:  303-555-1869 ¦
 ====================================================
```

Joe Bloe has created a text file containing his address, Internet address, CompuServe address, and phone number. You can really track this guy down now. He could also have included a mini resume, if he'd wanted, telling you what he does.

The finger command will also display the contents of the *first line* of the .project file, another text file the user may have created to provide a little more information—the .project file is likely to be updated periodically, while the .plan file contains more permanent information.

The finger command won't always work. Some hosts simply don't allow it—many Internet system administrators believe that it provides too much information, and poses a security risk.

## Search for Newsgroup Users

In Chapter 15 you will learn about the newsgroups, "areas" in which public messages can be posted and read, on thousands of different subjects. In order for you to be able to read these newsgroups, your service provider must "subscribe" to them.

A quick way to create a .plan file is to make a copy of your e-mail signature file. Some mail programs automatically pull text out of a file called .signature, and drop it into the end of your messages. You could use this UNIX command to use the same file as your finger file: **cp .signature .plan**. Press **Enter**, and you're finished.

MIT subscribes to most of them. And each time a newsgroup message comes into MIT, their system grabs the From: line and saves it. If you think the person you are trying to track down might have used the newsgroups, you might want to search MIT's database, by sending an e-mail message to **mail-server@ rtfm.mit.edu**. For instance:

```
teal% mail mail-server@.mit.edu
Subject: send usenet-addresses name/pit manager.
Cc:teal%
```

In place of *name* in this example, substitute the name you are searching for. An hour or two after sending the message, you'll probably get a list back in an e-mail message, showing the matches.

There are a few problems with this method, of course. You have to know an exact match from the From: line. You can't use a partial name, for instance, and can enter only one name, with no spaces. And many people use aliases (in the sense of "fake names") when they post messages in the newsgroups.

You'll sometimes see messages telling you to "finger" someone for more information. When you use the finger command on their address you'll see the contents of the .plan file. This is a quick and easy way to distribute information.

## Using KIS

You can use the Knowbot Information Service (KIS) to search a variety of directories at once. A *knowbot* is a program that can search the

Internet for requested information. We may be seeing more of them in the future—they'll search for anything, not just names—but for now they are in an experimental stage. That includes KIS, though it's usually functioning. Unfortunately its scope is rather limited. At the time of writing, it could search the whois directory at nic.ddn.mil, and the X.500 directory that fred searches, and can use the UNIX **finger** command on a named host, all of which you can do for yourself (we'll look at whois and X.500 in the next chapter). It can also search the MCIMail directory, which may be useful if you know the person you are trying to contact uses MCIMail, and RIPE, a directory of European Internet users.

To begin, you'll have to use Telnet:

```
teal% telnet info.cnri.reston.va.us 185
Trying 132.151.1.15 ...
Connected to info.cnri.reston.va.us.
Escape character is '^]'.

                Knowbot Information Service
KIS Client (V2.0).    Copyright CNRI 1990.    All Rights Reserved.
The KIS system is undergoing some changes.
Type 'news' at the prompt for more information
Type 'help' for a quick reference to commands.
Backspace characters are '^H' or DEL
>
```

Now, the simplest way to use KIS is to enter a name (mine, for instance) and press **Enter**:

```
> kent
Connected to KIS server (V1.0). Copyright CNRI 1990. All Rights Reserved.
The ds.internic.net whois server is being queried:
--------------------------------------------------
Kent, Bert (BK168)                  KENT@ABA.COM
   ABA, Inc.
   2500 Coors Road
   Santa Clara, CA 91234
```

```
   (408) 555-1500
   Record last updated on 18-Oct-90.
__________
Johns, Jeffrey R. (JRJ71)            Johns@MCS.KENT.EDU
   Kent State University
   Department of Mathematics and Computer Science
   Kent, OH 44242
   (216) 555-4004
   Record last updated on 19-Oct-92.
________________________________________________
```

As you can see from the list that is (eventually) displayed, KIS searches the entire entry, not just the user's name. So we've found Jeffrey Johns, because he's at Kent State University.

> **By the Way . . .**
>
> KIS has a lot to do when it carries out a search. It has no directories of its own, so it is sending requests out across the Internet for information. That means a search can be *very* slow. Be patient. I've also found that even when you are not searching (when you are just entering commands or reading the online manual), it can be pretty sluggish.

If you'd like to use KIS, spend a few moments reading the user manual—type **help** and press **Enter** at the > prompt. Then, after reading what you are shown, type **man** and press **Enter** to see some more. You can, for instance, specify an organization name, use a first and last name, and so on. To search the RIPE directory for the name **Kent** you would do this:

```
>service ripe
>kent
```

To search MCIMail the first line of this would be **service mcimail.** (To see a list of the service names, type **services** and press **Enter**.)

As with some of the other directory services, KIS also lets you search using e-mail. Send a message to **netaddress@nri.reston.va.us** or **netaddress@sol>bucknell>edu**, and type the command in the body of the message (the same commands you'd use if you were using KIS directly). You might want to try this rather than sit and wait for KIS to do its work.

## Using Netfind

There's another system you might want to try, Netfind. You can use Netfind by telneting to any of these hosts:

archie.au (AARNet, Melbourne, Australia)

bruno.cs.colorado.edu (University of Colorado, Boulder)

dino.conicit.ve (Nat. Council for Techn. & Scien. Research, Venezuela)

ds.internic.net (InterNIC Directory and DB Services, S. Plainfield, NJ)

lincoln.technet.sg (Technet Unit, Singapore)

macs.ee.mcgill.ca (McGill University, Montreal, Quebec, Canada)

malloco.ing.puc.cl (Catholic University of Chile, Santiago)

monolith.cc.ic.ac.uk (Imperial College, London, England)

mudhoney.micro.umn.edu (University of Minnesota, Minneapolis)

netfind.oc.com (OpenConnect Systems, Dallas, Texas)

netfind.vslib.cz (Liberec University of Technology, Czech Republic)

nic.nm.kr (Korea Network Information Center, Taejon, Korea)

nic.uakom.sk (Academy of Sciences, Banska Bystrica, Slovakia)

redmont.cis.uab.edu (University of Alabama at Birmingham)

Like this:

```
teal% telnet macs.ee.mcgill.ca
Trying 132.206.61.15 ...
```

```
Connected to Finnegan.EE.McGill.CA.
Escape character is '^]'.
SunOS UNIX (finnegan)

login: netfind
Password: (I typed my Internet address here.)

==========================================================================
Welcome to the Microelectronics And Computer Systems Laboratory
Netfind server.
==========================================================================
I think that your terminal can display 24 lines.  If this is wrong,
please enter the "Options" menu and set the correct number of
lines.

Top level choices:
        1. Help
        2. Search
        3. Seed database lookup
        4. Options
        5. Quit (exit server)
```

You'll probably want to read the Help file to get a good idea of the different forms of search that you can use. Then, when you are ready to search, you can use option 2. If you'd like to search a list of host names, you can use option 3. (You enter a portion of the hostname, and Netfind searches for matches within various different hostnames.) Let's search for my name. I'll enter my last name, and the city in which I live:

```
--> 2
Enter person and keys (blank to exit) --> kent lakewood
Please select at most 3 of the following domains to search:
    0. amc.org (amc cancer research center, lakewood, colorado)
    1. burner.com (the back burner bbs, lakewood, colorado)
    2. cobe.com (cobe laboratories, inc, lakewood, colorado)
    3. ecog.edu (eastern co-operative oncology group, lakewood, colorado)
    4. lakewood.com (lakewood microsystems, lakewood, new jersey)
```

Unfortunately it didn't find me. Notice that it searched for Lakewood in both the hostname and the host description. The next step is to pick up to three of these to search again. You'll be prompted to enter up to three numbers. If those domains have "nameservers," you'll be able to see more information, perhaps information on the person you are looking for. But there's a good chance that the one you select *won't* have more information.

This search didn't do me any good—none of the hosts were mine. Let's try another way, by entering my name and host name:

```
Enter person and keys (blank to exit) —> kent csn
Please select at most 3 of the following domains to search:
 0. csn.com (colorado supernet, inc, colorado supernet, inc,
    colorado supernet, inc.)
 1. csn.es (consejo de seguridad nuclear, dpto. informatica,
    justo dorado, madrid, spain)
 2. csn.net (colorado supernet, inc, colorado school of mines,
    golden, colorado)
 3. csn.org (colorado supernet, inc)
 4. csn.duke.edu (duke university, durham, north carolina)
Enter selection (e.g., 2 0 1) —>0
```

The first entry is Colorado Supernet, though not the domain I'm using. And in fact when I entered 0 and pressed Enter (on the last line of this example), Netfind was unable to find any information on me. Well, that's life. There's a good chance Netfind *won't* have what you're looking for, but it's worth a try.

## The Least You Need to Know

- You may think you've got the right e-mail address—but you could be wrong.
- Check the header of the returned message carefully—it should tell you why it was returned, and who didn't receive it.
- The easiest way to get someone's e-mail address is to talk to them. Pick up the phone. Or get it from someone who knows them.
- If you know the person is at the host that returned the e-mail, send e-mail to the postmaster and ask about him. Address the message to **postmaster@*hostname***.
- The **finger** command's a useful way to track someone if you know the hostname.
- If you know the user uses the newsgroups, try MIT's system—they might have his address.
- KIS can help you search for MCIMail users and European users.
- Netfind is a good way to check hostnames. It may be difficult to find individuals, though.

**Blank (this) subliminal (book)**
**message (is) page (great).**

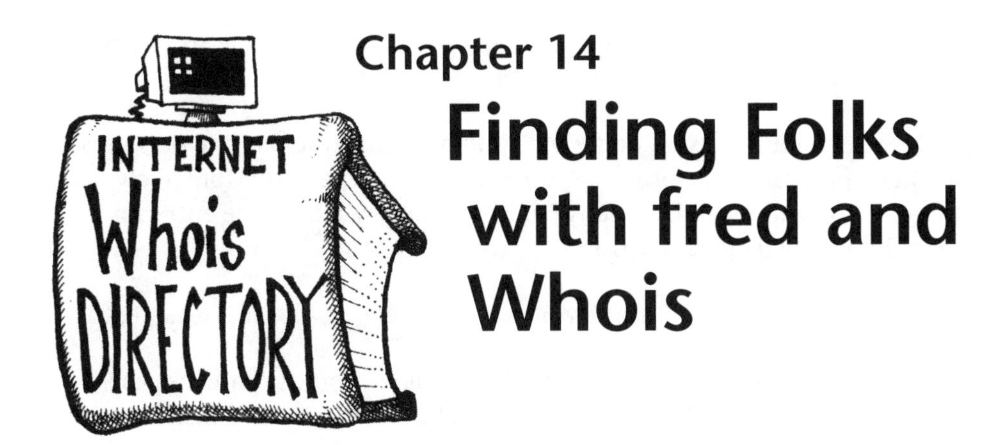


# Chapter 14
# Finding Folks with fred and Whois

## In This Chapter

- Using Whois to find "Interneties"
- Using fred to simplify X.500

In the last chapter we looked at a number of ways to track down people on the Internet. We're going to look at a couple more: *fred*, which searches the X.500 system, and *whois*. Hold on tight!

# Using Whois

If you are searching for a person you know to be involved in maintaining the Internet network or in network research, they may be listed in the Whois directory on the InterNIC Registration Services host (run by the DDN Network Information Center). You can use the Whois directory several ways: using the **whois** command, using Telnet, and using e-mail.

## The Whois Command

The **whois** command is very easy to use. Simply type **whois *name*** at the UNIX shell, and press **Enter**. This may be a first name, last name, or login name. And if you are not sure of the complete name, end it with a period: **whois ken.** will find Ken, Kent, Kentworth, etc. And you don't need to worry about capitalization.

You can only use one name at a time—you can't enter a person's first and last names.

If you enter an unusual name the system might find just one person, so it will display all the information it has about that person. More likely, though, it'll find several or many, so it will display a one-line entry for each. You'll see listings like this:

```
Bloe, Joe (BJ31)   joebloe@apotpeel.com          (303) 555-1869
```

The **BJ31** in parentheses is the person's *handle*. You can now use the whois command with the handle to get full information. For instance:

```
whois bj31
```

will find the person's full information—his e-mail address, USPO address, telephone number, and the date the record was last updated. (In some cases this command may not work. Instead, try **whois \!*handle*** or **whois !*handle*.**)

There are now a number of "whois servers," directories that work in the same way as the InterNIC Registration Services directory. There are servers at Pacific Bell, GTE Laboratories, many universities, several at NASA, and so on. There's a current list at the back of this book in Section B.

In Chapter 18 you'll learn how to use FTP to transfer files across the Internet. You an use FTP to go get the latest Whois list. Go to **sipb.mit.edu**. Log in as **anonymous**. Then go to the **/pub/whois directory**, and get the file called **whois-servers.list**.

If you want to search the directory on one of these servers you must use a different format of the whois command: **whois -h *hostname name***. For instance:

```
whois -h wpi.wpi.edu kent
```

This will search the server at the Worcester Polytechnic Institute (wpi.wpi.edu) for the name Kent. Unfortunately, not all systems will let you use the whois command to do this—they only let local users work with them.

## By Telnet and Mail

If you find you can't use the Whois directory from your system, you have two other options. You can Telnet to the directory at **nic.ddn.mil** (possibly to another whois server, but most probably won't let you in). You'll learn more about Telnet in Chapter 17, so check there for details. (Note: you won't need a login name or password to get into Whois at this server.)

You can also use e-mail to use Whois. Send a message to **whois@internic.net**, like this:

```
teal% whois@internic.net
Subject:
whois kent
.
Cc:
teal%
```

The body of the message is the whois command. After a while you'll get a report back to your e-mail system, showing what Whois found.

## Using X.500 and fred

Some time ago a group called the International Standards Organization came up with a standard called *X.500*, a method for letting computers search directories. It uses a "hierarchical" system to track down system users—the computer (or you) will provide the country, organization, and person; X.500 follows this path down the directory to the exact person in whom you are interested. Unfortunately, it's not widely used (and is difficult to use anyway).

You're in luck, though: there's a program called **fred** which makes X.500 easier to use for real people. You have to Telnet to a fred server first. (You'll learn about Telnet in Chapter 17. But don't worry, I'll tell you all you need to know for now.) There are two such servers: **wp.psi.com** and **wp2.psi.com**.

Okay, so what's *fred*? FRont End to Dish, of course. Don't ask what it means.

(If you can't get one to work, try the other.) To get to fred, type **telnet** ***server*** and press **Enter**; then, when asked to log in, type **fred** and press **Enter**. Like this:

```
teal% telnet wp2.psi.com
Trying 38.146.90.2 ...
Connected to wp1.psi.net.
Escape character is '^]'.
SunOS UNIX (wp1.psi.net)
login: fred
Last login: Tue Nov  9 13:50:18 from teal.csn.org
SunOS Release 4.0.3c (WP_PSI_BOOTBOX) #3: Mon Mar 8 12:14:31 EST
1993
You have new mail.
Welcome to the PSI White Pages Pilot Project

Try   "help" for a list of commands
     "whois" for information on how to find people
    "manual" for detailed documentation
    "report" to send a report to the white pages manager

To find out about participating organizations, try
    "whois -org *"
  accessing service, please wait...

fred>
```

Now you can search for people or organizations. Let's begin by searching for the organization of which the person is a member. Type **whois** ***partialname*** **organization -org ***. For instance, **whois a* organization -org *** will find seven organizations, as you can see below.

```
fred> whois a* organization -org *
7 matches found.
 13. Advanced Decision Systems     +1 415-960-7300
 14. ALCOA   +1 412-553-4545
 15. Anterior Technology   +1 415-328-5615
 16. Apple Computer, Inc.   +1 408/996-1010
 17. Argonne National Laboratory   +1 708-252-2000
 18. ATT     +1 212-387-5400
 19. Auburn University     +1 205-844-4512
```

Notice that each entry has a number in the left column. These numbers are assigned to each entry that fred finds for you during your session. (As you can see from this example, I've already done some searching—otherwise Advanced Decision Systems would have been number 1.) To find out more about one of these, you can type **whois *number***. For instance, **whois 18** would show you this:

```
fred> whois 18
ATT (18)                                               +1 212-387-5400
     aka: AT&T
     aka: American Telephone and Telegraph Company
ATT
  32 Avenue of the Americas
  New York
  New York 10013
  US
Comments about the ATT Directory should be sent to sri@qsun.att.com
Locality:    New York, New York
Name:     ATT, US (18)
Modified: Wed Jun 16 19:09:32 1993
      by: manager, att,
            US (21)
fred>
```

If it's a very long listing, it might stop in the middle; press **Enter** to continue. Notice also the *aka name*—this is another name you can enter in a search for this organization ("aka" means "also known as"). Sometimes you'll find that the aka name is much shorter than the original. (Not all entries have an aka name.)

Now, assuming this is the one you want, you can ask about a particular person. In this case I'm going to search for names beginning with J.

```
fred> whois j* -org 18
3 matches found.
 20. Joe Bloe
joeb@att.comfred>
 21. Jay Harvey
jayh@qsun.att.com
 22. Andrew Josephson                          Ajos@qsun.att.com
fred>
```

Now I can find more information about Joe Bloe:

```
fred> whois 20
Joe Bloe (20)                                  joeb@qsun.att.com
Member of Technical Staff
Bell Laboratories
Name:      Joe Bloe, Experimental Potato Division,
             ATT,
             US (20)
Modified: Tue Sep 29 14:13:54 1992
      by: Manager, ATT,
             US (21)
fred>
```

If you want to get fancy with fred, get hold of the fred manual. You can read the manual by typing **manual** and pressing **Enter**. You'll be able to move from page to page by pressing **Enter**, and stop the manual by pressing **Ctrl-C**.

I've just shown you the easiest way to use fred. There are many other ways—you could, for instance, look up a name in every organization beginning with a particular letter, or search phonetically.

When you are finished with fred, use the **quit** command to end the session. If your system seems to hang, press **Ctrl-]**. You'll find yourself back at the **telnet>** prompt. Type **quit** again to get back to the UNIX shell.

## The Least You Need to Know

- Use Whois if you know the person is involved with running the Internet or researching Internet issues.
- fred can help you search for users according to the organization of which they are a part.
- To save time waiting while whois or fred work, send the commands by e-mail.

# Part III
# Boldly Going Around the Internet

*There's more—much more—to the Internet than just sending messages to people. In this part of the book, you're going to learn how to navigate the treacherous and poorly-documented depths of the Internet.*

*We'll start off looking at how to use the* newsgroups, *groups of people with similar interests who take part in an electronic "discussion" about those interests. There are thousands of different subjects, hundreds of thousands of different conversations going on over the Internet. You're also going to learn how to travel across the Internet and grab computer files—books, magazine articles, programs, clip art, sounds, fonts . . . there are literally millions of computer files publicly available on the Internet.*

*Finally, you'll learn how to use programs on other computers with* Telnet, *whether you want to search a database, play chess, or just have a good old-fashioned (new-fashioned?) conversation with someone elsewhere.*

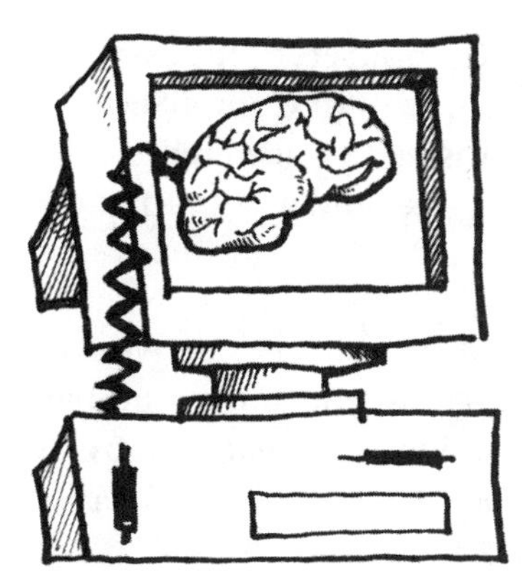

# Chapter 15
# Newsgroups: The Source of All Wisdom

## In This Chapter

- What you can find in the newsgroups
- About newsgroup subscriptions
- Finding out what newsgroups exist
- How USENET functions
- Using newsreaders
- Subscribing to newsgroups
- Reading messages

Since it would be wise to know what we're talking about, let's start out this chapter with a few definitions. (Wait! Don't leave! It won't be boring, I promise.)

Are you familiar with bulletin board systems (BBSs)? They're computerized systems for leaving messages, both public and private. Other computer users can read your messages, and you can read theirs. There are tens of thousands of small BBSs spread around the world, each with its own area of interest. Many computer companies have BBSs for their clients to get technical support. Many professional associations have BBSs for their members to leave messages for each other, and take part in discussions.

What, then, is an information service such as CompuServe? It's essentially a collection of many bulletin boards (called *forums* in CompuServe-speak). CompuServe has about 1,000 such BBSs. Instead of needing to know 1,000 telephone numbers, you can dial just one, and access any number of the BBSs in series.

So what is Internet? As we've already seen, it's a collection of networks hooked together. It's huge, and consequently, it has an enormous number of discussion groups. In Internet-speak these are called *newsgroups*; there are thousands of them, on any conceivable subject. My service provider *subscribes* to about 4,000 (more about subscribing in a moment), and there are many more scattered around.

True to its UNIX heritage, Internet uses the word *news* ambiguously. Often, when you see a reference to *news* in a menu or an Internet document, it refers to the messages left in newsgroups (not, as most real people would imagine, journalists' reports on current affairs).

If you've never used a newsgroup (or another system's forum or BBS or whatever), you may not be aware of the power of such communications. This sort of messaging system really brings computer networking alive, and it's not all computer nerds sitting around with nothing better to do. (Check out Internet's alt.sex newsgroup—these people are not your average introverted propeller-heads!) I've found work, made friends, found answers to research questions (much quicker and cheaper than I could have done by going to a library), and read people's "reviews" of tools I can use in my business. I've never found a lover or spouse online, but I know people who have (and anyway, I'm already married).

## So What's Out There . . .

You can use newsgroups for fun or real work. You can use them to spend time "talking" with other people who share your interests—whether they happen to be "making and baking with sourdough" (see the **rec.food.sourdough** group), kites and kiting (**rec.kites**), or S&M (**alt.sex.bondage**). Or you can do some serious work online, finding a job at a nuclear physics research site (**hepnet.jobs**), tracking down a piece of software for a biology project (**bionet.software**), or finding good stories about police work in the San Francisco area for an article you are writing (**clari.sfbay.police**). Here's just a tiny fraction of what is available:

**alt.ascii-art** Pictures created with ASCII text characters—such as Spock and the Simpsons.

**alt.comedy.british** Discussions on British comedy, in all its wonderful forms.

**alt.current-events.russia** What's going on in Russia right now. (Some messages are in broken English, some in Russian, but that just adds romance.)

**alt.missing-kids** About missing kids.

**alt.polyamory** A newsgroup for those with "multiple lovers."

**alt.sex** Discussions on Hillary Clinton's sexual orientation, nude beaches, oral sex, and anything else related to sex, marginally or otherwise.

**bit.listserv.down-syn** Discussions about Down's Syndrome.

**comp.research.japan** Computer research in Japan.

**misc.forsale** Goods for sale.

**rec.skydiving** A group for skydivers.

**sci.anthropology** People interested in anthropology.

**sci.military** Science and the military.

**soc.couples.intercultural** Interracial couples.

If you are looking for information on just about any subject, the question is not "I wonder if there's a newsgroup about this?" It should be, "I wonder what the newsgroup's name *is*, and does my service provider subscribe to it?"

Okay, so you *do* have a subject about which you want to start a newsgroup. Spend some time in the **news.groups** newsgroup to find out about starting a USENET newsgroup, or talk to your service provider about starting a local newsgroup.

## . . . But Can You Get to It?

There are so many newsgroups out there that they take up a *lot* of room. A service provider getting the messages of 3,000 newsgroups may have to set aside 500 MB of hard disk space to keep up with it all. So service providers have to decide which ones they will *subscribe* to.

Nobody subscribes to *all* the world's newsgroups, because many are simply of no interest to most Internet users, and many are not widely distributed—some are of regional interest only, some of interest to a specific organization. So system administrators have to pick the ones they want, and omit the ones they don't. Undoubtedly some "censor" newsgroups, omitting those they believe have no place online.

I'll give you an idea of what is available, but I can't specify what is available to *you*. You'll have to check with your service provider to find out what they have. And if they don't have what you want, ask them to get it. They can't know what people want unless someone tells them.

## Okay, Gimme a List!

Okay, we've given you a list. On the disk there's a file called NWSGROUP.TXT in a file called NWSGROUP.EXE (The instructions in Part V tell you how to get to it). In this text file you'll find a short summary of each of over four thousand newsgroups. If you don't have a DOS machine available, you can go to the **news.announce.newusers** newsgroup to find messages containing various lists. (You'll find out how to get to a newsgroup in a moment.)

As you'll see from the lists, some newsgroups are *moderated*. That means there's someone reading all the messages, and deciding which ones actually get posted. The intention is to keep the newsgroup focused, stopping the discussions from "going astray." Of course it may look a little like censorship (the extent of the resemblance depends on what you want to say or read).

# Where's It All Coming From?

Where do all these newsgroups come from? They are created on computers all over the world. Any host can create a newsgroup, and just about all do. Each will have newsgroups of local interest—about the service provider's services, about local politics, local events, and so on.

But a large number of newsgroups are part of a system called USENET. Like Internet, USENET is an intangible, a network of networks. It's not owned by anyone, and doesn't own anything itself. It's independent of any network (including Internet)—in fact it's older than Internet. It's simply a series of voluntary agreements to swap information. Most widely-available newsgroups go through USENET.

# What's in a Name?

Let's take a quick look at how newsgroups are named. Newsgroup names look much like host addresses, a series of words separated by periods. This is because, like hosts, they are set up in a hierarchical system (though instead of going right-to-left, they go left-to-right). The first name is the top level. These are the top-level USENET groups:

**comp** Computer-related subjects.

**news** Information about newsgroups themselves, including software used to read newsgroup messages, information about finding and using newsgroups.

**rec** Recreational topics—hobbies, sports, the arts, and so on.

**sci** Science—discussions about research in the "hard" sciences, as well as some social sciences.

**soc** A wide range of social issues, such as discussions about different types of societies and subcultures, as well as sociopolitical subjects.

**talk** Debate about politics, religion, and anything else that's controversial.

**misc** Stuff. Looking for jobs, selling things, a forum for paramedics. You know, *stuff*.

Not all newsgroups are true USENET groups. Many are local groups, though they may be distributed internationally—through USENET (don't worry about it, it doesn't matter). Such newsgroups are known as *Alternative Newsgroups Hierarchies*. So there are other top-level groups, such as these:

**alt** "Alternative" subjects, often subjects that many people would consider "inappropriate" or pornographic. Or just weird. Or simply interesting stuff, but the newsgroup has been created in an "unauthorized" manner to save time and hassle.

**bionet** Biological subjects.

**bit** A variety of newsgroups from the Bitnet network.

**biz** Business subjects, including advertisements.

**clari** Clarinet's newsgroups from "official" and commercial sources—mainly UPI news stories and various syndicated columns.

**courts** Related to law and lawyers.

**de** Various German-language newsgroups.

**fj** Various Japanese-language newsgroups.

**gnu** The Free Software Foundation's newsgroups.

**hepnet** Discussions about high-energy and nuclear-physics.

**ieee** The Institute of Electrical and Electronics Engineers' newsgroups.

**info** A collection of mailing lists formed into newsgroups at the University of Illinois.

**k12** Discussions about K-through-12th-grade education.

**relcom** Russian-language newsgroups, mainly distributed in the former Soviet Union.

**vmsnet** Subjects of interest to VAX/VMS computer users.

You'll see other groups, too, things like the following:

**brasil** Groups from Brazil (it's spelled with an "s" in Portugese).

**podunk** A local interest newsgroup for the town of Podunk.

**thisu** This University's newsgroup.

(Okay, I made up the last two, but you get the idea.)

## Reaching The Next Level

Well, these are the top-level groups. Below each level is another. For instance, there's **alt.3d**, a newsgroup about three-dimensional imaging. It's part of the alt hierarchy because, presumably, it was put together in an unauthorized way—the people who started it didn't want to go through the hassle of setting up a USENET group, so they created an alt group instead, where anything goes.

Another alt group is **alt.sex**, where anything really does go. And this group is a good example of how newsgroups may have more levels. Because it's such a diverse subject, one newsgroup wasn't really enough. So instead of posting messages to the alt.sex group, you can choose your particular pecadillo. There's

**alt.sex.bestiality.barney** (described as "for people with big, purple newt fetishes"),

**alt.sex.fetish.feet** (self-explanatory)

**alt.sex.motss** (member of the same sex)

**alt.sex.pictures** (described as "Gigabytes of copyright violations")

and so on. If you're into it, chances are good that there's a newsgroup for it.

If you really care how this information ends up on your service provider's computer, here goes. Computers acting as *news servers* collect the newsgroups from various other places—other servers that are part of the USENET agreements, computers with local newsgroups, Clarinet (a commercial "real" news service that carries a lot of news from United Press International), "gateways" to other networks (such as Bitnet), and so on. Then they make the information available to your system. Each server administrator has to make agreements with other administrators to transfer this data—usually (though not always) across the Internet.

The same hierarchy is used in all areas. For instance, there's **bionet.genome.arabidopsis**, **bionet.genome.chrom22** (a "discussion of Chromosome 22"), and for those of us interested in the eucaryote chromosomes, **bionet.genome.chromosomes**.

## Use a Newsreader!

Now you know what newsgroups are, how are you going to use them? News messages are stored in text files. Lots of text files. The best way to read the messages you want to read is to use a *newsreader* to help you sort and filter your way through all the garbage.

You'll probably have several types of newsreaders available. For instance, I can use tin, nn, trn, and rn. (Remember, Internet was developed by UNIX-types—there's a UNIX law somewhere that says program names must *not* use recognizable and easily-understood words.) These newsreaders vary in their ease of use, of course. Chances are, though, that most of you won't be running across a "user-friendly" news reader anytime soon.

You can also use the World Wide Web to read some newsgroups—if the ones you want are on the web, you may prefer to read them there. See Chapter 23 for more information.

You may also have a menu system that helps you find your way to the newsgroups. To find the newsgroups on my service provider's menu, I select *12 News and Weather*, and then see this menu:

```
                News and Weather

-->  1.   Colorado Weather Underground/
     2.   National Weather Service Forecasts/
     3.   Post to Usenet Newsgroup*
     4.   Read Usenet News*
     5.   Select a Usenet Newsreader*
     6.   Select an Editor*
     7.   UPI News/
```

If you don't want to use a newsreader, you don't have to. You can **grep** for keywords in the files in your service provider's /usr/spool/news directory. You're on your own, though. Don't expect any help from me. (**grep**, you may remember, is a UNIX command used for searching text files. See Chapter 9.)

Remember that there's some confusion on Internet as to the difference between personal messages and news. So this menu contains options that will get you to information about the weather (options 1 and 2), actual news reports (7), and the options related to the newsgroups, (message "forums"). In this chapter we're interested in the newsgroups.

The other options let me select a text editor to be used for writing newsgroup messages, select the newsreader I want to use, write a message to a newsgroup, and read the newsgroup messages.

## Using rn

I decided to describe the rn newsreader, because it's probably the reader used most commonly, and it's similar to another popular reader, nn. However, it's by no means the best. You may have something better available; ask your service provider, try several, and pick the one you find easiest. Those of us who've been involved in the world of DOS and Windows for the last few years will find that what Interneties describe as an "easy-to-use" newsreader may not actually *be* easy to use (though it's probably easier than the other choices). Chances are (at least for the moment), you'll have a rather clunky user interface that uses a multitude of special codes that you have to type. Other newsreaders are being developed, and things will get easier.

The following sections will help you use rn, if that's what you have, or at least give you an idea of what the other systems can do.

> **By the Way . . .**
> All these rn commands are difficult to remember, so I've put them on the tear-out reference card at the front of the book.

## Checking the Subscription List

Before we get started, let's see the groups to which you are subscribed; your service provider subscribes to lots, but hopefully *you* are not subscribed to all of them. Anyway, you can add or remove subscriptions.

This information is stored in a file called **.newsrc**. (The . before the name means it's a hidden file.) The file isn't created until you start your newsreader, so type **rn** and press **Enter**; when it starts, type **q** to quit.

Now, let's make sure the file has been created in your home directory. At the UNIX prompt, type **cd** and press **Enter** to make sure you are in the home directory, and then type **ls -a .newsrc** and press **Enter**. If the file is in your home directory, it will be listed.

Now you can open the file in the text editor you use. If you use vi, for instance, type **vi .newsrc** and press **Enter**. You'll see something like this (though the entire file probably won't be in alphabetical order):

```
alt.clintons.health.care.plan.is.a.crock:
alt! 1-0
alt.1d! 1-795
alt.3d! 1-1421
alt.abortion.inequity! 1-2760
alt.activism! 1-11625,14909
```

```
alt.activism.d! 1-1400
alt.adoption! 1-2208
alt.aeffle.und.pferdle! 1-130
".newsrc" 4147 lines, 104462 characters
```

This file lists all the newsgroups you have available. In this case you can see there are 4147 lines in this file (a *lot* of groups).

Now, any group that ends with ! is a group to which you are *unsubscribed,* a group you won't automatically get. Any group ending with : is one to which you *are* subscribed, one you *will* get.

You can move through this list using the **down arrow** or by pressing **Ctrl-f** in vi (remember, we described vi in detail in Chapter 11). If you find you are subscribed to everything, you would be wise to change all the : to !, so you are subscribed to none—then you can pick the ones you want to subscribe to individually. Even if your service provider selected various groups for you, you may want to unsubscribe and pick your own.

Use your text editor to do a search-and-replace. In vi, you will type : %s/:/!/ and press **Enter**.

Now you can select the groups you want to subscribe to. You can scroll through one by one, and change each ! to a :, but that would take a long time. Instead, pick the groups you want to join (use the list on our disk, or ask your service provider for a list), then search for each one you want to join.

In vi you would type **:/*groupname*** and press **Enter**. When you find the one you want, replace the ! with :. In vi, place the cursor over the ! and press **r:** to replace.

When you've finished subscribing to the groups you want, quit the editor, saving your work. (In vi, press **Esc** three times, then type **ZZ**.)

## Let's Get Started

Okay, let's start rn. Either you will select the newsreader from a menu, or start it from the UNIX shell. To start from the shell, simply type **rn** and press **Enter**. You'll probably see a short introduction. You'll find three important facts from this introduction:

1. To enter a command, you just type the appropriate letter—you don't need to press **Enter**.
2. To see a list of commands, type **h**. This will show the commands appropriate for your current location in the news reader.
3. Press **Spacebar** to tell rn to carry out the "default" command; the normal command, usually the "yes" response.

When you continue, rn may show you a list of new newsgroups. As it names each one, you can decide what you want to do with the group. For instance:

```
Newsgroup zer.z-netz.wissenschaft.physik not in .newsrc—
subscribe? [ynYN]
```

This is telling you that the newsgroup **zer.z-netz.wissenschaft.physik** has been added by your service provider, and that it doesn't appear in the .newsrc file. You can type any of these responses:

**y** to subscribe to the new group

**Y** to subscribe to *all* the new groups

**n** to *not* subscribe to the new group

**N** to *not* subscribe to any of the new groups.

If you press N or n, the group is still added to the end of the .newsrc file, but with an ! instead of a :. If you do decide to subscribe to a group, rn will ask you where you want to put the group: at the top of the list (type ^), at the bottom of the list (**$**), before a named newsgroup (***-name***), after a named newsgroup (***+name***), or in a particular position (type the position number). If you're not sure where to put it, you can type **L** to see a list of the newsgroups and their numbers. Its position will affect the sequence in which the newsgroups are presented to you when you start your newsreader.

When you've finished with the new groups, rn will show a list of your subscribed groups, and tell you how many unread messages each has. You'll see something like this:

```
Unread news in alt.sex.wizards                          1230 articles
Unread news in alt.silly.group.names.d                     3 articles
Unread news in alt.society.revolution                     55 articles
Unread news in bit.listserv.scuba-l                      823 articles
Unread news in soc.culture.yugoslavia                   1793 articles
etc.
******** 1230 unread articles in alt.sex.wizards—read now? [ynq]
```

The **etc.** means there are more newsgroups than shown here. You'll see how to get to them in a moment.

Now, what are your options? You can type **y** or press **Spacebar** to begin reading the first unread article in the first newsgroup, **n** to get rn to display the same question about the next newsgroup with unread messages, or **q** to leave rn.

There are *lots* of other options—I'm only going to mention a few of the most useful. You can tell rn to unsubscribe (type **u**). You can tell it to list the articles in the newsgroup (type =). Or type **N** for the next group; **n** for the next group with unread messages; **P** for the previous group; **p** for the previous group with unread messages; **$** for the last group; **1** for the first group; ^ for the first group with unread messages. You can even subscribe to another group by typing **g *groupname***.

## Just Read It

Let's take a look at the first unread article in the first newsgroup. Just type **y**:

```
Article 3165 (187 more) in bit.listserv.scuba-l:
From: jpayne@NMSU.EDU (James S. Payne)
Subject: Sea of Cortez Dive Report
Date: 26 Oct 93 16:11:40 GMT
Lines: 30
Comments: Gated by NETNEWS@AUVM.AMERICAN.EDU
Return-Path: <@AUVM.AMERICAN.EDU,
             @BROWNVM.BROWN.EDU:owner-scuba-l@BROWNVM.BROWN.EDU>
Return-Path: <@BROWNVM.BROWN.EDU:jpayne@NMSU.EDU>
Mime-Version: 1.0
```

```
Content-Type: TEXT/PLAIN; charset=US-ASCII
In-Reply-To: <9310261549.AA03041@dante>

As I promised here is a dive report on conditions around San
Carlos, Sonora, Mexico.  We were there from Oct. 15-24.
Water temperature is currently running between 74-78 degrees.
Gary's Dive Shop has 85 degrees posted, but I don't think he ever
changes it.  During a dive to 110' we found temps of 71.  One day
at Isla San Pedro we had 80 degrees, but it didn't last long.
```

(So you thought we were going to take a look at alt.sex.wizards, did you? Sorry, you'll have to check it out yourself.)

As you can see, the first part of the message is the usual header stuff—you can see the article number and newsgroup name, address of the person who sent it, the Subject title, and the date. You can generally ignore the rest of the header. It shows how the message got to the newsgroup.

What now? Here are a few things you may want to do:

**Unsubscribe** You weren't sure what the newsgroup was all about, but now you've seen it, you know you don't want it. Type **u** to "unsubscribe," so you won't come to this group next time.

To continue with the "news" analogy, messages that are posted to Internet newsgroups are called *articles*.

**Read the rest of the message** Press **Spacebar** to read the rest of the message (or press **Enter** to see the next line). If you're at the end of a message and press **Spacebar**, you'll move directly to the next one. You can move back up one page by pressing **b**, or to the top of the message by pressing **Ctrl-r**.

**Go to another article** Press **N** to go to the next article, or **n** to go to the next *unread* article. (This is the same thing when you first start. Your newsreader knows which messages you have seen, and assumes you've *read* them. As you view each one, it's *marked* as read.) Press **Ctrl-N** to go to the next unread article *with the same subject*. To go the other way—backwards—substitute P. That is, **P** for the previous article, **p** for the previous unread article, or **Ctrl-P** to go to the previous unread article with the same subject.

But there's more. You can also go to the last message you were viewing by pressing -. Or, if you know the number of the message you want to go to, simply type the message's ***number*** and press **Enter**. To go to the first unread message, press ^, or press **$** to go to the end of the newsgroup (for example, pressing **$P** displays the last message).

As you move from message to message, your newsreader automatically marks the ones you have seen as "read." That pulls them out of the way, so they won't appear when you move back up the list of messages using **p**.

**Viewing a List** You can save a lot of time by avoiding messages in which you have no interest. Instead, select the ones you want to see from a list. Press = to see a list of the unread articles:

```
3167 Re: New free dive record
3168 Re: Definition of Curmudgeon
3169 Re: catching tropical fish
3170 NED =
3171 Re: catching tropical fish
3172 Re: goodbye !!!
3173 Definition of Curmudgeon
3174 Re: Sea of Cortez Video
3175 NO SUBJECT
3176 The pros and cons of shrimpin
```

You'll see a screenful of subjects at a time; press **Spacebar** to see more. Unfortunately rn doesn't let you select directly from this list (though other newsreaders do). Still, it shows the message numbers, so you can type a number and press **Enter** to go right to a particular message.

Notice, by the way, that some message titles start with **Re:**. This means that they are replies to an original. It's these Re: messages that the Ctrl-N and Ctrl-P commands follow.

**Marking Messages as Read** You can mark messages, to indicate various conditions. If you decide you don't want to read a message right now, but will want to come back to read it later, press **m** to mark it as "unread." (If you simply went onto the next message by pressing Spacebar or N, for example, the message would be marked as "read.") In your next rn session, the message will still be marked as unread. (If you don't do this, when you come back next time the message won't be available.)

To mark a message as "read" *temporarily*, press **M**. This removes the message from the list of unread messages, but when you leave the newsgroup the message will be set back to "unread." Also, you can use the **Y** command to "yank" the message back, so it's marked as "unread" again, and appears in the listing.

You can mark all the messages related to a particular subject heading as "read" by pressing **k**—that moves them all out of the way when you are using the **n** command or **Spacebar** to move through the list. This process may take a little while, as rn has to search all the messages (you can end the process by pressing **Ctrl-C**).

**Going to another newsgroup** To leave this newsgroup, press **q** once to quit the message you're in, then press it again to return to the newsgroups list; rn will show you the name of the next group in sequence, and ask whether you want to read its messages.

**Using rot13** You'll sometimes find *rot13* messages. These are messages that can't be directly read—you can't be breezing through your messages and suddenly come across the text of a rot13 message, because it has been *encrypted*—it just looks like garbage. If you want to read the message, you'll have to make a point of telling the newsreader to convert it. In rn you'll press **Ctrl-x** to start the message in rot13 mode, or simply **x** to display the next page of the message in rot13. To start the message over, turning rot13 *off*, press **Ctrl-R**.

Okay, so what's the point? It's a way of saying "this message is probably offensive to some people, so if you are easily offended, don't read it." It makes sure nobody can claim they accidentally "stumbled" over an offensive message—they had to choose to read it.

*rot13* is a very simple encryption method—it's intended to make you think before you view a message, not to keep you out. The name of the method means "rotation 13." The letters of the alphabet have been rotated 13 characters—a becomes n, b becomes o, c becomes p. If you had the time, you could convert a rot13 file yourself.

## The Least You Need to Know

- A newsgroup is an "area" in which people with similar interests leave public messages—a sort of online public debate or discussion.
- There's a newsgroup on just about any subject you can imagine. If there *isn't*, there probably will be soon.
- Newsgroup names use a hierarchical system—each group may have *sub*-groups within it.
- The NWSGROUP.EXE file on the disk contains a text file that lists over 4,000 newsgroups.
- Your service provider probably has several news-readers you can choose from. Try them all and pick the best.
- The .newsrc file defines which newsgroups you are subscribed to.

# Chapter 16 More on Newsgroups—and LISTSERV

## In This Chapter

- Saving e-mail messages as text files
- Replying to messages
- Beginning a newsgroup discussion
- LISTSERV? What's That?
- Subscribing and Unsubscribing to LISTSERV groups

In the last chapter, you learned everything you need to know to get started with Internet's newsgroups. But of course there's more. (There's *always* more!) How about saving messages in a text file, or replying to them? And in the remote case that you can't find a newsgroup related to your interests, you may also want to know about the LISTSERV groups, another 4,000 or so groups that use e-mail to exchange information.

> **By the Way...**
>
> That's right, an additional 4,000 groups. Has it sunk in yet just how massive the Internet really is? The traffic volume is just staggering. That's why this book was such a great purchase to make—you'll never find your way around all alone.

# Save That Message!

You'll sometimes come across newsgroup messages that you want to save—I recently found a long message containing lots of interesting quotes, for instance. To save the message, you can type **s *filename***, You'll see something like this:

```
End of article 682 (of 683)—]what next? [npq] s quote.txt
File /home/clients4/peterk/News/quote.txt doesn't exist—
        use mailbox format? [ynq] y
Saved to mailbox /home/clients4/peterk/News/quote.txt
```

The file will be saved in the News directory. It doesn't much matter whether you type **y** or **n** here—either way you'll get a text file containing the message (if you type **y**, you'll get an extra line of garbage showing you where the message is from).

There's also a **w** command. It's the same as **s**, but it strips out all the message header stuff that you probably don't want anyway (you may want it if you are planning to contact the message's "poster," the author, so think about it before you use this command).

If you are using a dial-in terminal connection, you might prefer to use your telecommunications program's ability to save incoming text to a file. Or, if you are working in an "environment" in which you can copy text using the mouse (such as Windows or the Macintosh), copy the text into another application, such as a text editor or word processor.

## Replying to Messages

There are several ways to reply to a message you've just read. Press **f** to reply, or **F** if you want to reply and include the original message in your reply—this is very common, as it reminds the recipient of what he said, and lets new readers see what you are replying to. You can type your message *within* the original message, so you can break it down piece by piece, and reply to each individual point. With a little thought, this allows you to make the original writer (now the recipient) look like a total fool—a common practice in the newsgroups. (Internet's news-group-members are often rude, mean-spirited, and childish, it seems, depending on the group. The messages in alt.current-events.usa are probably much more heated than in, say, rec.games.chess.)

If you want to reply directly to the person who wrote the message, using e-mail instead of the newsgroup, you can type **r**. Type **R** to include the original message in the response.

*Flaming* is the act of writing an insulting message to or about another newsgroup member. Though you'll read that it's not polite, it's common (and *maybe* safer than saying it in person).

If you are working in rn, you will be leaving the "cbreak mode," that is, you'll now have to press **Enter** after typing a command. You may also see a message such as this:

```
This program posts news to thousands of
machines throughout the entire civilized world.  Your message will
cost the net hundreds if not thousands of dollars to send
everywhere.  Please be sure you know what you are doing.
Are you absolutely sure that you want to do this? [ny]
```

Of course you are, so type **y** and press **Enter**. You'll see:

```
Prepared file to include [none]:
```

If you have a text file you want to include in the message, type the name here and press **Enter** (if you don't, simply press **Enter**). Now, if you *did* include a file, you'll be asked if you want to

```
Send, abort, edit, or list?
```

To define which text editor you want to use, you should use this command *before* you open your newsreader: **setenv EDITOR *editorname*.** For instance, **setenv EDITOR vi** tells your system to use vi as the text editor.

You can type **s** to send the included file, **a** to end the operation, **e** to go into the text editor, or **l** to display the message you've just created (remember to press **Enter**). If you didn't include a file, you'll simply go straight to the text editor.

Once you're in your editor, type the message, then close the editor, saving your information. You'll see the same **Send, abort, edit, or list?** line. Type **s** and press **Enter** to send it on its way, and to return to the newsreader.

## Starting a Discussion

You can start your *own* newsgroup discussions, of course. Let's say you are searching for some information, or simply want to "talk" with "your own kind" (whatever or whoever they might be). First you'll decide on the newsgroup you want to post the message to. Of course, different systems use different methods to post news. The rn newsreader doesn't have a direct way to post news. On my system, I have to use the **Pnews** command. Like this:

```
teal% Pnews
Newsgroup(s): alt.politics.usa.misc

Your local distribution prefixes are:
    Local organization:    local
    Organization:   csn
    City:    boulder
    State:   co
    Country: usa
    Continent:      na
    Everywhere:     world

Distribution (world): world
Title/Subject: GOP bought election in New Jersey?

This program posts news to thousands of machines throughout the
entire civilized world.  Your message will cost the net hundreds if
not thousands of dollars to send everywhere.  Please be sure you
know what you are doing. Are you absolutely sure that you want to
do this? [ny] y
Prepared file to include [none]:
```

Then it pops into the text editor, which may look something like this:

```
   PICO 1.7        File: /home/clients4/peterk/.article    Modified

Newsgroups: alt.politics.usa.misc
Subject: GOP bought election in New Jersey?
Summary:
Followup-To:
Distribution: world
```

```
Organization: Colorado SuperNet, Inc.
Keywords: GOP NEW JERSEY ELECTION


What's this talk this morning about the GOP buying an election?
Anyone out there heard about this? Anyone know where I can find
more information?

              [ line 11 of 13 (84), character 363 of 365 (99) ]
^G Get Help ^O WriteOut ^R Read File^Y Prev Pg  ^K Del Line
^C Cur Pos ^X Exit ^J Justify  ^W Where is ^V Next Pg  ^U UnDel
Lin^T To Spell
```

When I close my editor (using **Ctrl-X** in this case), I'm asked if I want to save the message, and in what file. (It's saved in a file before sending—just press **Enter** when asked if the filename is correct.) Then I'll see a message like this:

```
Send, abort, edit, or list?
```

I type **s** and press **Enter**, and it's on its way.

# But Wait! There's More!

There are many more newsreader commands than we've looked at—you can operate on an entire range of messages at the same time, for instance, and create macros. And other newsreaders may be more convenient, or have other useful commands. Some let you scroll up and down the list of messages, marking the ones you want to read. What I've described in this and the last chapter will give you an idea of what a newsreader *should* be able to do as a minimum. To get an idea of what yours can do, read the manual of whatever newsreader you are using.

# A Word of Warning

Newsgroups can be *very* addictive. You can find messages about anything that interests you, angers you, or turns you on. If you are not careful, you can spend half your life in the newsgroups. You sit down in the morning to check your favorite newsgroups, and the next thing you know you haven't bathed, haven't eaten, and forgot to pick up the kids from school.

Hang around the newsgroups and you'll find people who are obviously spending a significant amount of time writing messages. These people are usually independently wealthy (that is, they work for large corporations who don't mind paying for them to talk politics over the Internet, or who don't know that they *are* paying for them to do so). If you have a job, a family, and a life, be careful.

## Using a LISTSERV Group

There's another form of "newsgroup" you might want to take a look at, the Bitnet LISTSERV discussion groups—also known as "lists" and "conferences." These come from the Bitnet network. There are well over 4,000 of them, and, as we'll see, they are based on e-mail.

For example, there's:

CHRISTIA@FINHUTC, a Christian discussion group.

ISO8859@JHUVM, a group that discusses ASCII/EBCDIC-character set issues (what fun!)

L-HCAP@NDSUVM1, a group for people interested in issues related to handicapped people in education.

PHILOSOP@YORKVM1, the Philosophy Discussion Forum.

The subjects handled by the LISTSERV groups are often of a technical nature, related to networks and computer hardware and software. But there are plenty of non-technical subjects as well. Groups belonging to the African American Student Network, the American Association of Teachers of German, the Forum da Associacao Brasileira de Estatistica. Groups on Chinese music, Dungeons and Dragons, American dialects, aircraft, agriculture, and plenty more.

LISTSERV works like this. Each group has an e-mail address. You begin by subscribing to the group you are interested in (I'll explain how in a moment). The e-mail address then acts like a *mail reflector*. You may remember we mentioned these in Chapter 12—they receive mail and then send it on to everyone on their lists. So every time someone sends a message to a group of which you are a member, you get a copy of the mail. And every time *you* send a message to a group, everyone else on the list gets a copy.

### The LISTSERV Address

The term LISTSERV actually refers to the software used to administer these groups; there are several different versions, though they work in very similar ways.

Let's take a look at the LISTSERV address. It's made up of three parts: the group name itself, the LISTSERV *site*, and **.bitnet**. For instance, the address of the group College Activism/Information List is **actnow-l@brownvm.bitnet. Actnow-l** is the name of the group, and **brownvm** is the name of the site.

A *site* is a computer that has the LISTSERV program and handles one or more LISTSERV groups. In fact, a site may have dozens of groups. The brownvm site, for instance, also has the ACH-EC-L, AFRICA-L, and AGING-L forums, among about 70 others.

## So Where's the List?

Some groups are listed as *peered.* A *peered* LISTSERV group is the same as a *moderated* newsgroup—someone's checking the mail and deciding what stays and what's trashed.

I've put a list of the LISTSERV groups on the bundled disk (see the info in Section C for more information). If you want to find the latest list, or if you don't have a DOS computer, you can get Bitnet to sent you a current list. Send an e-mail message to **listserv@bitnic.educom.edu**. In the *body* of the message (not the subject) write **list global**. That's all you need. You'll automatically get an e-mail message containing the new list.

## Let's Do It—Subscribing

Once you've found a LISTSERV group to which you want to subscribe, you must send an e-mail message to the LISTSERV site (not to the group itself), asking to subscribe to the list. You'll send a message with the following text in the *body* of the message (not the subject).

SUBSCRIBE *group firstname lastname*

For instance, if I wanted to subscribe to the **actnow-l** list at the **brownvm** LISTSERV site, I could use UNIX mail to send a message like this:

```
teal% mail listserv@brownvm.bitnet
Subject:
SUBSCRIBE actnow-l Peter Kent
.
Cc:
teal%
```

Notice that you send the message to **listserv@*sitename*.bitnet**. And that the SUBSCRIBE message only contains the name of the group, not the entire group address.

You may (or may not) receive some kind of confirmation message from the group. Such a message would tell you that you have subscribed, and provide background information about the group and the different commands you can use.

Once subscribed, just sit back and wait for the messages to arrive. Or send your own—simply address mail to the full group address (in the preceding case, to **actnow-l@brownvm.bitnet**).

## Enough Already!—Unsubscribing

When you're tired of receiving all these messages, you'll have to *unsubscribe*. Send another message to the LISTSERV address. This time, it'll look like this:

```
teal% mail listserv@brownvm.bitnet
Subject:
SIGNOFF actnow-l
.
Cc:
teal%
```

Again, make sure you address it to **listserv@**, not the group name itself. And make sure the group name, but not the entire group address, appears after SIGNOFF (the instruction to unsubscribe).

Even if you've got only a mail connection to Internet, you can still subscribe to LISTSERV groups. You may not want to, though. *Some mail connections charge for each message you receive.* Join a busy group and you'll go broke.

## Getting Fancy with LISTSERV

There are a few neat things you can do with LISTSERV. By sending e-mail messages to the LISTSERV site, you can tell the LISTSERV software how you want to handle your messages. You can ask LISTSERV to send you an acknowledgment each time you send a message—by default most groups *won't* do this. You can find information about another group member—or tell LISTSERV not to provide information about you to other users. You can tell LISTSERV to stop sending you messages temporarily—perhaps when you go on vacation—and tell it to send only the message subjects, rather than the entire messages. You can request a specific message, and even search the archives for old messages.

And you can combine these commands. For instance:

```
teal% mail listserv@brownvm.bitnet
Subject:
list
query groupname
info ?
.
Cc:
teal%
```

Remember that when you want to send a message to be read by other group members, you must address it to the *groupname@sitename*.bitnet. For all other purposes—to subscribe, unsubscribe, change user options, get more information, and so on—send the message to listserv@*sitename*.bitnet.

This tells LISTSERV to send you a list of the groups handled by this site (**list**), tells you what options you have set (**query *groupname***), and sends you a list of information guides (**info ?**). It's a good idea to use this last command to find out what user documentation they have available, then use the **info**

***documentname*** command to get the site to send you specific documents. (At some sites sending e-mail to the LISTSERV address with the message, **INFO REFCARD** will get you a document outlining the commands.)

## The Least You Need to Know

- In rn, use the **s *filename*** command to save a newsgroup message.
- Reply to messages with the **f** command, or **F** if you want to include the original message.
- You may be able to start a discussion from your newsreader—check the documentation. If not, you may have a **Pnews** command or similar that lets you send a newsgroup message from the UNIX shell.
- Subscribe to a LISTSERV group by putting this command—**SUBSCRIBE *group firstname lastname***—in the *body* of a message to **listserv@*sitename*.bitnet**.
- To unsubscribe, send this in the body of a message: **SIGNOFF *groupname***.
- When you join a group, send **info ?** in the body of a message to find out what documentation they have available.

# Chapter 17

# TELNET: Inviting Yourself onto Other Systems

## In This Chapter

- Starting a telnet session
- Setting up your terminal
- Ending a telnet session
- IBM telnet sites
- Using HYTELNET
- Telneting from a menu

There are millions of computers connected to the Internet, and some of them have some pretty interesting stuff. Wouldn't it be neat if you could "reach out" and get onto those computers, to take a look at the games and databases and programs on computers the other side of the world?

Well, you can. At least you can get onto computers whose administrators *want* you to get on, and there's a surprisingly high number who do. A special program called *telnet* lets you turn your computer into a telnet *client* to access data and programs on a telnet *server* somewhere. Because you are logging into a computer other than the one you connect to normally, "telneting" is sometimes known as *remote login*.

Many Internet users have private telnet accounts—a researcher, for instance, may have several computers he works on regularly, and may have been given a special login name and password by the administrators of those computers. But many computers also allow "strangers" into their systems. This is done on a purely voluntary basis, dependent on the goodwill of the people who own or operate a particular computer. If a telnet server is open to the public, anyone can get on the system and see what's available.

## Let's Go Telneting!

Internet has a simple menu system, called *Gopher*, that can help you find and connect to telnet sites. Gopher's a great way to see what's available, to cruise around in *Gopherspace* looking for telnet sites. Take a look at Chapter 21 for more information. And we'll look at an example of a service provider's menu system based on Gopher later in this chapter.

*Telneting*, as it's known, is surprisingly easy. All you need to know is the host name of the computer you want to reach, and (perhaps) a login name it will accept. Then you'll issue this command:

**telnet *hostname***

When you connect to the computer, you may be prompted for a login name. You can enter the one you know is acceptable, or, if you don't have a login name, just type your own name. In some cases you won't even have to log in—the computer just lets you straight in without any kind of checks.

Let's take a quick look at how it works. I'm going to telnet to the Conversational Hypertext computer, an experimental system owned by the Government of Canada. It contains databases that you can "talk" to—you type questions in plain English, and the databases answer you.

You may not even need to know a hostname—I'll show you an example of a menu-based telnet session a little later.

```
teal% telnet debra.doc.ca
Trying 142.92.36.15 ...
Connected to debra.dgbt.doc.ca.
Escape character is '^]'.
SunOS UNIX (debra.dgbt.doc.ca)

login: chat
Last login: Wed Nov 10 18:11:32 from vaxa-
eth.isc.rit
SunOS Release 4.1.2 (debra) #2: Wed Dec 30
16:00:32 EST 1992
```

You'll see some more introductory screens, telling you what the system is and does. Then you'll see a list of choices:

```
  There are information files available
on the following topics:
    - AIDS (Acquired Immune Deficiency
      Syndrome)
    - Epilepsy
    - Alice (A simulated conversation)
    - Maur (A simulated conversation
      with a dragon)
    - Spectrum Management Program of
      Industry and Science Canada

  Please specify which information file
you would like:

Select an Information File:
```

Let's have a word with that dragon. We type **Maur** and press **Enter**, wait for a few moments—then:

```
[This is an experimental simulation of a
[conversation with a dragon, and it is
[STILL UNDER CONSTRUCTION.
[
[If you don't already know, communicate
[with the dragon with plain English.
[Adventure game commands like
["run away" will NOT work.
[Also please note that you CANNOT browse
[in this conversation, as you can in
[other databases.
[
[A word of warning:
[This dragon is mean and nasty.  Be
[creative and inventive and try
[to come out of it alive - it IS
[possible.
```

How do you know what to use as a login name? Often you'll see a telnet site listed in a directory, file, or e-mail somewhere. This will often tell you to use a particular login name. For instance, in the following example we will use **chat** as a login name, which tells the computer that you are a "member of the public" who wants to use the chat program. If you're not sure what to use, try anonymous.

Can't see what you type when you are in a telnet session? See the **set echo** command later in this chapter.

You may need to specify a *port number* in addition to a host name. Simply leave a space, then type the number. For instance: **telnet eve.assumption.edu 5000** takes you to a telnet site where you can play chess with other users.

```
Press <Return> to continue.
It seems like you have been wandering through these dark tunnels
for years.  They hadn't seemed so bad when you and your companions
had entered the deserted mine, led by a rumour that the Hero's
Crown might have come to rest here.  But you have been separated
from your friends by a rockslide, and have ended up following
narrow passages and shafts leading forever downwards.  You are out
of food, too, and your stomach is grumbling. You break out of your
thoughts, noticing that the light from your torch is no longer
reflecting off of damp, rough-hewn walls. Instead, the flickering
light of the torch is swallowed up by the darkness of some sort of
large cavern.  You glance back over your shoulder, and realize you
can no longer tell where you entered the cavern.  Putting aside
your misgivings, you begin to stride forward once more.  All at
once, a sibilant voice comes out of nowhere, filling your head
without a sound being made.

The voice says:
Well, well, a visitor.  It has been a long time since anyone has
come down this way.
You say:  who's there?
```

It may take a while, but eventually you'll see this:

```
The voice says:
Long ago my name would have meant something to you.  Whole villages
fled at my coming; at least they tried...  my name is Maur.
You say:  Maur? What kind of stupid name is that?

Maur says:
Yes, Maur.  You are rather irritating, you pitiful human!  I may
very well burn you to a crisp this instant!
You say:  I'd like to see you try, you over-inflated pile of $%#@
Maur says:
See for yourself.  (About ten meters into the gloom, ahead of you
and to the right, two huge red reptilian eyes flick open.  In the
faint light of your torch, you see what you thought to be a huge
black boulder, as tall as you and half again as wide, raise itself
from the rocky floor of the cave.  You realize now that it is the
head of an absolutely enormous dragon.)
```

Well, I think the computer got a little confused by my last statement. Still, it's an experimental system.

Once connected through telnet, what you see depends on what sort of system is set up on that computer. It might be a series of menus that let you select options, or it might be a prompt at which you type. You're simply logging onto a different computer, and each system varies a little.

Telnet can be slow, *very* slow, sometimes. You may on occasion type and not see what you have typed for several seconds, or even several minutes. It depends on the amount of network traffic going that way, the number of people working on the machine at that time, and the amount of traffic on your service provider's computer. If you find a particular task *too* slow, you should probably come back later. If it's *always* slow at that telnet site, maybe you can find another site with the same services.

## What Type Is Your Terminal?

Sometimes you'll be prompted to enter a terminal type before you start a telnet session. If you enter a terminal type that the other system doesn't recognize, you may not be able to see what's displayed on your screen. The most common terminal type, one that virtually all systems can use, is *VT100*. (Some communication programs have VT102 instead of VT100—they're pretty much the same.) Make sure you set your communication software to the same terminal type that you tell the telnet site to use.

## Waving Goodbye to the Telnet Site

Once you've logged on to a telnet site, you're in that computer's system, and each system's different. How do you leave the telnet site? Try **quit**, **exit**, **Ctrl-d**, or **done**. One of those, in that order, will probably end the session and return you to the telnet> prompt, or all the way to the UNIX prompt if you used the **telnet *host*** command to start the session. If none of these work, try **Ctrl-]** followed by **close**.

# Commanding Telnet to Do Your Bidding

As you've seen, you can start telnet and go to a computer directly from the UNIX prompt. You can also start telnet and go to the telnet> prompt simply by typing **telnet** and pressing **Enter**. If you do this you'll have to use the **open** command. You can't just type **telnet *hostname*** at the telnet> prompt; you'll have to use **open *hostname*** instead. Here are a few other commands you should know:

**close** Closes the connection to the telnet server. Use this if you get stuck somehow on the other computer and it doesn't seem to let you log out; press **Ctrl-]** and then type **close**. If you issued the **telnet** command from the UNIX shell prompt, you'll go back there. If you used the **open** command, you'll go back to the telnet> prompt.

**Ctrl-]** Use this to send an *escape character*, a way to halt a telnet session temporarily, while still remaining in telnet. If the telnet server just locks up, for instance, and you can't even issue the **close** command, try **Ctrl-]** instead. Then use the **close** command to actually close the session with that telnet site, or press **Enter** to return to the session. Ctrl-] won't always do the job. Some computers use a different character, but there will normally be some kind of notice (when you log in) explaining what to use.

**set escape *character*** This command changes the escape character to whatever you choose. You might want to use this in the case of a telnet session in which you log into one machine, then use telnet from there to *another* machine. (You probably won't do so often.) If you used **Ctrl-]**, it would take you all the way back to the first machine, instead of the second. So you can set a different character for just the first session. Press **Ctrl-]**, then type **set escape *character***, then press **Enter** to return to the session and telnet to the next site. (You can type ^ to indicate the Ctrl key—**^a** for Ctrl-a, for instance—or simply type the command then press **Ctrl-a**.)

**set echo** Telnet usually works with *remote echoing*: when you type, the characters are sent to the server, which then sends them back; only then are they displayed on your screen. If they are *not* sent back—you notice that you don't see the command when you type it, but the command is still used by the telnet server—you can turn *local echoing* on with this command. Press **Ctrl-]** to get back to the telnet> prompt, then type **set echo** and press **Enter**, and press **Enter** again to return to the session. Repeat to turn local echoing off. Or use the set echo command if you see everything you type *twice*, to turn off local echo.

**?** This command displays a list of telnet commands. But you can only issue it at the telnet> prompt—again, press **Ctrl-]** before typing **?**.

z This command lets you suspend the telnet session, do something on your own system, then return to where you were in the telnet session. To use this system, first press **Ctrl-]**. You'll get back to the telnet> prompt. Then type z and press **Enter**. You'll be back at the UNIX shell prompt. How you return to the telnet session depends on the type of system you are running. You'll probably use the **fg** command at the UNIX shell. In some other shells, you may have been working in a "subshell," and have to close it before you can return automatically to the telnet session. And some systems simply won't work with the z command (try it and see).

**quit** or **q** Use this to end your telnet session and return to the UNIX shell. You may also be able to use **Ctrl-d**.

# IBM Mainframe Telnet Sites

Some telnet sites are on IBM mainframes running "3270" software. If you try to telnet to a site and find the connection is instantly closed (even before you get to the login prompt), it *may* be a 3270 site (though there's no guarantee of it). If you log in and see this:

```
VM/XA SP ONLINE-PRESS ENTER KEY TO BEGIN SESSION
```

you've definitely reached a 3270 site. Leave the site (press **Ctrl-]**, then type **q** and press **Enter**). Now use this command: **tn3270** ***host***. For instance, you might have telneted with this command:

```
telnet vmd.cso.uiuc.edu.
```

You saw this:

```
Trying 128.174.5.98 ...
Connected to vmd.cso.uiuc.edu.
Escape character is '^]'.
VM/XA SP ONLINE-PRESS ENTER KEY TO BEGIN SESSION .
```

Leave the session, then do this:

```
teal% tn3270 vmd.cso.uiuc.edu
```

You'll see this:

```
VM/XA SP ONLINE

               University of Illinois  Computing Services Office
               3081-KX Serial 24222           VM/XA SP 2.1 9205

                    ¦¦       ¦¦   ¦¦¦      ¦¦¦   ¦¦¦¦¦¦¦¦
                     ¦¦     ¦¦    ¦¦¦¦    ¦¦¦¦    ¦¦    ¦¦
                      ¦¦   ¦¦     ¦¦ ¦¦  ¦¦ ¦¦    ¦¦     ¦¦
                       ¦¦ ¦¦      ¦¦  ¦¦¦¦  ¦¦    ¦¦     ¦¦
                        ¦¦¦       ¦¦   ¦¦   ¦¦    ¦¦    ¦¦
                         ¦        ¦¦        ¦¦   ¦¦¦¦¦¦¦¦

               Bitnet: UIUCVMD        Internet: vmd.cso.uiuc.edu
                                            IP: 128.174.5.98

 Fill in your USERID and PASSWORD and press ENTER
 (Your password will not appear when you type it)
 USERID   ===>
 PASSWORD ===>

 COMMAND  ===>
                                                          RUNNING   VMD
```

Now you are into the site using the 3270 mode. You can type **?** and press **Enter** to see a help screen, and **logoff** and **Enter** to end the session.

In 3270 mode you usually type something at a prompt and press **Enter** or a function key (a *PF key* in 3270-speak). If you find a 3270 site you need to work with, see if your service provider can find you some program documentation that explains how to work in this mode.

## The HYTELNET Directory—Finding What's out There

To get a taste for what's available in the world of telnet, telnet to **access.usask.ca** and log in as **hytelnet**. You'll see this:

```
                    Welcome to HYTELNET version 6.6.x
                      Last Update: November 15, 1993

          —>  What is HYTELNET?  <WHATIS>
                 Library catalogs        <SITES1>
                 Other resources <SITES2>
                 Help files for catalogs <OP000>
                 Catalog interfaces      <SYS000>
                 Internet Glossary       <GLOSSARY>
                 Telnet tips      <TELNET>
                 Telnet/TN3270 escape keys      <ESCAPE.KEY>
                 Key-stroke commands     <HELP>

   Up/Down arrows MOVE       Left/Right arrows SELECT     ? for
HELP anytime

          m  returns here     i  searches the index       q  quits

                HYTELNET 6.6 was written by Peter Scott
               E-mail address: aa375@freenet.carleton.ca
```

You'll notice that **<WHATIS>** is highlighted. You can move the highlight up and down with the **arrow** keys, and press **Enter** to select an option. Return to this menu by pressing **m**. And when you get down the "menu tree" you can use the **left arrow** to move back to the previous menu.

Play around in here—you'll find descriptions of various resources—electronic books, NASA databases, library catalogs, the Biotechnet Electronic Buyers Guide, the Business Start-Up Information Database, and on and on—and which telnet site you have to go to find them.

# Easy Street: Telneting From a Menu

If you're lucky, your service provider has set up some kind of menu system—possibly based on Gopher (explained in Chapter 21)—that leads you to various telnet sites. On the system I'm working with, for instance, **<TEL>** appears at the end of various menu options, as an indication that the option will use telnet to take me somewhere. For example, if I select

**15. Tools for Information Retrieval**, I see several options with the <TEL> indicator. There's

```
1. HYTELNET Directory of Telnet Accessible Resources <TEL>
```

(we just learned about HYTELNET); there is also

```
4.  Services - An Interactive Directory of Internet Resources <TEL>
```

(which takes you to **library.wustl.edu**, where you can access library databases all over the world). Then there's this one:

```
6.  World Wide Web (WWW) <TEL>
```

You'll learn more about WWW in Chapter 23.

What happens when I select **1. HYTELNET Directory of Telnet Accessible Resources <TEL>**? I see the following box pop up:

```
+------HYTELNET Directory of Telnet Accessible Resources------+
|                                                              |
|  Warning!!!!!, you are about to leave the Colorado SuperNet |
|  Supermenu and connect to your selection.  If you get stuck |
|  press the control key and the ] key.  If you immediately   |
|  return to SuperMenu the line may be busy.                   |
|                                                              |
|  Connecting to access.usask.ca using telnet.                 |
|                                                              |
|  Use the account name "hytelnet" to log in                   |
|                                                              |
|                               [Cancel - ^G] [OK - Enter] |
|                                                              |
+--------------------------------------------------------------+
```

Notice that this tells me where I'm going (**Connecting to access.usask.ca using telnet**), and also tells me how to log in (**Use the account name "hytelnet" to log in**). All I need to do is press **Enter**, and away I go—within a few seconds, I find myself at the HYTELNET login prompt.

## The Least You Need to Know

- Start a telnet session by typing **telnet *hostname*** or **telnet *hostname port*** and pressing **Enter**.
- To connect to a telnet site while at the telnet> prompt, type **open *hostname*** or **open *hostname port***.
- Get back to the telnet> prompt without ending the session, by pressing **Ctrl-d**.
- To close the telnet session and return to the telnet> prompt try **quit**, **exit**, **Ctrl-d**, or **done**.
- Use the **close** command to close the connection to the telnet site.
- Press **Ctrl-]** to return to the telnet> prompt, then use the **z** command to temporarily suspend the session. In most cases you'll use the **fg** command to return.
- Close telnet using the **quit**, **q**, or **Ctrl-d** commands.
- Telnet to an IBM mainframe with the **tn3270** command.
- Take a look at HYTELNET to find out what's available by telneting.

**This page requires the Alpha Books Secret Decoder/Mood Ring, available in fine stores everywhere in Upper Volta.**

# Part IV
# Finding People, Finding Files

*The Internet has a major problem. Because it's so huge, because it's not owned by anyone, there's no single index that will show you what's available and where it is. So I'm going to show you how to track down what you are looking for—or just cruise across the Internet on a voyage of discovery—in this section.*

*Also in this section, you'll meet some important allies: Archie, a program that lets you search over a thousand different computers for a particular file; Gopher, a menu system that can lead you across the world; the Wide Area Information Server, a simple method for searching databases; and the World Wide Web, a simple hypertext system that lets you follow topics from continent to continent.*

# Chapter 18
# Grabbing the Goodies—Downloading Files with FTP

## In This Chapter

- Using a menu versus a UNIX prompt
- Clues that will help you find files
- Knowing your file formats
- Searching with grep
- Grabbing files from here and there
- Dealing with compressed files

Let's say you've discovered a really neat file on a computer in Albania, or Australia, or Alabama, or somewhere. Perhaps someone told you where it was, or you saw a message in a newsgroup about it. It might be a public domain or shareware program, a document containing information you want for some research you're working on, a picture, a book you want to read. Just about anything. Now, how do you get the file from that computer to your computer?

You'll use a system called *file transfer protocol*, or *FTP* for short. In fact you'll often see the term **ftp** or **FTP**. In a directory or mail message, you might be told to "ftp to such and such a computer to find this file." That simply means use the FTP system to grab the file.

In some cases, you may have specific permission to get onto another computer and grab files. A researcher, for instance, may have been given permission to access files on a computer owned by an organization involved in the same sort of research (another university or government department, for instance).

In other cases, though, you'll just be rooting around on other people's systems without specific permission. Some systems are open to the public; anyone can get on and grab files that the system administrator has decided should be publicly accessible. This is known as *anonymous ftp*, because you don't need a login name to get onto the computer—you simply login as *anonymous*. For a password, you normally enter your mail address.

What if you know the file you want, but have no idea where to look for it? A quick way to track down a file is using Archie—I'll explain all about Archie in Chapter 20.

Before we get started, a word about *when* you should use FTP. Many systems don't like people digging around during business hours. They would rather you came in during evenings and weekends. So you may see a message asking you to restrict your use to after hours, or the FTP site may even not let you in at all during certain hours.

FTP is relatively easy to use, once you know what you are doing. But like everything else on the Internet, it's not designed to *look* like it's easy to use. There's no fancy graphical user interface (or even a menu system) built into FTP—though there is something called *Gopher* which can automate FTP for you to some degree (more of which in a moment).

## Menus, If You're Lucky

If you're lucky, your service provider has set up some kind of menu system to make FTP easy to work with, possibly using a Gopher to help you find your way through the Internet to FTP sites (we'll look at Gophers in detail in Chapter 21). On my service provider's menu system, I can select

```
8.  File Transfer (FTP)/
```

to see an FTP menu. From there I can do various things, including "Connect to a specific ftp host" and view "Ftp sites in alphabetical order by hostname." The first option expects me to enter the FTP site name. The second displays hundreds of different FTP sites, in alphabetical order. It even has a word or two indicating what I might find there. For instance:

```
                              a FTP sites

—> 1.  a.cs.uiuc.edu 128.174.252.1   TeX, dvi2ps, gif, texx2.7,/
   2.  a.psc.edu 128.182.66.105  GPLOT, GTEX/
   3.  aarnet.edu.au 139.130.204.4   Australian AARNET network/
   4.  ab20.larc.nasa.gov 128.155.23.64 amiga, comp.sources.amiga,/
   5.  acacia.maths.uwa.oz.au 130.95.16.2     unknown/
   6.  acfcluster.nyu.edu 128.122.128.11 VMS UUCP, news, DECUS library/
   7.  acns.nwu.edu 129.105.49.1    virus info/programs, maps/
```

Whichever way I use to get to one of the FTP sites, the system handles all the logging on for me, and displays file directories in the form of a menu, thus:

```
        a.cs.uiuc.edu 128.174.252.1   TeX, dvi2ps, gif, texx2.7,

     1.  .cshrc.
     2.  .hushlogin.
     3.  .login.
     4.  adm/
     5.  bin/
     6.  dev/
     7.  etc/
     8.  files.lst.
     9.  files.lst.Z <Bin>
     10. lib.
     11. ls-lR.
     12. ls-lR.Z <Bin>
     13. msgs/
 —>  14. pub/
```

E-Z

Remember, these commands are "case-sensitive." That is, an uppercase D is not the same as a lowercase d.

I can select the **pub** directory just as I would select any menu option. If I want to read a text file, I just select it from the menu (and to *get* the file, i.e. copy it back to the service provider's computer, I press **qs** while reading the file). To see information about a file, I just put the arrow on it and press =. And to transfer a binary file, I just select it from the menu.

I can even download a file directly from FTP to my computer! I select the file I want to get, then type **D**. I see something like this:

```
+————medit001.zip—————+
|                             |
|  1. Zmodem                  |
|  2. Ymodem                  |
|  3. Xmodem-1K               |
|  4. Xmodem-CRC              |
|  5. Kermit                  |
|  6. Text                    |
|                             |
|  Choose a download method:  |
|                             |
|  [Cancel ^G]  [Choose 1-6]  |
|                             |
+—————————————————+
```

I select my *transfer mode*, and away I go. (We'll look at file transfers in more detail in the next chapter.)

This system makes running around an FTP site *much* easier than using FTP itself (as you'll soon realize while you read on). I can view directories and text files more easily, transfer files back to my service provider's computer more easily, and even transfer them back to my system easily. Still, you may not have such a system available; even if you do, you may still find you want to use FTP yourself sometimes. You may not be able to get to some systems or some files using the menu system. So we're going to take a detailed look at FTP and how to use it.

# Hitting the FTP Trail

Okay, you've discovered that a file you want lies somewhere on a computer in, say, London. You've got the hostname of the FTP site, but you don't know exactly where on the computer the file lies. We'll track it down (maybe). To get started, go to the UNIX prompt and type

```
ftp hostname
```

The hostname may be a name (leo.nmc.edu) or a number (192.88.242.239).

then press **Enter**. Actually, to start the FTP program you can simply type **ftp** and press **Enter**, but including a hostname starts FTP *and* tells FTP to connect to the named host. Let's say you mistyped the name, though. You'll see an *unknown host* message, then notice that the prompt has changed to **ftp>**. To try to connect to a host from the ftp> prompt, you'll have to use the **open** command:

```
open hostname
```

OOPS!

Made a mistake when you typed the login? You'll get a message saying that the login failed. Don't worry, you're not stuck. Type **user anonymous** (or type the login name you've been assigned instead of "anonymous") and press **Enter**. Although this won't always work (the remote system may close the connection), it's worth a try.

and press **Enter**. Let's see an example:

```
ftp> open ftp.demon.co.uk
Connected to newgate.demon.co.uk.
220 newgate.demon.co.uk FTP server (Version 5.60 #1) ready.
Name (ftp.demon.co.uk:peterk): anonymous
331 Guest login ok, send ident as password.
Password: (type your e-mail address as the password)
230 Guest login ok, access restrictions apply.ftp>
```

You can ignore most of what FTP tells you. The numbers that appear before each line are of absolutely no use to you, for example. FTP likes to talk, but most of the time you don't need to listen.

We used the **open** command to connect to this host, because we were already running FTP. Notice that this hostname (**ftp.demon.co.uk**) starts with *ftp*. Many ftp sites start their hostnames with ftp, which means to get to them from the UNIX prompt you would have to type *ftp ftp.etcetera* (ftp ftp.demon.co.uk, in this case).

We saw a message saying that we had connected, another line saying that the system was ready, and then a line asking for our Name. We logged on using the name **anonymous**. In some cases you may want to ftp to a system that doesn't let just anyone in—in this case, you'll have to get permission from the system administrator, and use the login name provided. If you log in using **anonymous**, the system will usually ask you to enter your real "ident" or something similar—enter your e-mail address as the password. (You can see in our example where the remote system asked for the **Password**, but because it doesn't "echo it back" to us, you can't actually see what I typed.)

After entering your login name, you'll see a line telling you that you got through (**Guest login ok**), and probably see a message telling you that **access restrictions apply**. This simply means you're going to go only where the system administrator wants you to go, and do what he wants you to do, no more.

Remember that UNIX uses a forward slash to separate directory names, unlike DOS, which uses a backslash.

Finally, you'll see the **ftp>** prompt again. You're on. Now what?

# Finding That Pot o' Gold

Now you're on, you want to find the file you know lies somewhere on this system. Where do you start? Well, FTP has a number of commands available to you, some of which are the same as the standard UNIX commands. You might start with **pwd**. That will show you where you are: you are probably in the root directory ( / ).

Next you might use **dir**. This will show you a list of files and directories—the actual form of the list will vary between systems. (FTP's *dir* command simply tells the system to send the information, and the system decides in which format to send it.) You can also use the **ls** command to do a simple, name-only listing.

This is not quite the same as in DOS, by the way. DOS files have not only a name, but an *extension*, three characters that appear at the end of the name preceded by a period. For instance in THISFILE.TXT, the TXT is the extension. *UNIX filenames don't have extensions.* Sure, a name might have a period in it, but it might have *several* periods—a period does not signify the beginning of an "extension."

There's a problem with FTP's listing commands, though—a long directory will shoot by you faster than you can read it. There are a few ways around this problem (none are ideal, of course, but you're in the UNIX world now; this is normal).

First of all, you can use the command **ls -l "|more"** to show the list a page at a time, Alternatively, you could do a multi-column listing—type **ls -C** and press **Enter**, and the listing will be placed in several columns across your screen (though you'll get filenames only, no detail).

You could then limit the listing to only those files in which you are interested, and you can use the * *wildcards* to limit the search a little. If you type **dir *thisfile*** and press **Enter**, for instance, you'll see information about *thisfile*. Or you could type **dir *txt** and press **Enter**, you'll see a listing of all the files that end in the characters *txt*. The * simply means "anything might be here."

You could also type **dir p*** to search for all files beginning with *p* (or **dir P*** for all files beginning with *P*). However, the **dir** command also lets you specify which directory you want to list, in this manner: **dir *directoryname***. So if there are any directories beginning with *p* (or *P*), you'll also see a listing of the files in those directories.

You can also do a "recursive" directory listing. Type **ls -lR** and press **Enter**; FTP will display a list of all the files and subdirectories in the current directory, *plus* all the files and subdirectories in *those* directories, and

Perhaps the easiest way around this problem is to use your communications program to bypass it. For instance, most communications programs let you copy all the incoming data to a text file. If you are using a Windows communications program, you could then go to File Manager and double-click on the text file to open and read it (assuming it's got the extension .TXT). And some communications programs let you scroll back to see earlier in the session, so if the text runs past, you can scroll back up to view it.

Some systems let you run multiple sessions, in multiple "windows." You won't be able to do this if you have a dial-in terminal connection, but you may be able to do it if you have (for instance) a SLIP connection, depending on the software you are using. If so, you can transfer a file to your system, then read the file in another window; you don't have to leave FTP.

so on. This will often be much too big and fast to read online, so type **ls -lR *filename*** to copy it to a file—it will be placed in a file on *your* system (so you will have to close FTP to read the file), but it may help you track down what you want a bit more quickly.

## Look for Clues

Some system administrators will place clues to help you figure out what can be found where. You may see a file called **README**, **READ.ME**, **README.TXT**, **INDEX**, or something similar. This quite likely gives you a listing of what you can take, and where it is.

Also, did you see a directory named **pub**? That's the *public* directory, where the system administrator has probably placed all the files that outsiders are likely to want. You might go into that directory and see what's there, or simply type **dir pub** to list the contents of the pub directory.

You'll often find that directories have names that describe their contents (hey, we may be working with UNIX, but not *everything* has to be difficult): **slip** will probably contain SLIP software, **mac** will have Macintosh software, **xwindows** will have X Windows software, **windows** will have Microsoft Windows software, **gif** will contain GIF-format graphics, and so on. If you know what you are looking for, you can often figure out what the directory names mean.

### Why Don't You Read the Index?

Let's say you find an index file of some kind, a file named README or INDEX or whatever. How can you read this? Unfortunately, you *can't* use the

UNIX **cat** and **more** commands (at least not directly). Here's what you *can* do:

**get *filename* -** The **get** command is normally used to transfer a file from the remote system back to yours. But if you place a space and a hyphen after the filename, then press **Enter**, the remote system will display the text file. If it's short, that's great—you can easily read it. If it's not, you might try pressing **Ctrl-S** to stop the text flow, and **Ctrl-Q** to restart it (though that might not work).

You tried Ctrl-S and Ctrl-Q. You are back at the **ftp>** prompt, but now your keyboard doesn't seem to work. Press **Ctrl-Q** again.

**get *filename* "|more"** This command sends the file to the **more** command, so (if you are lucky) you can read the file in the usual UNIX way: press **Spacebar** to move from page to page. To stop displaying the file, press **Ctrl-C** (not **q**).

**get *filename*** If neither of these systems work, and if you can't use your communications program to save incoming text in a text file for you, your only hope is to transfer the file back to your system, and go back and read it there. We'll look at how to transfer files in a moment.

## grep to It!

There's another useful command for finding information: **grep**. We looked at grep in Chapter 9. You can use grep while working in FTP, but in a slightly different way; you combine it with the **get** command. For instance:

```
get wizoz10.txt "¦grep Dorothy"
```

This will search through a file called **wizoz10.txt** to see if the word **Dorothy** appears anywhere. If it does, grep will display each line in which it may be found. If there are lots of such lines, you can press **Ctrl-C** to end the list. You may also be able to use **Ctrl-S** and **Ctrl-Q** to stop and restart the list, though there will probably be quite a time lag.

You can use some (though not all) of grep's permutations. For instance, if you are not sure of the capitalization of the word you are looking for, type

```
get wizoz10.txt "¦grep -i dorothy"
```

Now grep will find the lines whether the word is **Dorothy** or **dorothy** (or DOROTHY, or DoRoThY, or whatever). Remember, however, that using the **-i** "switch" will also get you lines containing words of which the specified word is just one part. For instance, if you were searching for **she** with the **-i** switch, you'd get lines containing **she**, and lines containing **sheet**.

Unfortunately you won't be able to search for a "string" of words. This command, for instance,

```
get wizoz10.txt "¦grep "she was in""
```

would find all lines with the letters "she."

## Moving Around

You can move around the remote computer's directory system in a way very similar to that in which you move around in directories on your *own* system. You'll use the **cd** command, though it doesn't work *quite* the same in FTP as it does in plain ol' UNIX. You can't just type **cd** and press **Enter** to move to a "home" directory; if you try this, the FTP site will probably prompt you for a directory name. So it's a good idea to use the **pwd** command now and again to figure out where you are, then you can always use **cd** to get you back there. For instance, if you were in the / directory (the "root") when you got onto the FTP site's machine, you can type **cd /** and press **Enter** to go back to it from your adventures in its subdirectories.

### Changing *Your* Directory

While you are working in FTP, the **cd** command changes the directory on the FTP site's machine. There's also **lcd**, a "local change directory" command that changes the directory on *your* host machine (such as from C: to A:). That's useful when you want to transfer files, because it lets you define into which directory you want to place the file. The **lcd** command works the same as the usual cd command, as I described in Chapter 9.

# Grabbing Files—What Format?

When you've found a file you want, you'll use the **get** command to grab it. But first, let's consider the *type* of data you are going to grab. The data might be *ASCII* or *binary*. (Okay, ASCII files are *also* binary files—all computer files are stored as a collection of binary digits—but we're concerned here with how the files are going to be transferred. Read on and you'll understand the distinction.)

## ASCII or Text Files

By *ASCII* we mean a file that contains plain text—no pictures, no sounds, no program. Plain text is just that—it's not a word processing or spreadsheet file (with all the fancy formatting that comes with such files), it's just letters, numbers, and a few special characters. These include punctuation, %, $, #, and so on. Most documents you find on the Internet are ASCII files; many that end in **.txt** or **.doc** are probably ASCII files, but so are many that *don't*.

FTP assumes automatically that you want to transfer your files in ASCII (text) format. (If you want to use binary format, you'll have to tell FTP first. We'll get to that in a moment.)

Now, when FTP sends a file using an ASCII-type transfer, it doesn't really send the *file* at all—it sends the individual letters, numbers, and characters. The machine receiving the data then saves it in a text file in the appropriate format. A UNIX machine saves it in a UNIX format, a Macintosh saves it in Mac format, and so on. Different computers store information in different ways, so a Macintosh can't read a UNIX text file. But if you use an ASCII transfer, you're not transferring the file itself—you're transferring the *text*, which is stored in the receiving computer's format.

## Binary Files

Sending a binary file is different. The sending machine looks at every *bit*, and sends exactly the bits—the ones or zeros—it sees. It doesn't care what the data means. In effect, it tells the machine receiving the data that "this is a *1*, this is a *0*, this is a *0*, this is a *1*, this is a *1*," and so on. With an ASCII transfer, it would be telling the receiving computer that "this is a *p*, this is an *l*, this is an *e*, this is an *a*," and so on.

A *bit* means a *binary digit*, the smallest piece of data that can be stored by a computer. Each bit is represented by a single number, a one or a zero. The *binary* number system has only two digits, one and zero, thus *binary digit*. It takes eight bits (known as one *byte*) to store one letter, number, or character.

Why is this distinction important? Because when FTP transfers an ASCII file, it makes sure that the machine reading the file can put it in a format that can be used on that machine. But when it transfers a binary file, it really doesn't care; it transfers the file exactly as it appears at the FTP site, and assumes that the user—you—will know what sort of machine the file can be used on. So if you are transferring a DOS program, you will be using the program on a DOS machine, not a UNIX computer or a Macintosh.

## Decisions, Decisions: Choosing the Transfer Type

By default, FTP will carry out ASCII transfers. (You can check to be sure by using the **type** command, and FTP will tell you the type of transfer it's going to use.) To change to a binary transfer, use the **binary** command. FTP, characteristically obtuse, will then display **Type set to I**. Don't worry, **I** (for *image*) means binary.

If you try to send a non-text file by an ASCII transfer, FTP will get upset. It might lock up; it could even lock up *your* computer. Use ASCII transfer for text files, and binary transfer for everything else.

To convert back to an ASCII transfer, use the **ascii** command. This time FTP displays **Type set to A**.

But how do you choose what type of transfer to use? Generally this is easy. If you are transferring a document, use ASCII. If you are transferring just about anything else—a program, picture, sound, word processing document, spreadsheet, database—you'll use binary.

There are some exceptions, of course:

**Database file** These *might* be text files. If the file was created by a mainstream database program (such as dBase, Access, FoxPro, or whatever), it's a binary file. But it's quite possible to create a database in an ASCII file, using commas, tabs, or other characters to separate the data.

**Spreadsheet file** A spreadsheet file is almost certainly a binary file (although, again, it's *possible* to create a spreadsheet file as an ASCII file).

**Word processing file** A word processing file is, almost by definition, a binary file, because it contains all sorts of formatting codes. Virtually all word processors (Word, WordPerfect, Q&A Write, WordStar, etc.), create files that should be regarded as binary files. Don't confuse word processors with *text editors*; though a text editor is a program that lets you write (as is a word processor), it stores the text in an ASCII file. The earliest word processors were little more than text editors, and stored their data in an ASCII format.

**Program file** Programs are almost always transferred as binary files. However, program *source code* is generally ASCII. Programs themselves *may* be text files if they are *scripting* files. For instance, DOS "batch files" and UNIX "script files" are ASCII.

*Source code* is what a programmer actually writes; it's just words and numbers in a text file. Source code is then *compiled* into the *program file* (the file that actually does the work).

**E-mail file** Internet e-mail messages are stored as ASCII.

**Compressed file** A compressed file, one that has been "squeezed" to take up less room, is always a binary file.

**UUENCODed file** A file that has been converted to ASCII using UUENCODE or something similar (as we discussed in Chapter 12), is, of course . . . ASCII.

**PostScript file** These files, used to print on laser printers or to store graphics, are ASCII files.

**UNIX tar file** A file ending with **.tar** is a *tape archive* file created with the UNIX **tar** command. This command is used to store various files in a single .tar file (which may or may not be on tape!). These are binary files.

## If You're Not Sure What It Is . . .

. . . then you might try these rules-of-thumb:

- If you think the file's a text file (and you've no reason to think otherwise), transfer as ASCII. To be sure, you can use the **get *filename* "¦more"** command first.

- If you think the file's a program, database, spreadsheet, or word processing file (and you've no reason to think it might be ASCII), transfer as binary.
- If you know it's a graphic, sound, unencoded, or tar file, it's binary.
- If you know it's PostScript, e-mail, or compressed, it's ASCII.

UNIX actually has a command that helps you find out the type of file—not surprisingly, it's the **file** command. For instance:

```
teal% file dis212.exe
dis212.exe:     data
teal% file doswincs
doswincs:   ascii text
teal% file /bin/spell
/bin/spell:     executable shell script
teal% file disk/
disk/:          directory
teal% file nos212.zip
nos212.zip:     data
```

Problem is, you can't use this in FTP.

## Getting the File

When you're ready to get the file, transfer using the **get** command: **get *filename***. For instance, **get README** will transfer the file called README. Simple. Or rename the file while you're transferring it, with **get *filename newfilename***.

You can also get more than one file at a time by using the **mget** command: **mget *filename filename etc***. For instance:

```
ftp> mget dm930119.doc dm930119.exe
```

This tells FTP to get both **dm930119.doc** and **dm930119.exe**. I could also use a *wildcard*, like this:

```
ftp> mget d*
```

This tells FTP to get all the files starting with **d**. Of course, you could do it the other way around; **mget *.txt** would get all the files with **.txt** at the end. You can use wildcards in other ways, too. For instance, the **?** replaces a single character, so **get dm93811?.exe** would get dm938111.exe, dm938112.exe, dm938113.exe, and so on. But be warned: *the rules for using wildcards vary from system to system.*

When you finally press **Enter** and FTP starts to get your files, you'll be able to confirm that you want each one; FTP will name each file before transferring it, and ask whether you really want it (for instance: "mget dm930119.doc?"). You can type **y** and press **Enter** to continue, or **n** to skip to the next file.

Here's another pair of handy commands. Before doing a file transfer, use the **hash** command; this tells FTP to display hash marks (#) to show that it's actually doing something during transmission (so you don't think it's locked up). And use the **prompt off** command if you are using **mget**, so FTP doesn't ask you to confirm each file transfer.

## You *Might* Be Able to Do This . . .

Most people will use *anonymous FTP* most of the time. That is, they'll be "guests" on someone else's system, able to do little more than look around and "get" files that have been placed there for public use.

You've transferred a UNIX program file and found that you can't use it. You need to change the permissions on the file, so you can *execute* it. Type: **chmod u+x filename**.

In some cases, though, you may be working on a system with which you have more *rights*. You may be able to place files there, for instance (using the **put** and **mput** commands), create new directories, or even delete files. The **put** and **mput** commands work in the same way as the **get** and **mget** commands. And the other commands are the same as in UNIX. (See Chapter 9 for more information.)

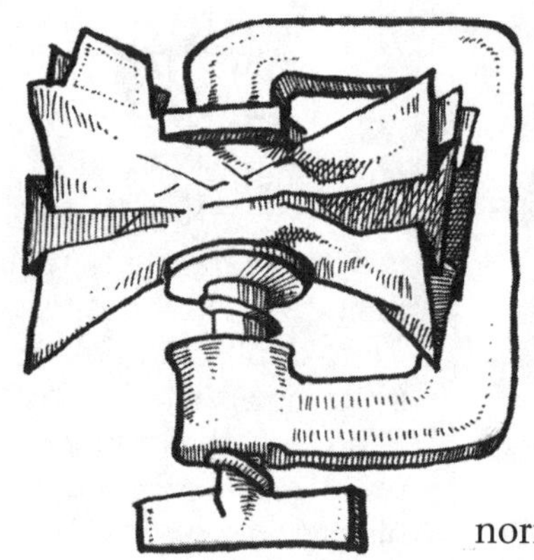

# Compressed (Squeezed) Files

Many files on FTP sites are *compressed*. That is, special programs have been used to "squeeze" the information into a smaller area. These files can't be used in their compressed state, but it's a great way to store and transmit them, because it saves disk space and transmission time. Files can be reduced down to as little as 2% of their normal size, depending on the type of file and the program used (though 40% to 75% is probably a more normal range). If you decide you need one of these compressed files, transfer it as binary. You'll then have to *uncompress* it at some point.

If you are a DOS user, you'll find that most of the compressed DOS files are in **.ZIP** format, a format created by a program called PKZIP. There *are* other programs, though—you may also see **.ARJ** (created by a program called ARJ) and **.LZH** (created by LHA).

Here are some other compressed formats:

An *archive file* is one that contains one or more other files, generally in a compressed format. Archive files are used for storing infrequently used files or for transferring files from one computer to another.

| | |
|---|---|
| .Z | UNIX, compress |
| .z | UNIX, pack |
| .shar | UNIX, sh (shell archive) |
| Sit | Macintosh, Stuffit |
| .pit | Macintosh, Packit |
| .zoo | zoo210 (available on various systems) |
| .tar | UNIX tar |
| .arc | DOS, PKARC (an older method, predating PKZIP) |

You may even see programs that have been compressed *twice*. For instance, you might find a file called **sliphack.tar.Z**. First you should use the UNIX **uncompress** program (**uncompress sliphack.tar.Z**). The files inside this file are extracted. You'll then find that one or more of those files are .tar files, so you'll use the **tar** program:

**tar xvf sliphack.tar**

This command simply tells tar to extract the files from sliphack.tar, and display the file names as it does so. If you just want to see what's inside, use **tar tf *filename***.

You may occasionally run into *shell archives*, files that end with **.shar**. These are UNIX files that have been archived with a shell script (a script in UNIX is kinda like a batch file in DOS). You run the script to extract the files: **sh *filename***.

Finally, there's something called *self-extracting archives*. Various programs, such as PKZIP and ARJ, can create files that can be *executed* (run) to extract the archived files automatically. This is very useful for sending a compressed file to someone when you're not sure if they have the program to uncompress the file (or would know how to use it). For instance, PKZIP can create a file with a **.EXE** extension; such a file can be run directly from the DOS prompt, just by typing its name and pressing **Enter**. When you do so, out pop all the compressed files.

There's a major problem with shell archives. They are actual programs, and you don't know for sure what they are going to do when they run. At a minimum, put the .shar file in its own directory before you run it, to limit the damage it might do should it "get loose." Ideally, you should know where the thing came from, and be sure it's okay before you use it. (See the next chapter for more information about viruses, mean little programs that can make your life a misery.)

While digging around in an FTP site, you'll often notice files with the same name except for the last few characters—you might find **thisdoc.txt** and **thisdoc.zip**, for instance. The first is a simple ASCII text file, the next is a ZIP file—which, you'll notice, is much smaller than the first. If you know you can uncompress the file once you've got it, get the compressed version. It'll save time and money.

To impress your friends with your familiarity with the command line, you can type **qui** or even **by** and press **Enter** to leave FTP.

## So Long, Farewell

How do you leave FTP? Well, to leave the current FTP site you are logged onto, you can type **close** and press **Enter**. This will take you back to the ftp> prompt (if you used the **open** command to start the session), or to the UNIX prompt (if you used the **ftp** command to start the session). To leave the FTP site *and* close FTP at the same time, you can use the **quit** or **bye** commands. Or press **Ctrl-D.**

### The Least You Need to Know

- If your service provider has a menu system for FTP, get to know it. It can save *lots* of time and trouble.
- Start an FTP session from the UNIX prompt by typing **ftp *hostname***. Start from the ftp> prompt by typing **open *hostname***.
- Use the **cd** and **pwd** commands to move around in the directories.
- The **ls -x** command lists all the files in several columns, so you can see them all.
- Read a text file using this command: **get *filename* "|more"**.
- Transfer a file back to your system using the **get *filename*** command.
- If the file's anything other than a text document, use the **binary** command *before* using the **get *filename*** command to set FTP to a binary transfer. Use **ascii** to change it back.
- Close the FTP session using the **close** command.
- Close the FTP session and close FTP itself with **qui** or **by** or **Ctrl-D**.

# Chapter 19
# More Neato FTP Stuff

## In This Chapter

- Grabbing the CIA World Factbook
- File transfers with xmodem or zmodem
- Speeding logins with .netrc
- Meeting Your FTP hosts
- FTP by mail
- Avoiding computer viruses

By this time, you should know that "FTP" is a *file transfer protocol*, not a rude noise. (For your reference, the rude noise would look something like "pfttph." Go ahead and pronounce it if FTP has been a struggle up to now.) Anyway, in the last chapter we spent a lot of time getting an overview of FTP and what it does. In this chapter, we're going to look at a few more details. But first, let's actually *do* something with FTP.

## Grabbing Files From Project Gutenberg

In this example, we're going to take a look at Project Gutenberg's files, and grab a free copy of the CIA's *World Factbook*. It's large (about 1 MB in compressed form, about 2.5 MB uncompressed), so if you see something you'd rather have, grab that instead.

Here we go. The commands that *you* type are in **bold**. The rest is what you'll see from the other computer. First, let's start by FTPing to the host that has Project Gutenberg's files:

```
teal% ftp mrcnext.cso.uiuc.edu
Connected to mrcnext.cso.uiuc.edu.
220 mrcnext.cso.uiuc.edu FTP server (Version 5.1 (NeXT 1.0) Tue Jul
21, 1992) ready.
Name (mrcnext.cso.uiuc.edu:peterk): anonymous
331 Guest login ok, send ident as password.
Password: (I typed my e mail address here; you won't see it, so
type carefully.)
230 Guest login ok, access restrictions apply.
ftp>
```

I don't really know were everything is, so let's take a look at the directory. (I'm not going to show you the entire directory.)

```
ftp> dir
200 PORT command successful.
150 Opening ASCII mode data connection for /bin/ls.
total 137
-rw-r—r—    1 187      micro       1579   Jun  4    2000 README
-rw-r—r—    1 109      micro       1798   Jan  4    2000 README.bak
drwxrwxr-x  2 root     micro       1024   Oct  4    1999 amiga
dr-xr-xr-x  2 root     micro       1024   Jul 14    2000 bin
```

Did you notice the README file? Let's take a look at what it has to say:

```
ftp> get README "¦more"
200 PORT command successful.
150 Opening ASCII mode data connection for README (1579 bytes).
This is an '040 NeXT cube with a 660 Meg hard drive.  In this
public directory is an NFS mount of the ftp directory on
ftp.cso.uiuc.edu,
128.174.5.59, labelled "ux1".  It contains a lot more than 660 Meg.
Files/directories of interest:
amiga
        A few files for Amigans.  Look in ux1/amiga for more.
```

```
apple2
              For necromechanomaniacs.
Bible
              A copy of the KJB can be found on uxc.cso.uiuc.edu
drivers.zip
              A bunch of packet drivers for PC versions of Telnet.
cwp.zip
              Chinese Word Processor.  This is NOT a product of the
              University of Illinois, and we're NOT doing support for
              it.
               It is nonetheless useful, and it's here.
etext
              Michael Hart's Project Gutenberg electronic text
               collection.
```

There's more, but we're interested in the **etext** directory. Let's go there now, and take a look at what's in it.

```
ftp> cd etext
250 CWD command successful.
ftp> dir
200 PORT command successful.
150 Opening ASCII mode data connection for /bin/ls.
total 54
-rw-r—r—     1 24      wheel    14300   May 1    07:03   0INDEX.GUT
-rw-r—r—     1 24      wheel      300   Sep 28    2000   ETEXT92
-rw-r—r—     1 24      wheel     9214   Jul 19    1998   LIST.COM
-rw-r—r—     1 24      wheel     4420   Jun  3    2000   NEWUSER.GUT
drwxr-xr-x   3 24      wheel     1024   Apr 29   17:00   articles
```

Again, there's more, but let's take a look at 0INDEX.GUT.

```
ftp> get OINDEX.GUT "¦more"
200 PORT command successful.
550 OINDEX.GUT: No such file or directory.
```

Oops! I typed an O (capital "oh") instead of a 0 (zero). Let's try again.

```
ftp> get 0INDEX.GUT "¦more"
200 PORT command successful.
```

```
150 Opening ASCII mode data connection for 0INDEX.GUT (14300
bytes).
etext93:
total 36522
-rw-r—r—   1 hart      1166473    Mar  1     1993     2sqrt10.txt
-rw-r—r—   1 hart       552131    Mar  1     1993     2sqrt10.zip
-rw-r—r—   1 hart       247391    Jun 29    17:10     32pri10.txt
-rw-r—r—   1 hart       124130    Jun 29    17:10     32pri10.zip
-rw-r—r—   1 hart       637842    Aug 31    22:56     7gabl10.txt
-rw-r—r—   1 hart       276240    Aug 31    22:57     7gabl10.zip
-rw-r—r—   1 hart       38818     Mar 31     1993     alad10.txt
```

It turns out that this file is a list of the Gutenberg files—not much use to us right now, because we don't know which is which. When we did a **dir** earlier on, though, we saw another file called **gutmar3.3**. Let's see what that says.

```
ftp> get gutmar3.3 "¦more"
200 PORT command successful.
150 Opening ASCII mode data connection for gutmar3.3 (14005 bytes).
****This is the Project Gutenberg Newsletter for March, 1993***
Our Goal, To Give Away One Trillion Etexts By December 31, 2001
*[10,000 titles to 100,000,000 people equals 1,000,000,000,000]
```

This file has more background information. Later on in the file, though, we find a listing of some of the books available, including this line:

```
Jan 1993 The World Factbook          (world192.xxx)
```

This file doesn't show a complete listing, unfortunately; to find that, we'd probably have to spend more time digging around. Still, it's shown us that *The World Factbook* is in a file called **world192.xxx**, and was put there in January of 1993. (The gutmar3.3 file lists other things, too: *Dr. Jekyll and Mr. Hyde, Far From the Madding Crowd,* Sophocles' *Oedipus Trilogy, The Time Machine* by H.G. Wells, The 1990 U.S. Census, *Alice in Wonderland,* and more.)

So, let's go get that *World Factbook*. First we'll go to the **etext93** directory, where the documents added in 1993 are stored.

```
ftp> cd etext93
250 CWD command successful.
```

Now we'll look for the *World Factbook*. This command will list all the files beginning with **world**:

```
ftp> dir world*
200 PORT command successful.
150 Opening ASCII mode data connection for /bin/ls.
total 9432
-rw-r—r—   1 24     wheel    2473400   Jul  6  2001  world192.txt
-rw-r—r—   1 24     wheel    1006254   Jul  6  2001  world192.zip
-rw-r—r—   1 24     wheel    2423749   Jun 19  2001  world92.txt
-rw-r—r—   1 24     wheel     992943   Jun 19  2001  world92.zip
-rw-r—r—   1 24     wheel    2638067   May 1  19:43  world93.txt
-rw-r—r—   1 24     wheel    1080105   May 1  19:46  world93.zip
226 Transfer complete.
remote: world*
414 bytes received in 0.15 seconds (2.7 Kbytes/s)
```

The gutmar3.3 file told us that the *World Factbook* was in world92.xxx. The *xxx* means the last three characters may vary; as you can see, there's a **.txt** version (ASCII text) and a **.zip** version (compressed using PKZIP). But you'll notice also that there's a version called **world93.txt**, probably the next year's version. Let's look:

```
ftp> get world93.text "¦more"
200 PORT command successful.
150 Opening ASCII mode data connection for world93.txt
(2638067 bytes).
**Welcome To The World of Free Plain Vanilla Electronic Texts**
**Etexts Readable By Both Humans and By Computers, Since 1971**
*These Etexts Prepared By Hundreds of Volunteers and Donations*
Information on contacting Project Gutenberg to get Etexts, and
```

This file goes on with introductory stuff, but finally, we see:

```
*The Project Gutenberg Edition of the 1993 CIA World Factbook*
Central Intelligence Agency
The World Factbook 1993
```

That's it, exactly what we're looking for. We can browse through the file a little way, but when we're ready to transfer it back to our own system, we press **Ctrl-c**.

```
^C
426 Transfer aborted. Data connection closed.
226 Abort successful
local: ¦more remote: world93.txt
12679 bytes received in 3.9 seconds (3.2 Kbytes/s)
```

We're ready to transfer the file. We'll transfer the ZIP version—it's much smaller, and we can "unzip" it when we get back (that's assuming you've got a DOS-based PC and a copy of PKUNZIP. If not, you'll want to use the text version.) First, though, we have to change to a binary format, using the **bin** or **binary** command (*if you're transferring text, don't use this command*).

```
ftp> bin
200 Type set to I.
ftp> get world93.zip
200 PORT command successful.
150 Opening BINARY mode data connection for world93.zip (1080105
bytes).
226 Transfer complete.
local: world93.zip remote: world93.zip
1080105 bytes received in 28 seconds (38 Kbytes/s)
```

We've finished in FTP, so let's get out:

```
ftp> bye
221 Goodbye.
```

Now, if you've got a dial-in terminal connection, you have to get the file from the service provider's computer back to yours. So let's look at *file transfers*.

# File Transfers

If you have a dial-in terminal account, you are working at home or your office on your computer, which is connected to your service provider's computer. When you *get* files using FTP, where do they go? Back to your directory on the service provider's computer. Now you've got to get them back to *your* computer. How?

Well, there are a few ways. Most communication programs will let you do an *xmodem* transfer, so we'll look at that first.

## Xmodem

Most communications programs can work with xmodem to transmit files. It's quite easy. First, make sure your communication program is set up to receive files by xmodem. If you are using Windows Terminal, for instance, you will select **Binary Transfers** from the **Settings** menu, then click on the **Xmodem** option button.

Now, at the UNIX shell, you'll type the xmodem command, starting with **xmodem**, and followed by one of these:

**sb** Send binary—use this if you are sending a binary file (see the last chapter for a discussion of binary Vs. ASCII).

**st** Send text—use this if you are sending a text (ASCII) file to an MS-DOS computer.

**sa** Send Apple—use this if you are sending a text (ASCII) file to an Apple computer.

Then follow these by the filename. So, for instance:

```
xmodem st zap.txt
```

This would send the file named **zap.txt** in ASCII format to your computer. After typing the command and pressing **Enter**, you'll see this:

If you are going the other way—sending files from your computer to the service provider's computer—you'll use the **rb**, **rt**, and **ra** commands (Receive Binary, Receive Text, and Receive Apple).

```
XMODEM Version 3.9 (November 1990) — UNIX-Microcomputer File
Transfer Facility
File zap.txt Ready to SEND in text mode
Estimated File Size 2K, 15 Sectors, 1845 Bytes
Estimated transmission time 2 seconds
Send several Control-X characters to cancel
```

You then tell your communications program to receive the file; in Windows Terminal, you would select **Receive Binary File** from the **Transfers** menu (even if you are sending a text file, you are using a binary transfer method to send it). You'll have to tell your communications program what filename to use. When the transfer is complete, you'll be returned to the UNIX shell prompt.

There are a lot of options available with the xmodem command (to read the xmodem manual pages, type **man xmodem** at the UNIX prompt and press **Enter**). You can tell it to send *xmodem/crc* when *receiving* files, for instance (though this isn't necessary when *sending* them, because the receiving software will request that type of error-checking; Windows Terminal uses xmodem/crc). You can also use the xmodem command to send files using another protocol, *ymodem*, which many communications programs can use.

Be careful when transferring files. These systems will usually overwrite files that have the same names as the ones being transferred. If you use zmodem, you can use the -p switch (as in **sz -p *filename***) to make sure files aren't overwritten; but test this first, as it may not work with some systems. See the next section.

## Zmodem

The xmodem and ymodem protocols are not necessarily your best options. *Zmodem*, for instance, is much better. It's quite a bit faster, and while xmodem can send multiple files with a bit of messing around (assuming your communications software can *accept* multiple files, which it may not be able to do), zmodem makes it much easier to send several files at once.

To run zmodem, begin by setting up your communications program to receive zmodem transfers (Windows Terminal can't use zmodem).

Then use this command:

```
sz filename
```

To see a summary of all the options, type **sz** and press **Enter** at the prompt.

You can actually send several files at a time. For instance, **sz *.txt** sends all the .txt files in the directory, **sz file1 file2** sends both file1 and file2.

The nice thing about zmodem is that once you issue the command, that's it—you don't have to tell your system anything about the incoming files. As long as you've got *zmodem receive* set up, it will detect when the service provider's computer is sending data, and even figure out the filenames, automatically. When transferring files from your computer to the service providers, zmodem is also very simple. You begin the transfer from your communications program; the service provider's computer detects it, and begins receiving automatically.

There are a few command *switches* you need to know about when using zmodem:

**-b** Sends the file in binary format. This is the default anyway, so you won't normally need to use this.

**-a** This, in effect, sends an ASCII file to a DOS machine—it converts the UNIX new line character at the end of each line to the DOS carriage return/line feed characters.

**-p** This tells your computer not to overwrite any existing files with the same name. But this option may not work with all systems, so experiment with it before you rely on it.

You can combine these. For instance, **sz -ap *filename*** to send a text file and ensure that it doesn't overwrite a file of the same name.

## By the Way . . .

If you want more information about zmodem, use the **man sz** command to see the online manual.

## Sending the CIA World Factbook

I'm going to use Zmodem to get the CIA *World Factbook* off my service provider's computer, because it's fast. If you don't have Zmodem, use Xmodem (type **xmodem -st world93.zip**, for instance, press **Enter**, then tell your communication program to get ready to receive the file).

```
teal% sz world93.zip
rz
*B0000000000
teal%
```

That's almost it. If you transferred the ZIP version, you now have to unzip it. Go to the DOS prompt, change to the directory containing the file (make sure that you have a copy of PKUNZIP in that directory), and type

```
C:\DOWNLOAD>pkunzip world93.zip
```

Now press **Enter**. (Okay, you don't *have* to put the files in the same directory if you type a full path for each one, but this is the easy way.) That's it. In a few seconds you'll have an (almost) free copy of the CIA's 1993 *World Factbook*. You can open it in any word processor, and use the search feature to track down anything you need to know about Albania, Australia, or Zimbabwe.

# Speedy Logins—Using the .netrc File

If you find yourself going to a particular FTP site frequently, maybe you should automate the login procedure. Use a text editor (such as vi) to create a file called **.netrc** in your home directory. Then enter this text:

```
machine hostname
login loginname
password password
```

Here's an example:

```
machine ftp.demon.co.uk
login anonymous
password peterk@csn.org
```

The next time you ftp to this site, here's what you'll see:

```
teal% ftp ftp.demon.co.uk
Connected to newgate.demon.co.uk.
220 newgate.demon.co.uk FTP server (Version 5.60 #1) ready.
331 Guest login ok, send ident as password.
230 Guest login ok, access restrictions apply.
ftp>
```

The .netrc logs in for you. It's quicker, and it doesn't make mistakes.

# But Mine Doesn't Work That Way . . .

I've explained standard FTP, but there are variations. As you may remember, I told you that when you use the **dir** command, FTP asks the host to send a directory listing, and the host decides what to send. That means you'll see some differences between systems. Here are a few things to remember:

## DEC VMS Systems

Filenames on VMS systems consist of the name itself, an extension, and a version number (e.g., READTHIS.TXT;5). You can ignore the version number. If the extension is .TXT, it's a text file you can read. If it's .DIR, it's not a file at all, it's a directory. To change directories, use the name without the extension (**cd files**, not **cd files.dir**). Also, VMS systems separate subdirectories with periods, not slashes; DIR1/DIR2/DIR3 appears as DIR1.DIR2.DIR3. And the **cd** command may not work normally for you on a VMS system. Instead of **cd ..**, You may need to use **cdup**. Also, you may have to name the subdirectory you want to move to (like this: **cd [dir1.dir2.dir3]**), though the normal **cd dir1/dir2/dir3** may work on some systems.

## DOS Systems

If you are a DOS user, you'll feel right at home when ftping to a DOS host (there *are* a few). DOS names consist of a name (up to 8 characters), and extension (up to three). In directory listings, directories will be indicated by **<dir>**. Also, you may be able to change *disks* to get to more directories while working on a DOS system (type **cd *n:*** where *n* is the disk letter). And while DOS uses backslashes to separate directories (dir1\dir2\dir3), you must use the forward slash when using the cd command in FTP (cd dir1/dir2/dir3).

## IBM/VM Systems

VM machines store files on disks rather than in a directory system. And *each disk* requires that you log in. So to change to another disk, you type **cd *login.disk***, where *login* is your login name for that disk, and *disk* is the disk itself. Then type **account *password***. (If you are using anonymous ftp, you won't need the password.) Filenames on VM systems have two parts—the name itself and a file *type*. These parts are separated by spaces. When you use the **get** command, however, you'll separate the two parts with a period (**get *name.type***).

## Macintosh

On a Macintosh system, directories (or *folders* in Mac-speak) are shown by a slash at the end of a name. And filenames may contain spaces. To work with a file that has spaces in its name, enclose the entire name in quotation marks (as in **get "this file" "|more"**). When you transfer such a file, you should rename it while transferring (**get "this file" thisfile**).

# FTP by Mail?

If you don't have access to FTP (as many Internet mail-only users don't), there's still hope for you. It's possible to work by mail using *FTPmail*. Digital Equipment Corporation (DEC) kindly maintains a system that will FTP to any site for you. You just send FTPmail an e-mail message telling it what you want it to do, and away it goes. You'll send your message to **ftp@decwrl.dec.com**.

If you'd like to try this, send an e-mail message to this host. Don't include a subject, and just write **help** at the beginning of the first line of the message. You'll get a list of commands back. For instance, it will explain how to find a listing of a particular directory (using the index command).

Note that you might find FTPmail tricky to use. You need to know *where* (in which directory) the file you want is. That's not always easy, because people aren't always specific when they tell you to get something from an FTP site—either they don't remember exactly where a particular file is, or figure that you'll be able to find it anyway. Even if they are specific, the file may get moved, or they may get the *case* wrong—remember that you need to spell the filename *exactly* as it really is, using uppercase and lowercase correctly. FTPmail is like working blind, but it may be worth a try if it's your only option.

To get a file from FTPmail, you'll put something like this in the body of a message:

```
connect hostname
chdir directorypath
binary
get filename
quit
```

Of course, if you want the file sent as ASCII, you'd omit the *binary* command. See the FTPmail help document for more information.

## More Files by Mail: Special Servers and LISTSERV

There are two other ways to get files by mail: using various special servers scattered around the Internet, and using special LISTSERV servers (we looked at LISTSERV in Chapter 16). These are mail servers set up specially to distribute files. You may see these sites mentioned elsewhere, with instructions to get a particular file from a particular mail address.

In the case of the Internet servers, you'll send a message with the subject that looks like this:

```
send filename
```

The *body* of the message is left blank. The filename may need to include the directory path. If you're not sure what is where, send a message with **help** as the subject.

When you are trying to grab mail from LISTSERV servers, you'll put the commands in the *body* of the message, not the subject:

```
get filename filetype
```

The files distributed by the LISTSERV servers use the IBM VM filename format, in which each filename has two parts—the name itself, and the file type. To get a file, you'll have to know both parts.

## It's Alive! Viruses and Other Nasties

If you haven't been alone in a cave for the past six or seven years, you've probably heard about computer viruses. A *virus* is a computer program that can reproduce itself, and even convince unknowing users to help it spread. It spreads far and wide, and may create damage. As with the real things, the effects of a virus can range from almost-unnoticeable to fatal (to your system). A virus may display a Christmas tree on your screen, or destroy everything on your hard disk.

Viruses hide out in a variety of places. *Boot sector* viruses hide in a disk's boot sector, the part of the disk read into memory when the computer starts; from there, they can then copy themselves onto the boot sectors of other disks. *File* viruses hide out in program files, and copy themselves to other program files when that program is run.

Viruses and other malevolent computer bugs are real, and they do real damage. In 1988, 6,000 computers connected to the Internet were infected with a worm. (The Internet has grown tremendously since then—the numbers would surely be higher today.) Just recently, a service provider in New York had to close down temporarily after its system became infected.

Unfortunately, security on the Internet is lax. Some computer BBS services (such as CompuServe) check their own systems for viruses regularly. But on the Internet it's up to each system administrator (and there are thousands of them) to keep their systems clean. If just one does a bad job, a virus can get through, and be carried by ftp all over the world. Some system administrators are reacting by closing off some Internet services (not allowing users to ftp files, for instance).

The term *virus* has become a "catch-all" for a variety of different digital organisms. Such as *bacteria* (which reproduce and do no direct damage except using up disk space and memory); *rabbits* (which reproduce very quickly); *Trojan horses* (viruses embedded in otherwise-useful programs); *bombs* (a program that just sits and waits for a particular date or event before wreaking destruction—often left deep inside programs by disgruntled employees); and *worms* (programs that copy themselves from one computer to another, independent of other executable files, and "clog" the computers by taking over memory and disk space).

## Tips for "Safe Computing"

If you are just working with e-mail and perhaps ftping documents, you're okay. The problems arise when you transfer programs. (That's not to say your directories on your service provider's system can't get infected, but if you don't transfer programs back to your own computer, it won't get infected; if you don't ftp programs to your service provider's system, you won't introduce viruses. Even so, another user may.)

If you *do* plan to transmit programs, perhaps the best advice is to get a good anti-virus program—they're available for all computer types. Each time you transmit an executable file, use your anti-virus program to check it. And make sure you keep good backups of your data. Backups can also become infected with viruses, of course—but if a virus hits, at least you can reload your backup data and then use an anti-virus program to clean the files (some backup programs check for viruses while backing up).

## The Least You Need to Know

- Send a binary file with xmodem using this command: **xmodem sb *filename***.
- To send a text file with xmodem, use **st** instead of sb. To send text to an Apple computer, use **sa**.
- Zmodem is generally quicker and easier to use than xmodem.
- Send binary files with zmodem using this command: **sz *filename filename filename***.
- Send text files using this command: **sz -a *filename filename filename***.
- The .netrc file lets you automate your FTP logins; FTP will enter the appropriate loginname and password for you, automatically.
- Not all FTP hosts are UNIX machines. VMS, DOS, and Macintosh hosts work in a similar (but slightly different) way.
- Viruses are real and dangerous. Use anti-virus software to check files you transfer.

# Chapter 20
# Archie the File Searcher

## In This Chapter

- How Archie indexes files
- Using an Archie Telnet site
- Searching for files
- Sending Archie lists home via e-mail
- Searching for file descriptions
- Using your service provider's Archie client
- Mail Order Archie

FTP is all very well, but how do you know where to go to find the file you want? Sometimes you'll see the FTP site mentioned in e-mail or a document you found somewhere. But what if you know the file you are looking for, but have no idea where to go to find it?

Archie to the rescue. Designed by a few guys at McGill University in Canada, *Archie* is a system that indexes FTP sites, listing the files that are available at each site. Archie lists several million files, at over a thousand FTP sites, and provides a surprisingly quick way to find out where to go to grab a file in which you are interested.

**By the Way . . .**

Though Archie finds files, many files contain data—and because Archie has a *descriptive-index search*, that means you can search for a particular *subject*, and find files with information about that subject. See later in this chapter.

# More Client/Server Stuff

As with certain other Internet systems, Archie is set up using a "client/server" system. An Archie *server* is a computer that periodically takes a look at all the Internet FTP sites around the world, and builds a list of all their available files. Each server builds a database of those files. An Archie *client* program can then come along and search the server's database, using it as an index.

It's generally believed in Internetland that it doesn't matter much which Archie server you use, because they all do much the same thing—some are simply a few days more recent than others. This isn't always true. Sometimes you may get very different results from two different servers. If one server finds two "hits," another might find seven, for instance.

# Getting to Archie

There are several ways to use Archie:

- Use an Archie client on your service provider's computer, either from a menu option or a shell command.
- Use telnet to get to an Archie server site.
- Use e-mail to send questions to an Archie server site.

If your service provider's system has an Archie client setup, you should use it when you can (instead of telneting to an Archie server) because it will cut down on network traffic. However, this arrangement has limitations; it may be much slower than telneting to a server, and you won't be able to do everything you could do if you telneted. We'll take a look at the telnet method first.

# Telneting to Archie's Place

Here are the current Archie servers:

**United States:**

| | | |
|---|---|---|
| archie.ans.net | 147.225.1.2 | USA, ANS |
| archie.internic.net | 198.49.45.10 | USA, AT&T (NY) |
| archie.rutgers.edu | 128.6.18.15 | USA, Rutgers U. |
| nic.sura.net | 128.167.254.179 | USA, SURAnet |
| archie.unl.edu | 129.93.1.14 | USA, U. of Nebraska |

**Other Countries:**

| | | |
|---|---|---|
| archie.au | 139.130.4.6 | Australia |
| archie.edvz.uni-linz.ac.at | 140.78.3.8 | Austria |
| archie.univie.ac.at | 131.130.1.23 | Austria |
| archie.uqam.ca | 132.208.250.10 | Canada |
| archie.funet.fi | 128.214.6.100 | Finland |
| archie.th-darmstadt.de | 130.83.22.60 | Germany |
| archie.cs.huji.ac.il | 132.65.6.15 | Israel |
| archie.unipi.it | 131.114.21.10 | Italy |
| archie.kuis.kyoto-u.ac.jp | 130.54.20.1 | Japan |
| archie.wide.ad.jp | 133.4.3.6 | Japan |
| archie.kr | 128.134.1.1 | Korea |
| archie.sogang.ac.kr | 163.239.1.11 | Korea |
| archie.nz | 130.195.9.4 | New Zealand |
| archie.rediris.es | 130.206.1.2 | Spain |
| archie.luth.se | 130.240.18.4 | Sweden |
| archie.switch.ch | 130.59.1.40 | Switzerland |
| archie.ncu.edu.tw | 140.115.19.24 | Taiwan |
| archie.doc.ic.ac.uk | 146.169.11.3 | UK |

All Archie servers are in English, no matter what country they're in, but the introductory text may be written in the host's native language.

Which should you use? Depends. *The closer the better,* generally, because you are generating less network traffic—your message only has to travel over, say, a few hundred miles of the network rather than thousands. But you'll find you won't be able to get onto some of these servers. Some may be too busy; Archie is a very popular service, and some servers receive more attempts to get into the system than they can handle. Once they have more than a certain number of people using the system, they simply deny access.

Other systems have a policy of denying *everyone* access between certain hours—8:00 a.m. and 8:00 p.m., for instance. You can use the server later, or try another.

How, then, to get to one of these? For instance, type

```
teal% telnet archie.rutgers.edu
```

and press **Enter**. When asked to log in, simply type **archie** and press **Enter**.

To find the latest list of Archie servers, send an e-mail message to an Archie server, like this: **archie@*archieserver*** (for example, **archie@archie.rutgers.edu**). In the body of the message, type **servers** on the first line.

## Searching a Server Via Telnet

Before you begin searching for a filename, you ought to figure out the *type* of search that you want to use:

**exact** You must type the exact name of the file for which you are looking.

**regex** You will type a UNIX *regular expression.* That means that Archie will regard some of the characters in the word you type as *wildcards*. If you don't understand regular expressions, you're better off *avoiding* this type of search.

**sub** Archie will search *within* filenames for what you type. That is, it will look for all names that are the same, or that *include* the characters you typed. If you are searching for "textwin," for example, it will find "textwin" *and* "textwindows." Also, when using a sub search, you don't need to worry about the case of the characters—Archie will find "textwindows" *and* "TextWindows".

**subcase** This is like the sub search, except you need to get the *case* of the word correct—if you ask for "textwin," Archie will find "textwindows," but not "TextWindows".

You'll probably want to use the sub search. It will take a little longer than others, but it's more likely to find what you are looking for.

Each server expects to see a different type of search. If you type **show search** and press **Enter**, Archie will show you which one it assumes you are going to use. In fact, when you first log into Archie, you may see

```
# 'search' (type string) has the value 'regex'
```

or a similar line. To set the search to another form, type **set search *type*** (**set search sub**, for instance).

## So Where's My File?

Now, down to the nitty gritty. Where's the file you want? We are going to use the **prog** command to search. Let's search for "textwin." First, we're going to set the search type to *sub*. Then we'll search.

```
archie> set search sub
archie> prog textwin
```

**prog** is the original Archie command used to find a file. Newer versions can also accept the **find** command. Both do the same thing—it doesn't matter which you use.

When Archie begins, you may see something like this:

```
# Search type: sub.
# Your queue position: 3
# Estimated time for completion: 00:19
working... ¦
```

Or perhaps you'll just see this, which shows you how many files it has found, and the percentage of the index it's searched so far:

```
# matches / % database searched:    7 /80%
```

Either way, if you are lucky and Archie finds something, eventually you'll see something like this:

```
Location: /contrib/src/pa/ups-2.45/mips-ultrix/ups
FILE      rwxr-xr-x        23  Oct 28 06:43   textwin.c -> ../../
src/ups/textwin.c
FILE      rwxr-xr-x        23  Oct 28 06:43   textwin.h -> ../../
src/ups/textwin.
Location: /contrib/src/pa/ups-2.45/src/ups
FILE      r—r—r—        18985  May 20  1992   textwin.c
FILE      r—r—r—         2542  May  3  1991   textwin.h

Host csn.org   (128.138.213.21)
Last updated 19:45  4 May 1993
Location: /pub/dos
DIRECTORY rwxrwxr-x       512  Mar 29 04:01   textwin

Host faui43.informatik.uni-erlangen.de   (131.188.1.43)
Last updated 08:17  7 May 1993
Location: /mounts/epix/iwiftp/public/portal/amiga/amok/amok58
FILE      rw-r—r—       10132  Feb 15 20:29   TextWindows.lzh
Location: /mounts/epix/iwiftp/public/portal/amiga/amok/amok68
FILE      rw-r—r—       10928  Feb 15 20:30   TextWindows_1.1.lha
```

That's it—now you know where to go to find the files you are looking for. In this case, we found a program called TextWindows and one called textwin. Notice the words **FILE** and **DIRECTORY** on the left side of the listing. Archie searches for both files *and* directories that match your criteria. Above each listing there's also a **Location**, showing the directory (or subdirectory) in which you should look for this file. A line or two above there, you'll see the **Host** line: this is the host computer to which you should ftp to get the file. For instance, if you wanted to get the last file in our list, you would ftp to **faui43.informatik.uni-erlangen.de** (a computer somewhere in Germany), and go into the following directory:

**/mounts/epix/iwiftp/public/portal/amiga/amok/amok68**

You should know, however, that filenames are not always set in stone. With thousands of different people posting millions of different files on thousands of different computers, sometimes filenames get changed a little. It may be that all these files are actually the same program. Or maybe three or four different programs.

If the list is long, and shoots by before you can use it, use the **set pager** command, then do the search again. Now the list will stop after each page, and you can press **Spacebar** to see the next page, or **q** and **Enter** to stop the listing. Turn off this feature using **unset pager**. You can also send long lists home, using e-mail. More on this in a moment.

Sometimes you'll find clues, though. The TextWindows files are in directories that probably have something to do with the Amiga computer; notice that one of the directories in the "path" is **amiga**. One of the other **textwin** listings, though, is in a directory called **dos**, probably containing files used on DOS computers.

## Sending It Home

If you are doing a lot of Archie searches, or get a very long list, you can send the information "home" to your e-mail address. Type **mail *emailaddress*** and press **Enter**. The last list Archie found for you will be sent to your e-mail inbox. If you are going to use this feature several times, you can even store your e-mail address (temporarily). First, type **set mailto *emailaddress*** and press **Enter**. Now you can type the **mail** command alone, without bothering to include the e-mail address.

## "Whatis" the Descriptive Index?

Archie has a *whatis* search that you might try. This command searches a *descriptive index*, an index of file descriptions. Not all files indexed by Archie have a description, but many do. For instance, you might type:

```
archie> whatis cia
```

You would see a long listing of descriptions, including these:

```
libhoward              libhoward portability library
linpack                Gaussian elimination, QR, SVD  by Dongarra,
                       Bunch, Mol er, Stewart  (argonne)
mazewar                A game for Suns (SunView)
metrics                Tools for generating software metrics
xfernews               xfernews software
xtank                  Multi-player X11 tank war game
xtrek                  Multi-player X11 "Startrek" war game
```

You may not be able to figure out how your keyword fits with some of these files, but no matter, as long as some of them look like what you want. Notice the word on the left side of each line. If you want to find out where the listed file is, type **prog *name***. For instance, **prog xtank** would list the X11 "Startrek" files.

When you are finished working in Archie, type **exit** and press **Enter**.

## But Wait! There's More!

You can, of course, do more with Archie. You can view a list of all the FTP sites included in this particular Archie server's index: type **list** and press **Enter**. You can get into what may be a rather confusing "help" system (**help**), list Archie servers (**servers**—though the list may not be up to date), limit the number of files Archie will find (**maxhits *number***), and plenty more.

If you want to learn more about Archie, spend a frustrating half hour in the help system. (Type **help** and press **Enter**; you may have to then press **q** to get to the help> prompt. Then type **?** and press **Enter** to see a list of help topics. You can now type the name of a command and press **Enter** to view information about that command. Press **Spacebar** to go to the next page, **q** to return to the help> prompt. To get back to the archie> prompt, type **done** and press **Enter**.)

## Working with Clients

Many service providers have loaded Archie clients. That means you don't have to worry about finding a client or a server; you can just select **Archie** from a menu or use a UNIX command to use it. On the system in which I work, for instance, I can select

```
8. File Transfer (FTP)/
```

from the menu, then select

```
5. Search FTP sites (Archie)/
```

to get to Archie. I can select from two types of searches—*Exact search* or *Substring search*—and then I'll see a box in which I type the filename for which I want to search.

You may also be able to type **archie** ***searchstring*** at the command prompt to start your search.

Using your service provider's client will be a little different from using the Archie server itself. You won't use the **prog** command, for instance, and you won't set the type of search *before* searching; you'll specify it at the same time. For instance:

```
teal% archie -s textwin
```

This would do a *sub* search for **textwin**; that is, it would look for any filename that contains the letters **textwin**, and it wouldn't care about case—it would find **TextWindows** or **textwin**. (For a description of the four search types—exact, regex, sub, and subcase—see the telneting section earlier in this chapter.)

So here's how you can enter a command. You'll always start with **archie**, and you'll finish with the name you are searching for. Everything in-between is optional. You can select the type of search with these options:

-e Archie will do an *exact* search.

-r Archie will do a *regex* search.

-s Archie will do a *sub* search.

-c Archie will do a *sub case* search.

If you *don't* use one of these, Archie will do an exact search. (What, then, is the point of having an -e option, if omitting it does an exact search anyway? Because you could include -e and one of the other three. That way, Archie can do an exact search, and do one of the other searches if it doesn't find anything. Note, however, that you can't combine the other three.)

There are a few more options:

**-h*hostname*** You can, if you wish, tell the Archie client which Archie server to use. Each client is set up with a default server, but if you have a reason to search a particular server, you could enter **-h*hostname*** to tell it which one to go to.

**-m*number*** Tells Archie to limit the number of files it will find. If you use **-m1**, for instance, it will stop when it finds the first match. If you don't use this option, it will stop at the 95th match.

-l You'll see a simplified output, with one line (consisting of a time and date, file size, host name, and file or directory name) for each entry.

> **By the Way . . .**
>
> Unfortunately, using Archie from your service provider's system can prove *very* slow—you might imagine it's locked up (who knows, it might have!). Maybe you can set Archie running and find something else to do for five (or ten) minutes. If you get tired waiting, **Ctrl-c** should stop it.

## Saving It in a File

If you wish, you can copy the search results into a file by following the name you are searching for with **>*textfilename***. For instance:

```
archie -s textwin >textw.txt
```

This will do a *sub* search for the name *textwin*, and copy the output into a file called *textw.txt*. This is useful when you are likely to get a big list, or if you want to save the information and use it later.

## Mail-Order Archie

If you don't want to spend time looking for an Archie server you can use, or waiting while it works, you may want to send an e-mail message to an Archie server, and wait for the response. You could also use Archie by mail if you don't have access to telnet (as some Internet users don't).

Using Archie by mail is actually quite simple. You send a message to **archie@*archieserver***. You can choose whichever Archie server you want.

Leave the **Subject** blank, but put the commands in the **body** of the message. Each command must be on a separate line (you can put as many commands in a message as you wish), and the first character of each command must be the first character on its line. For instance, here's a message created with UNIX mail:

```
teal% mail archie@archie.rutgers.edu
Subject:
servers
prog textwin
whatis war
.
Cc:
teal%
```

The first command, **servers**, asks Archie to send you a list of Archie servers (remember, this list may not be complete—you may want to try several different servers to get a complete picture). The **prog** command tells Archie to search for textwin. And the **whatis** command tells Archie to search for the description "war," as we saw earlier.

Here are a few more commands:

**set search *type*** As we saw earlier, this command tells Archie what type of search you want to do: exact, regex, sub, or subcase.

**compress** Tells Archie to compress the listing before sending it to you. You'll have to use uncompress it to read it (see Chapter 18 for more information about uuencoding). You may want to use this option if you expect the list to be very large.

**help** Sends a Mail Archie user guide.

**site *host*** You can enter a host IP address (the numbers that describe a host's location) or domain name), and Archie will send a list of all the files held at that FTP site.

**quit** This tells Archie to ignore everything that follows in the message. If you have a mail system that inserts a signature file automatically at the end of each message, use **quit** to make sure you don't get the help information each time you send an Archie request (if Archie sees any "command" it doesn't understand, it sends the help information automatically).

How soon will you get a response? Some responses may take just a few minutes. Others (even responses to commands in the same e-mail message) may take hours. Archie says that if you wait two days without any response, there's probably a problem, and you may want to try the **set mailto** command to make sure Archie has your correct e-mail address.

**set mailto *mailaddress*** If you find your Archie requests go unanswered, it may be because your mail program is not inserting enough information in the **From** line. You can use this command to enter the path to which you want Archie's response sent.

If you like the idea of working with Archie through the mail, send the **help** command to get the user's guide. There are plenty of little tricks you can use with this system.

## The Least You Need to Know

- Archie servers index available files at over a thousand FTP sites periodically. Archie clients can read the indexes.
- You can telnet to an Archie site and log in using the **archie** login name.
- It's important to know what type of search you are doing—type **show search** and press **Enter**. To change the search type, type **set search *type*** and press **Enter**. The *type* may be exact, regex, sub, or subcase.
- Use the **prog *filename*** command to search for a file.
- Use the **mail *emailaddress*** command to send a list to your e-mail inbox.
- Use the **whatis *description*** command to search for a file description.
- Your service provider probably has a client setup you can use from a menu or the UNIX prompt (though it may be slow).
- Using Archie by mail can be easy and convenient. Send the message to **archie@*archieserver***. Put the commands in the *body* of the message.

**Meditation page (Insert mantra here).**

# Chapter 21

# Digging Through the Internet With Gopher

## In This Chapter

- Finding a Gopher client
- Using your service provider's Gopher
- Gophering from the UNIX prompt
- Telnet Gophering
- Finding your way around Gopherspace
- Saving text documents and computer files
- Using Veronica to search in Gopherspace

Having seen how complicated the Internet can be, you may be happy to learn that it doesn't always have to be so difficult. You can use a *Gopher* to help you find your way around. No, a Gopher is not a furry garden pest—it's a menu system that helps you find Telnet and FTP sites.

The Gopher system is based on several hundred Gopher *servers* (computers that contain the indexes) and thousands of Gopher *clients* (computers that are running the Gopher menu software that accesses the server's indexes). All servers are public, so any client can access the information from any server.

Why "Gopher"? For three reasons. It was originally developed at the University of Minnesota—home of the "Golden Gophers." As most Americans know, "gofer" is slang for someone who "goes fer" things—and Gopher's job is to "go fer" files and stuff. And the system digs its way through the Internet, like a Gopher in a burrow. By the way, when you use Gopher you are traveling through *Gopherspace.*

Each time a client starts, it has to get the information it needs from the server. In other words, when you start the Gopher menu (I'll explain how in a moment), the menu software goes out onto the network and grabs all the information it needs from one of the servers. And you can even use *bookmarks* to create your own menu of places you frequent.

Where does all the information come from? Well, first a system administrator decides to make areas on his or her host computer available to the "public" (so users can come in and take files run databases, play games, and so on). Then the host administrator informs the Gopher server administrators, so they can add the information to their indexes.

## Which Gopher Do You Want to Use?

So there are hundreds of Gopher servers, and thousands of Gopher clients. Unless you install a client (which I'll explain in a moment), you don't have to worry about the servers. But which client are you going to use? You have a few options:

**Maybe your service provider's system is based on Gopher** Some service providers have based their own user interface on the Gopher system (the menu system we looked at in Chapter 8).

**You can run gopher from the UNIX prompt** While you may not see the Gopher menu when you log in, it may be available when you type **gopher** and press **Enter** at the UNIX shell.

**You can telnet to a Gopher site** Some computers will let you log in on a telnet connection and use their Gopher system. However, this practice is falling out of favor; it creates a lot of network traffic, and many administrators feel you should set up your own Gopher client (or get your system administrator to set up a Gopher client). Some systems that (until recently) allowed telnet users to use their Gopher system are now denying access to outsiders.

**You can set up your own Gopher client** If you have a permanent connection or a dial-in direct account, you can set up your own Gopher client. There's software available for just about any type of computer. We'll look at where to find it a little later.

# Using Your Service Provider's Gopher

Most Internet users will work with their service provider's own Gopher, the one already installed on their systems. When you log in, you may find you are already in Gopher. If you find yourself in a menu system that looks like the following, there's a good chance you are in a Gopher:

```
                    << SuperMenu Main Menu >>


 —>  1.  About SuperMenu.
     2.  Search SuperMenu Titles <?>
     3.  Commercial Services/
     4.  Communities/
     5.  Databases/
     6.  Education/
     7.  Events & Entertainment/
     8.  File Transfer (FTP)/
     9.  Help/
     10. Libraries/
     11. Mail/
     12. News and Weather/
     13. Phone Books/
     14. SuperNet Services/
     15. Tools for Information Retrieval/

Help ?  Quit q  Main-Menu m  Menu-Up u  BackPg <  NextPg > Page:1/1
```

Notice that some of the menu options have a slash (/) at the end—a typical Gopher indication that selecting this option leads to another menu, a *sub-menu*. Notice also the commands at the bottom. These are typical Gopher menu commands. And there's even an **About** option right at the top—if you select this option, at least on this particular system, you'd find that this is, indeed, a Gopher system.

## Starting from the UNIX Shell

If you don't see a Gopher menu when you log in, you may be able to start Gopher from the system prompt (the UNIX shell if you are working on a UNIX host). Simply type **gopher** and press **Enter**. We can hope your service provider has set up a Gopher client. If so, they will have defined the gopher command so that it goes out to a Gopher server somewhere, grabs the relevant information, and builds the Gopher menu for you. Again, you'll see something similar to the menu we just looked at.

You can also use this method to define where you want to go. For instance, **gopher yaleinfo.yale.edu 7000** will take you to a Yale University gopher site.

Maybe your service provider does it differently. Perhaps you don't run a command from the UNIX prompt; instead you might have to select a command from a different menu system. If you can't find Gopher, ask your service provider how to get to it, or check the documentation you got when you first got your account.

# Using Someone Else's Gopher—Through Telnet

It's possible your service provider's system administrator hasn't set up Gopher. If not, ask if he or she could do so. In the meantime, see if you can use someone else's Gopher. It used to be that you could telnet to another computer, and use Gopher from there. It's still possible, but with the incredible increase in Internet traffic in the past year, it's becoming more difficult. Some Gopher sites that used to allow public access now limit Gopher use to their own accounts. Still, if you want to telnet, you can try these sites:

**consultant.micro.umn.edu** Log in as **gopher**. This system says it will accept outside gophering, but if you try it you may not actually be able to do so; the system may simply "timeout" before you are connected. And they are trying to discourage telnet users from gophering. (This is the University of Minnesota, the home of the Gopher.)

**hafnhaf.micro.umn.edu** Log in as **gopher**. This is the University of Minnesota again.

**pubinfo.ais.umn.edu** This is the University of Minnesota yet again, but this host is a "3270" host, so you would get there using the **tn3270** command instead of telnet (**tn3270 pubinfo.ais.umn.edu**).

**library.wustl.edu** No login required (Washington University, St. Louis, Missouri).

**ux1.cso.uiuc.edu** Log in as **gopher** (University of Illinois).

**panda.uiowa.edu** No login required (University of Iowa).

**gopher.sunet.se** Log in as **gopher**. (This is in Sweden, though the menus are in English.)

**info.anu.edu.au** Log in as **info** (Australia).

**gopher.chalmers.se** Log in as **gopher**. (This is in Sweden, and the menus are in Swedish and English. Confusing if you don't speak Swedish, because—not surprisingly—the Swedish comes first.)

**tolten.puc.cl** Log in as **gopher** then press **Enter**. (This is in Chile, and it's mainly in Spanish, with a little English.)

**pinto.isca.uiowa.edu** (USA) and **ecnet.ec** (in Ecuador) You can, reportedly, gopher to these sites, though I haven't managed to get through. All the others, at the time of writing, did accept telnet gophering.

## Here We Go—Let's Gopher It!

Let's do a little gophering. In all my examples, I'm going to assume you are using the most common type of Gopher client, known as the *Curses* Gopher. If you have installed your own, or if your service provider is using something fancy, commands will vary, but the principles will be the same.

Whichever method you use—telneting or using your service provider's gopher—you're going to arrive at a screen that is something like this:

```
                    Internet Gopher Information Client 2.0 pl10
                      Root gopher server: hafnhaf.micro.umn.edu

—>  1.  Information About Gopher/
```

```
2.  Computer Information/
3.  Internet file server (ftp) sites/
4.  Fun & Games/
5.  Libraries/
6.  Mailing Lists/
7.  News/
8.  Other Gopher and Information Servers/
9.  Phone Books/
10. Search Gopher Titles at the University of Minnesota <?>
11. Search lots of places at the U of M <?>
12. UofM Campus Information/

Press ? for Help, q to Quit                                    Page: 1/1
```

While working in the Gopher menus, you don't need to press **Enter** to carry out a command (unless told to do so). For instance, to go to the previous menu, simply press **u**. No need to press Enter after the *u*.

The main menu screen may have some kind of system title— Washington University Libraries, Cornell University, Electronic Library Information System at ANU, or whatever. In the example, it simply shows the root server, the location of the Gopher server that is providing the information.

Below the title lines are the menu options, each one numbered. You can type the number you want to select, or move the arrow (—>) to it, and press **Enter** or the **right arrow** to select it. Move the arrow using your keyboard's **up** and **down arrow** keys; if they won't work, try the **j** and **k** keys. Here are some other commands you'll need:

| | |
|---|---|
| Return to the previous menu | **u** or **left arrow** |
| Return to the main menu | **m** |
| View the next page in long menus | **Spacebar** or > or + or **PgDn** |
| View the previous page in long menus | **b** or < or - or **PgUp** |
| Exit the Gopher (the system will ask you to confirm) | **q** |
| Exit Gopher immediately (no confirmation) | **Q** |

Play with these commands for a few minutes and you'll soon get the hang of it.

> **By the Way . . .**
>
> If you are telneting to a Gopher, you may find that the system responds very slowly. Gopher sites are often very heavily used—which is why they want you to get your service provider to set up a client, or set up one yourself.

## What Are the Symbols at the Ends of Menu Options?

Notice that each menu option has some kind of symbol or word at the end, as shown in the following list. The previous example shows only the first two of these, but you may see the others elsewhere.

| | |
|---|---|
| / | Indicates that selecting the menu option displays another menu (that it is a *directory*). |
| <?> | Select one of these menu options and you'll be able to enter a search word. |
| . (period) | Select this option and the Gopher will display a document. |
| **<TEL>** | Selecting this option telnets you to another computer system. |
| **<bin>** or **<PC Bin>** | A DOS file that has been compressed with an archive program such as PKZIP. |
| **<Movie>** | A video file. |
| **<Picture>** | A graphics file. |
| **<HQX>** | This leads to a BinHex file, a Macintosh file that has been converted to ASCII so it can be transferred as e-mail. |

There are plenty of other such indicators, some of which are numbers or letters. You can check what an item is by using the = command. Just place the arrow next to item and press = and you'll see something like this:

```
Name=disinfectant33.sea.hqx
Type=4
Port=70
Path=ftp:ftp.acns.nwu.edu@/pub/disinfectant/disinfectant33.sea.hqx
Host=gopher1.cit.cornell.edu
```

At the top it shows you the menu option name (which we know already, of course), but the next line shows the item *type*. These are the types you may see:

| | |
|---|---|
| 0 | A text file. Select it and you'll be able to read the file, page by page. The same as seeing a . (period) at the end of the menu option. |
| 1 | A *directory*, that is, selecting this option leads to another menu. The same as seeing a / at the end of the menu option. |
| 2 | A menu option that leads you to a CSO "phonebook" you can use to find Internet users. |
| 4 | A BinHex Macintosh file. |
| 5 | A DOS compressed file, such as a ZIP or ARC file. The same as seeing **<PC BIN>** at the end of the menu option. (You'll need the appropriate decompression utility to use the file, unless it's a self-extracting archive file—if it has the extension **.EXE**, it's self-extracting.) |
| 6 | A UUENCODed file. You'll need UUDECODE to convert the file to its original format. |
| 7 | Select this option and you'll be prompted to type a search word. The same as seeing <?> at the end of the menu option. |
| 8 | This menu option takes you to a telnet session. |

| | |
|---|---|
| 9 | Select this option and you'll be sent a binary file—you don't necessarily want to do this, unless your system is set up to receive such a file. |
| T | This menu option takes you to a tn3270 connection (an IBM 3270 equivalent of the telnet session). |
| s | A *mulaw sound file*. Your system may not be set up to use this. |
| g | A GIF graphics file. |
| M | An e-mail file in MIME file-transfer format. |

Some of the more fancy Gopher clients have various "viewers" that can accept the more unusual types of data. For instance, a client may have a *GIF viewer*, so if you select a GIF graphics file, you'll actually be able to see the picture on your screen. The basic "Curses" Gopher client cannot do that—in fact, you'd be well advised *not* to try getting data types that your Gopher client can't handle. At best it's a waste of time. At worst your computer may crash.

The information that appears after the type line varies, but will often help you find a file if you can't transfer the file using Gopher. You might find the host and path, for instance; then you may be able to use FTP to get to the host, and use the **cd** command to go directly to the directory containing the file.

## Saving Stuff

Of course, traveling through Gopherspace is all very well, but what about saving what you find? There are ways to save files and documents, depending on where your Gopher client is.

If you are using a client on your own computer (or your service provider's computer), you will be able to save stuff. If you are using a telnet Gopher session, your options are more limited. I'm going to assume you are working with your own or your service provider's Gopher; some of what I describe next won't work if you are telneting.

## Saving a Document

There are several ways to save a document. First, you can save it while you are reading it. Press **q** to stop reading it, and you'll see this:

```
--Press <ENTER> for next page, q to exit--q
Press 's' to save this file or any other key to continue:
```

Press **s** and you'll see this:

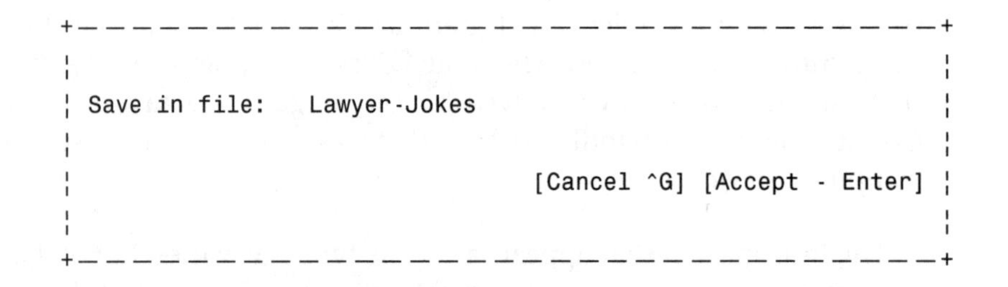

```
+------------------------------------------+
|                                          |
| Save in file:   Lawyer-Jokes             |
|                                          |
|           [Cancel ^G] [Accept - Enter]   |
|                                          |
+------------------------------------------+
```

Press **Enter** and that's it—you've saved the file (if you are working with your service provider's Gopher client, it's in your home directory).

You can use this method at the menu itself—just place the arrow (—>) next to the menu option, and press **s** (remember that menu options that end with . are documents).

If you are working on a dial-in terminal connection with your service provider's Gopher client, you may want to send the data back to your system. Type **D** to see the following box:

```
                    Humor

    1.  Alice in UNIX Land.
    2.  Backwoods Fusion.
```

```
     3.  Beer_vs_Cucum+————Lawyer Jokes—————+
     4.  Berkeley.    ¦                       ¦
     5.  C-Programming¦    1. Zmodem          ¦
     6.  C-Shell.     ¦  2. Ymodem            ¦
     7.  Car-Acronyms.¦  3. Xmodem-1K         ¦
     8.  Chai's C Bibl¦  4. Xmodem-CRC        ¦
     9.  Final Exam.  ¦  5. Kermit            ¦
    10.  Hacker Test. ¦  6. Text              ¦
    11.  How To Take N¦                       ¦
—> 12.  Lawyer Jokes.¦  Choose a download method:  ¦
    13.  McDonnell Dou¦                       ¦
    14.  Programming. ¦  [Cancel ^G]  [Choose 1-6]  ¦
    15.  Real Computer¦                       ¦
    16.  Real Programm+———————————————————————+
    17.  Real Software Engineers.
```

You've got your communications program set to a particular type of file transfer; you can type the number associated with it, and away you go. In the case of Zmodem, your program will start automatically for you. In other cases, you'll have to tell it to begin (see Chapter 19 for more information about file transfers). When the transfer is finished, press **Enter** to return to the Gopher menu.

You tried to download a file, but the menu option disappeared! You probably pressed **d** instead of **D**. The **d** command removes menu options (we'll learn more about that when we discuss bookmarks, in a moment). To get the menu option back, you'll have to go back one menu (**u**) and then return (**Enter**). (If you remove it from the main menu, though, you'll have to leave the Gopher client and restart it.)

## Saving Files

In some cases you can use Gopher in place of FTP to transfer files across the world. (If you telnet to a Gopher client, you won't be able to do this.) The procedures are similar to those used for grabbing text files. Simply select the option that leads to the file from the menu: type its number and press **Enter**, or place the arrow next to it and press **Enter** or **s**. You'll see the same **Save in File** box we looked at a moment ago. To download using a file transfer method such as Zmodem or Xmodem, place the arrow next to the option and press **D**.

## Searching for Entries

In long menus, you can search for a particular menu option by pressing / and then typing the word you are looking for. You'll see this (I'm searching for *bio* in this example):

```
       4.  ACM SIGGRAPH/
+-----------------------------------------------------------+
|                                                           |
| Search directory titles for   bio                         |
|                                                           |
|                          [Cancel ^G] [Accept - Enter]     |
|                                                           |
+-----------------------------------------------------------+
       12. Albert Einstein College of Medicine/
```

When you press **Enter**, the arrow will move to the first entry that matches what you typed—you can press **n** to move to the next matching entry. In this way you can search for all entries related to, in this case, biology—EMBnet Bioinformation Resource, Center for Genetic Eng. & Biotech, and so on.

## Create Your Own Menu—Placing Bookmarks

While you're working in the Gopher, you might want to place *bookmarks*. These let you create a list of menu options in which you are interested—you can travel around, marking the things you think you may want to check into further, then come back and examine each, one at a time.

Use these commands (remember, they're case-sensitive):

Add the selected menu item to the bookmark list with **a**.

Add the current menu to the bookmark list with **A**.

View the list of bookmarks with **v**.

Delete a bookmark from the list with **d**.

For instance, you find something you want to mark, and you press **a**. You'll see something like this:

```
        6.  C-Shell.
+-----------------------------------------------------------------+
|                                                                 |
| Name for this bookmark:                                         |
|                                                                 |
|  Lawyer Jokes                                                   |
|                     [Cancel ^G] [Erase: ^U] [Accept - Enter]    |
|                                                                 |
+-----------------------------------------------------------------+
        15. Real Computer Scientists.
```

You'll press **Enter** to place the bookmark. (If you wanted to enter a different name for the bookmark, you'd press **Ctrl-U** and then type the new one.)

Later, when you want to view all the bookmarks, just press **v**. You'll see something like this:

```
              Internet Gopher Information Client 2.0 pl10

                                  Bookmarks

 -->  1.  University of Western Sydney/
      2.  Empire of the Petal Throne/
      3.  Virtual Spaces at U Texas/
      4.  Guns n' Roses.
      5.  Killer Dwarfs.
      6.  X.500 Gateway/
      7.  Lawyer Jokes.
```

This is just like any other Gopher menu—you select items in the same way—but it's a menu that *you* created.

Of course, if you are using a menu on another system, these bookmarks will be lost when you leave the system. If you are using a Gopher client on your own computer—or even your service provider's system—the bookmarks will be saved, which is very convenient. In effect, you can build your own menu of frequently-used menu options, and view the menu at any time by pressing **v**.

Veronica is a perfect example of that American habit of picking a word to be an acronym, and *then* finding the words to fit it. Veronica means *Very Easy Rodent-Oriented Net-wide Index to Computerized Archives*. My bet is that it's named after Archie's girlfriend.

Finding your way back to somewhere you've been before in Gopherspace can be very frustrating. If you think you may *ever* need to return, create a bookmark, and enter your own title if you wish (something you're more likely to remember).

## Using Veronica

There are hundreds of servers in Gopherspace, and even a system that's intended to make the Internet easier to use could do with its own system to make itself easier to use. Enter *Veronica,* a frequently-updated index system that you can search.

Most Gopher systems will have a menu option for Veronica somewhere. Something like **3. Search Topics in Gopherspace Using Veronica/**. Select this option and you'll see something like this:

```
Search Gopherspace using Veronica


—>1.  Search gopherspace at NYSERNet <?>
  2.  Search gopherspace at PSINet <?>
  3.  Search gopherspace at University of Pisa <?>
  4.  Search gopherspace at University of Cologne <?>
  5.  Search Gopher Directory Titles at NYSERNet <?>
  6.  Search Gopher Directory Titles at PSINet <?>
  7.  Search Gopher Directory Titles at University of Pisa <?>
  8.  Search Gopher Directory Titles at University of Cologne <?>
  9.                                                        .
  10. *** 100% Experimental WWW indexer (NorthStar) ***/
  11.                                                               .
  12. FAQ:  Frequently-Asked Questions about veronica (1993/08/23).
  13. How to compose  veronica queries (NEW June 24) READ ME!!.
              Search Topics in GopherSpace Using Veronica
```

There are different Veronica servers, hosts that maintain Veronica databases. The four shown here are not the only ones—you may find different ones on your Gopher client.

Notice that there are two sorts of searches: you can search *all titles*, or *directory titles*. The former will search for *all* information stored in gopher servers—menu names (a menu is, in effect, the same as a directory), telnet connections, FTP connections, filenames, and so on. The directory-titles search only looks at the menus, not at the files.

A title search will, therefore, result in a larger number of "hits" than a directory-titles search, perhaps many more. Where the directory-title list might be one page long, the titles search might be a dozen.

To search using Veronica, simply select the menu option, and type the word or words for which you want to search into the box, thus:

You can even place the result of a Veronica search into your custom menu using the **A** command (to create a bookmark). If you are using your own Gopher client or your service provider's, this will be saved when you close the client, and will be there the next time you return. However, what is actually being saved is the *search statement*. Each time you select it from your Bookmarks menu, the search is carried out again; if you deleted any menu options last time, they'll be back again. Still, you can always add individual menu options to your Bookmarks menu using the **a** command.

```
+-----------------------------------------------------------------+
|                                                                 |
| Words to search for  Electronic books                           |
|                                                                 |
|                              [Cancel ^G] [Accept - Enter]       |
|                                                                 |
+-----------------------------------------------------------------+
```

Press **Enter**, and Veronica's off and running. In a few moments you'll see a new menu, like this:

```
 Search DIRECTORY Titles in GopherSpace via NYSERNet database:
electronic books
```

```
-> 1.  Phone Books/
   2.  E-mail Addresses and Telephone Books/
   3.  Online Books, Images, Journals, Preprints, Publishers,
       Tech Report../
   4.  Books/
   5.  Books and Literary Events/
   6.  Electronic Books/
```

(This search actually found me 12 pages of entries.)

If one of the hits interests you, select it as you would any menu option, and you'll be taken directly there. Or place the arrow next to it and press = to see some information about it—the hostname, for instance.

Veronica is a fantastic tool for finding information in Gopherspace. In effect, you are very quickly creating a menu of options in which you are interested—menu options that may be spread across several continents and dozens of countries.

As I've mentioned elsewhere in this book, experimenting with Internet software is *not* for the weak of heart or the inexperienced. As the READ-ME file at boombox. micro. umn.edu states, "there is minimal documentation for the software; but have faith, we are working on it." Still, if you use Gopher a lot, you might want to install your own client. If you don't, or if you hate "tinkering" with your computer and software, use someone else's client.

You will usually find plenty of entries that you *don't* want. For instance, when searching for Electronic Books, I found Phone and Address Books, E-mail Addresses and Telephone Books, and so on. You can remove an entry quickly by placing the arrow next to it and pressing **d**.

## Finding Gopher Software

If you have a dial-in direct account, you may want to find your own Gopher client software. You don't have to; you can run the gopher software made available by your service provider. But you may prefer to get some neat-looking software that fits the way you are used to working, Macintosh software that looks like Macintosh software, Windows software that looks like Windows software, and so on.

If you want to get the most recent releases of the gopher software, use "anonymous ftp" (or Gopher itself) to go to **boombox.micro.umn.edu**.

You'll find various subdirectories in the **/pub/gopher** directory. You'll find directories that contain various Gopher client and server programs for these systems: Macintosh, NeXT, PC, UNIX, Microsoft Windows, OS/2, VM/CMS, and VMS. (Don't forget, unless you've got a permanent or dial-in direct account, you can't download directly to your computer; you have to go through your service-provider's computer.)

## The Least You Need to Know

- Your service provider probably has a Gopher client set up. If so, use it; if you telnet to a Gopher client, you won't be able to save things back to your disk.
- Travel through Gopherspace by selecting menu options: type the number and press **Enter**, or move the arrow to the option and press **Enter**.
- Go back the way you came by pressing **u** or **left arrow**, or by pressing **m** to return to the main menu.
- To find out more about a menu option, place the arrow next to it and press =.
- To save a text document or file, place the arrow next to it and press **s**. To transfer it back to your computer (if using a dial-in terminal connection) press **D**.
- To search a menu press /.
- Create your own menu by creating bookmarks. Add a menu to your custom menu by pressing **A**. Add a menu option by moving the arrow to it and pressing **a**. View your custom menu by pressing **v**.
- Veronica is a powerful tool to search through thousands of miles of Gopherspace at once. Look for a Veronica menu option somewhere in your Gopher menu.
- Leave a Gopher client by pressing **q** or **Q**.

**List of computer nerds who made the list of the world's sexiest people.**

# Chapter 22
# Finding Your WAIS Around

## In This Chapter

- How to run WAIS
- Getting around in WAIS
- Searching and saving Info
- Using the directory of servers
- Using Gopher
- Installing a WAIS client

In the last chapter, I showed you how Gopher can help you dig your way around the Internet, burrowing for whatever may interest you. In this chapter, you'll learn about WAIS, the *Wide Area Information Server*, a system that helps you search for documents containing the information you want.

WAIS does the work for you (well, part of it). Rather than simply providing a menu that lets you "travel" around the world, WAIS provides a list of databases, lets you select the ones you want to search, and carries out a search for you. If it finds what you want, it can then save the documents, sending them to you via e-mail (or, if you're using a WAIS server on your computer or on your service provider's computer, saving them to a file). Not bad, eh?

While I was writing this book, the number of databases WAIS can search rose from 497 to 624!

WAIS can search through over 620 databases as I'm writing this—probably more by the time you read it. In the last year, the number more than quadrupled. Those 620 databases contain tens of thousands of documents, from the archives of various news groups to weather reports, zip codes, computer archaeology, and kids' software reviews. While most of the files contain text documents, you may also find sounds, graphics, and so on. As with other aspects of the Internet, you name a subject, and it's probably out there somewhere.

In case you're interested, WAIS uses the American National Standard Z39.50: Information Retrieval Service Definition and Protocol Specification for Library Applications standard, revised by the National Information Standards Organization. (No, you don't need to remember that.) Z39.50 is a method for connecting different computer systems and databases. It provides a standard for storing and accessing database information.

## Getting Started

As with Gopher, there are several ways to run WAIS:

- Telnet to **quake.think.com** or **nnsc.nsf.net** and run WAIS from there.
- Run WAIS on your service provider's system, from a menu option.
- Run WAIS from a Gopher menu option.
- Set up a WAIS client on your own computer, if you have a permanent or dial-in direct connection.

As usual, there are various types of WAIS interfaces available. The one you can get to by telnetting is *swais*, a UNIX-based WAIS server. There are WAIS systems available for just about any computer system: DOS, Windows, Macintosh, X Windows, NeXt, and so on. They all work differently, and some have more features than others. We're going to look at the swais version, because it's one of the simplest. Ask your service provider what *you* have available.

## Let's Try It!

Let's take a look at WAIS. We're going to use telnet to get to a WAIS server. You can telnet to **quake.think.com**, or **nnsc.nsf.net** and login as **wais**.

```
teal% telnet quake.think.com
Trying 192.31.181.1 ...
Connected to quake.think.com.
Escape character is '^]'.
SunOS UNIX (quake)

login: wais
Last login: Tue Nov 16 10:44:41 from forsythe.Stanfor
SunOS Release 4.1.1 (QUAKE) #3: Tue Jul 7 11:09:01 PDT 1992
Welcome to swais.
Please type user identifier (optional, i.e user@host): peterk@csn.org
TERM = (vt100) (press Enter)
Starting swais (this may take a little while)...
```

It's true—it *might* take a little while. Eventually you'll see this screen:

```
SWAIS                               Source Selection     Sources: 497
  #               Server                    Source               Cost
001: [            archie.au]  aarnet-resource-guide             Free
002: [ndadsb.gsfc.nasa.gov]   AAS_jobs                          Free
003: [ndadsb.gsfc.nasa.gov]   AAS_meeting                       Free
004: [       munin.ub2.lu.se] academic_email_conf               Free
005: [wraith.cs.uow.edu.au]   acronyms                          Free
006: [     archive.orst.edu]  aeronautics                       Free
007: [ ftp.cs.colorado.edu]   aftp-cs-colorado-edu              Free
008: [nostromo.oes.orst.ed]   agricultural-market-news          Free
009: [     archive.orst.edu]  alt.drugs                         Free
010: [     wais.oit.unc.edu]  alt.gopher                        Free
011: [sun-wais.oit.unc.edu]   alt.sys.sun                       Free
012: [     wais.oit.unc.edu]  alt.wais                          Free
013: [alfred.ccs.carleton.]   amiga-slip                        Free
014: [       munin.ub2.lu.se] amiga_fish_contents               Free
015: [         150.203.76.2] ANU-Aboriginal-EconPolicies $0.00/minute
016: [    coombs.anu.edu.au]  ANU-Aboriginal-Studies      $0.00/minute
017: [         150.203.76.2] ANU-Ancient-DNA-L           $0.00/minute
018: [         150.203.76.2] ANU-Ancient-DNA-Studies     $0.00/minute
Keywords:
<space> selects, w for keywords, arrows move, <return> searches, q
quits, or ?
```

## By the Way . . .

Important note: A day or two before we went to print, the WAIS server at quake.think.com changed its format. Instead of the list of databases, you will first see a message explaining the changes; press **q** to end the message. Then you'll see a single entry—the directory-of-servers. This is an experimental system—it may stay this way, it may not. If it is this way, see "A Good Server Is Hard to Find," on the next page.

This is the first page of many. The first entry will be highlighted. At the time of writing, there were 624 databases in this list; there will be more by the time you get there. Here's how you'll use the list:

| | |
|---|---|
| Move the cursor down one entry | **j** or **down arrow** or **Ctrl-n** |
| Move the cursor down one screen | **J** or **Ctrl-v** or **Ctrl-d** |
| Move the cursor up one entry | **k** or **up arrow** or **Ctrl-p** |
| Move the cursor up one screen | **K** or **Ctrl-u** |
| Move to a particular line | type the ***number*** and press **Enter** |
| Read about the highlighted database | **v** or **,** (comma) (type **q** and **Enter** to return to the listing) |
| Select an entry (or deselect a selected entry) | **Spacebar** or **.** (period) |
| Deselect all selections | = |
| Select an entry and move to keywords field | **Ctrl-j** |
| Search for a listing | Press / then type the ***word*** you are looking for and press **Enter** |
| Enter keywords on which to search | **w** and then press **Enter**. (Press **Ctrl-C** to cancel) |
| Search selected entries with keywords | **Enter** |
| Return to the listing | **s** |
| View the Help screen | **h** or **?** |
| Quit | **q** |

You'll use the various commands to move the cursor through the list, and press **Spacebar** or . (period) to select the entries you want to search. (You can select as many as you want.) If you see an entry you think might be useful, move the highlight to it, then press **v** or , (comma) to read a description of the database (press **q** and **Enter** to return to the list).

At the time of this writing, all database searches are free. However, notice that some database entries have $0.00/minute in the right column—you may be billed for searches in the future.

## A Good Server Is Hard to Find

One problem you'll find with WAIS is figuring out which databases contain what data. The names are often quite obscure. (For instance, what is bib-ens-lyon? It's the Ecole Normale Superieure de Lyon, and has databases on the sciences—geology, math, physics, chemistry, and so on.) But WAIS has a database called the directory-of-servers that you can use to narrow the search a little.

In fact, the directory-of-servers may be the first thing you see when you enter WAIS (as we noted earlier, at the time we went to press, the system administrators were experimenting with WAIS—the last I looked, they had removed the main list and replaced it with the single directory-of-servers, but this *may* change back to the former system). If so, just press **Enter** to select it and display the Keywords line, then type a general keyword: **biology**, for instance. Press **Enter** again, and WAIS will search for databases with biology-related subjects. When it has found matches, it will show you a list. You can move the highlight to an entry and press **Spacebar** to see a description of the database's contents. If it's one that you are interested in, press **q** to remove the database description, then press **u** to add the database to the main list. Continue in this manner, finding all the databases in which you want to search. When you've picked the databases you want, press **s** to return to the main listing. Back at the main list, deselect the directory-of-servers and select the databases you picked (highlight each entry and then press **Spacebar**). Then you can press **w**, press **Backspace** several times to clear the original search word, and press **Enter** to search. (By the way, you may not be able to see the original search word. Just press **Backspace** until the text cursor is immediately after **Keywords;**, and type a new search word.)

If, when you use WAIS, it has reverted to its previous format, you can reach the directory-of-servers by searching for it. First, type **/direct** and press **Enter**. This will take you to the first listing that begins with *direct*. Then move the highlight down until it rests on the directory-of-servers line. Again, press **Enter** to select it and display the Keywords line, then type a general keyword: **biology**, for instance. Press **Enter** again, and WAIS will search for databases with biology-related subjects. When it has found matches, it will show you a list. You can view the database descriptions using the **Spacebar**. If you want to search a particular database, though, you won't add it to the main list (if WAIS has reverted to its previous format, the database is already *in* the main list). Instead, you'll return to the main list (press **s**) and then go to that database and select it. (Check the help screen—press **?**. You may find that, with all these changes going on, there's some way to mark the database in the second list so it is already selected in the main list.)

## The Big Search

When you've selected the databases you want to search, press **w**. You'll see the prompt:

```
Keywords:
```

Type the keywords on which you want to search—**Albania**, or **Beethoven**, or **squash**, or whatever—and press **Enter**. For instance, I selected this database:

```
295: * [  info.curtin.edu.au]  k-12-software           Free
```

Then I entered these keywords:

```
Keywords: math spelling
```

You can continue selecting more databases, or just press **Enter** to begin a search. (When you press **Enter**, you'll find yourself back at the Keywords prompt, so you can enter new keywords. Simply press **Enter** again to continue without typing more keywords. Also, notice that if you press **Enter** while the highlight is on an unselected line, that line will be selected, and *then* you'll go to the Keywords prompt.)

## Picking Your Keywords

What sort of keywords can you use? You can enter several words, separated by spaces. Note that you can only do a simple keyword search this way—WAIS will search for each word you enter, so you can't do the sort of *Boolean* search that many computer databases use. For instance, in a Boolean search **MATH AND SPELL** would search for documents that contained both MATH and SPELL. With WAIS, though, the AND will be ignored (because it's a *stop* word, a common word that is not indexed), and it will find any documents that contain either MATH *or* SPELL (or both).

Keywords must start with a letter, not a number. And you may only use one type of punctuation character inside words—a period, for instance, as in "I.B.M."

> **By the Way . . .**
>
> Some words are *stop words* because they are common—*and, or, though*, and so on. Other words may be stop words because they are common in a particular database. The word *software* may be a stop word in a database that is related to computer programs, for instance.

A little while after beginning the search, you'll see something like this:

```
SWAIS                              Search Results
  #     Score       Source                 Title                              Lines
001:   [1000]  (  k-12-software) PACKAGE:THE SPELLING SYSTEM SUBJECT:En       -1
002:   [ 994]  (  k-12-software) PACKAGE:SPELLING MASTER SUBJECT: Englis      -1
003:   [ 952]  (  k-12-software) PACKAGE:COMPUTER MATH ACTIVITIES VOL 1-     -1
004:   [ 872]  (  k-12-software) PACKAGE:CARE SPELLING MANAGER SUBJECT:       -1
005:   [ 870]  (  k-12-software) PACKAGE:SPELLING MASTERY SUBJECT:Engli       -1
006:   [ 730]  (  k-12-software) PACKAGE:SPELLING WIZ SUBJECT:English A       -1
```

*continues*

```
SWAIS                                  Search Results
  #    Score      Source                      Title                        Lines
007: [ 719] ( k-12-software) PACKAGE:CARE SPELLING SUBJECT: English          -1
008: [ 698] ( k-12-software) PACKAGE:SPELLING MANAGER SUBJECT: Engli          1
009: [ 684] ( k-12-software) PACKAGE:SPELLING SUBJECT:English AREA:          -1
010: [ 675] ( k-12-software) PACKAGE:SPELLING STRATEGY SUBJECT: Engl         -1
011: [ 675] ( k-12-software) PACKAGE:MICROTUTOR - PRIMARY SPELLING S         -1
012: [ 672] ( k-12-software) PACKAGE:SPELLING BEE WITH READING PRIME         -1
013: [ 668] ( k-12-software) PACKAGE:THE SPELLING MACHINE SUBJECT: E         -1
014: [   0] (ANU-Australia-N)Search produced no result. Here's the Ca        45
```

Notice the **Score** column. The document with the most number of "hits"—the largest number of keywords—is given a score of 1000. The other documents are given a relative score. A score of 500 means half as many hits as the top document.

When you press **Enter** to begin a search, you may notice the Keywords: field is empty, though the text cursor is not at the left side—it's indented a little. Your keywords are still there, you just can't see them. Press **Enter** to continue; or **Backspace** all the way to Keywords: and type a new keyword.

## Reading and Saving the Info

You can now move through this list, in the same way you moved through the previous list. This time the list is of documents, not databases. When you press **Spacebar** or **Enter**, you'll be able to read the highlighted document.

What if you want to save the information? You can send the document to yourself—or anyone else, for that matter—using e-mail. Press **m**. You'll be prompted for an e-mail address. Type the address, press **Enter**, and it's on its way. If the WAIS client is on your service provider's computer, or on your own computer, you can use the **S** command to save the document in a file.

## Using Gopher

There's a simpler way to use WAIS—through a Gopher menu. This might be through your service provider's menu system (if they have set up a menu based on Gopher), or through a Gopher client you telneted to (see Chapter 21 for more information about Gopher).

For instance, on my service provider's system, I can select **15. Tools for Information Retrieval/**, followed by **5. Wide Area Information Servers (WAIS)/**. I then have the option of telneting to quake.think.com or nnsc.nsf.net. Or I can select **1. Search WAIS using Gopher/**. This selection leads me to several more options. I can select **2. List of all WAIS Sources/** (to see a list in numerical order), **3. WAIS Databases sorted by Letter/**, or **4. WAIS Databases sorted by Subject/** (an experimental system in Sweden). This is especially useful, because the menu system helps me find databases that are relevant to the subject I'm interested in—Archaeology, Religion, Math, and so on. Whatever I choose, eventually I can find my way to a particular database. Selecting the database displays a box into which I can type a search term.

To get back to the list of databases, press **s**.

Gopher is a very convenient way to search through WAIS, but it has one significant drawback. You can only search one database at a time. As we've already seen, if you telnet to a WAIS site, you can select any number of databases and search all of them at once.

To be more exact, you *may* be able to read the document. Sometimes documents will be displayed jumbled up slightly, so the lines are not consecutive. If that happens, try this. Go to the list and highlight the document you want to read. Then press I, type **more**, and press **Enter**.

# Be Your Own Client

The following info is for dial-in direct users only. The rest of you can skip right to the end of the chapter—or stick your fingers in your ears and hum, if you prefer.

If you just want a different user interface to work with, you need WAIS *client* software. If you want to set up your own indexed database and make it available to the Internet, you need WAIS *server* software.

If you decide you like using WAIS, but don't like the user interface you're forced to work with, you can set up your own WAIS client. You can find WAIS software in various places. Try ftping to **wais.com**, go into the **pub/freeware** directory, and search around for client software for your computer. There are directories for various types of systems, including Windows, NeXt, Sun, and Motif.

You may also be able to find WAIS software at **sunsite.unc.edu**, **think.com**, **quake.think.com**, and **cnidr.org**. Be warned though, that setting up WAIS software may be (will be?) a hassle.

## The Least You Need to Know

- Run WAIS from your service provider's menu, or from the UNIX shell.
- You can also telnet to a WAIS server at quake.think.com or nnsc.nsf.net.
- Press **m** to send a document to yourself via e-mail. If the WAIS client is on your service provider's system, save the document as a file with **S**.
- Refer to the directory of servers to narrow your search to those servers with information that interests you.
- WAIS only accepts simple keyword searches, not Boolean searches.
- To search the highlighted database, press **Enter**, type a keyword, and press **Enter** again.
- To search several databases at once, highlight each one and press **Spacebar**. Press **w** and type the keyword. Then press **Enter**.
- Probably the easiest way to search WAIS is through a Gopher menu.

# Chapter 23
# Think Global: World Wide Web

## In This Chapter

- Getting to a WWW browser
- Finding your way around the web
- Viewing topic lists
- Searching for info on the web
- From Web to Gopher, WAIS, FTP, and Whois

Here's another Internet tool that can help you search for what you need. The *World Wide Web* (*WWW*, *The Web*, or sometimes even *W3*) is a *hypertext* system that helps you travel around the world electronically, looking for information.

WWW is very easy to use, probably the easiest Internet system you'll find. Rather than searching for a keyword, as you would do with WAIS, with WWW you follow a "trail" of linked words. You select a topic that interests you, and view related information—from which you select another topic that interests you, and see information related to *that* topic.

What is *hypertext*? If you've ever used a Windows Help file, or a Macintosh HyperCard file, you've used hypertext. A hypertext document lets you jump from place to place in the document using *links* of some kind. Rather than reading the document from front to back, you can select a piece of text and move to a piece of related text elsewhere in the document.

You move from one topic to another; with any luck, you move closer to where you want to be. (You'll see exactly what I mean in a moment.) If you ever decide you've taken the wrong trail, you can quickly return whence you came.

The World Wide Web is made up of documents with built-in topics. Each topic has a bracketed number, like this: **[3]**. For instance, you are reading a menu of options, and see something like this:

> **The Virtual Library[1]**
> **A classification by information by subject. Includes links to other known virtual libraries.**

There's a **[1]** after the title, which means you can type **1** and press **Enter** to move to this "Virtual Library."

The topic number doesn't have to be in a header; it could appear after a word anywhere in a document's text—and a document may have dozens of these topics, each leading somewhere different.

## Getting to the Web

As usual, there are several ways to use the Web:

- You can telnet to a WWW browser.
- There may be a menu option in your service provider's menu system. This may be a shortcut that uses Telnet automatically, to get you to a WWW *browser*. Or your service provider may have installed a WWW browser on their system.
- From the UNIX shell, you can use a command that your service provider has set up to connect to a WWW browser automatically.
- If you are using a dial-in direct or permanent connection, you can install your own WWW browser.

Whichever method you use, you will be using a *browser*, a program that knows how to search through the hypertext files. We're going to look at the simplest browser, a text-based system (or *line-mode browser*) that you'll probably be using. There are others around, though, and some are quite fancy, appearing more like Windows Help systems, with underlined text—instead of bracketed numbers—to denote topics you can select.

# Off to the Alps—Using WWW

To use WWW, we're going to take a quick trip to Switzerland, to **nxoc01.cern.ch** (that's a zero before the 1, not an *o*) at the European Particle Physics Laboratory. We're going to use Telnet to get us there.

```
teal% telnet nxoc01.cern.ch
Trying 128.141.201.74 ...
Connected to nxoc01.cern.ch.
Escape character is '^]'.
                              GENERAL OVERVIEW

There is no "top" to the World-Wide Web. You can look at it from many
points of view. Here are some places to start:

The Virtual Library[1]
        A classification by information by subject. Includes links to
other known virtual libraries.
HTTP servers[2]         All registered WWW native "http" servers, by
                        location.
Servers by type[3]      if you know what sort of server you are
                        looking for.
About WWW[4]            About the World-Wide Web global infor-
                        mation sharing project

Starting somewhere else
To use a different default page, perhaps one representing your field of
interest, see "customizing your home page"[5].

                                                                 TBL [6]

1-6, Up, <RETURN> for more, Quit, or Help:
```

Notice that we didn't have to log in—when you telnet to here, you are placed into WWW automatically. And notice all the numbers in brackets. For instance, if you'd like to take a look at the *virtual library*, a system in which you'll be able to search through different subjects as a starting point, you would type **1** and press **Enter**. If you want to see a list of the WWW servers, you would type **2** and press **Enter**, and so on.

## The WWW Commands

WWW is one of the easiest Internet tools to use. Here are the commands you'll use when moving through the WWW. Type each command and then press **Enter**.

| | |
|---|---|
| Go down one page | Press **Enter** |
| Go to the previous page | **u** or **up** |
| Go to the last page | **bo** or **bottom** |
| Go to the first page | **t** or **top** |
| Go to a [*number*] reference | Type the number and press **Enter**. |
| Search a document for a keyword **find** ***keywords*** (only when you see FIND on the prompt line). | **f** ***keywords*** |
| See a list of [ ] references | **l** or **list** |
| Go to the previous document | **b** or **back** |
| Go to the first document you saw | **ho** or **home** |
| List the documents you've seen | **r** or **recall** |
| Go to a document in the Recall list | **r** ***number*** or **recall** ***number*** |
| View the next reference from the last document | **n** or **next** |
| Display the Help page | **h** or **help** |
| Display the WWW manual | **m** or **manual** |
| Quit | **quit** |

Just play with these commands while you're working in WWW, and soon you'll get the hang of it. Just type the topic number and press **Enter** to select a particular topic. Then move down the topic, whether it's a listing or document, by pressing **Enter**. Move back up a page by pressing **u** and then **Enter**. To go back to where you just came from, use **b** and **Enter**. You'll soon get the idea. Take a look at the chart included here, and try navigating through the web.

## Let's Explore

Let's take a look at what we find if you select **[1]** from the page we saw earlier (**The Virtual Library**). We'll see the beginning of a list, like this:

```
          The World-Wide Web Virtual Library: Subject Catalogue
   (25/119)
     This is a distributed subject catalogue. See also arrangement by
  service type[1] ., and other subject catalogues[2] .

     Mail www-request@info.cern.ch to add pointers to this list, or if
  you would like to contibute to administration of a subject area.

    Aeronautics             Mailing list archive index[3] . See also NASA
                            LaRC[4]

    Agriculture[5]          Separate list, see also Almanac mail serv-
                            ers[6] .
```

We have six "links" or topics in this small area alone. We can see a list of different services available by selecting **1**: World Wide Web servers, WAIS servers, Network News, Gopher, Telnet, and so on. We can also see other subject catalogues by selecting **2**; we'll see several other types of indexes of information we can work our way through.

Below the header stuff, we see the beginning of the catalogue itself, starting with **Aeronautics**. You'll notice that there are two topics related to Aeronautics, a mailing list index and some kind of NASA-related topic. If you select the first one, **[3]**, you'll find it simply tells you where to find the Aeronautics mailing list; you can then use FTP to go and get it. If you select **[4]**, you'll see a list of topics about NASA—**The NASA Vision**, **About Langley Research Center**, and so on. Each has its own number, of course. If you select **The NASA Vision**, for instance, you'll be able to read a document containing NASA's "statement of purpose."

The next item in the catalogue is **Agriculture**. Notice that this time there's a number next to Agriculture itself, and the words **Separate list** on the description line. This means that if you type **5** and press **Enter**, you'll see another list of agriculture-related-resources: **Agricultural Info from Penn State [1]**, **Agricultural Info from CSU Fresno[2]**, and so on. You can also type **6** and press **Enter** to see a list of e-mail addresses that can be used to receive "USDA market news, articles about the use of computer in agricultural science, and Extension Computing Technology Newsletters." At the end of the list, you'll see a (currently very sparse) description of how to use the e-mail commands.

Okay, so maybe you're not interested in agriculture. Just play with WWW, and go where your fancy takes you.

## Looking at a Topic List

You can view a list of all the topics or references in the current document. Type **l** and press **Enter**, and you'll see something like this:

```
     References from this document:-
[1]  http://history.cc.ukans.edu/history/ftp.html
[2]  http://history.cc.ukans.edu/history/archive.html
[3]  Electronic History Journals
[4]  http://history.cc.ukans.edu/history/hnsource_main.html
[5]  http://history.cc.ukans.edu/history/H-Net_news/Resources
[6]  http://history.cc.ukans.edu/history/adding_to_WWW_main.html
```

If you are in a very big listing or document, you may have dozens of topics, and they'll shoot right by you before you can read them. Still, in smaller documents the listing may be useful.

On the other hand, it may not. You are only interested in the numbers in brackets, and the names at the end of each line after the last /, if any. For instance, in that last example above, topic 3 was obvious. Some of the others are not. Topic 4 (**hnsource_main.html**) is not too clear, while number 6 is, perhaps, not too arcane.

After viewing the list, either type one of the numbers or **u**, and press **Enter** (**u** will just return you to the previous page).

> **By the Way . . .**
>
> The WWW sometimes gets a little confused. It's a new system—still in development—and sometimes little bugs appear. For instance, you may enter a command and see a long program listing instead of the information you are supposed to see. Or perhaps it simply won't jump to where it's supposed to go. Or maybe the **home** command won't take you back to the first document. If you run into problems, try another command—go to a different document, or in a different "direction"—and the system will eventually get working again. If it *doesn't*, you may have to leave and come back.

## Finding What You Want

In some areas, you may be able to enter keywords so you can search a document. For instance, you can search the CIA *World Factbook*. You'll notice that the prompt line has changed:

```
FIND <keywords>, Back, Up, Quit, or Help:
```

This is telling you that you can type **find** (or just **f**), followed by the keywords for which you wish to search. For instance, you could type

```
f kuala lumpur
```

to search for information on the capital of Malaysia. Here's what you'd see:

```
                                          kuala lumpur (in CIA)
                                 KUALA LUMPUR

   Index CIA contains the following 4 items relevant to 'kuala
   lumpur'. The first figure for each entry is its relative score,
   the second the number of lines in the item.

 1000   415  Malaysia  Geography Total area: 329,750 km2; land area: 328,550
km2[1]
  970   348  Madagascar  Geography Total area: 587,040 km2; land area:
581,540 km2[2]
  248   310  Brunei  Geography Total area: 5,770 km2; land area: 5,270 km2[3]
    1   351  *** HELP for the Public CM WAIS Server ***[4]
     [End]
```

How do you get to the *World Factbook*? These are the topics that take you there from the top of the **nxoc01.cern.ch** WWW browser right now (they may change slightly): select **The Virtual Library[1]**; press **Enter** until you get to the **Geography** listing (probably twice); then select the **CIA World Fact Book[30]** topic.

You have three listings—notice the topic numbers at the end of each line. (There's a fourth, which gets you to the WAIS help system, because WWW accesses the CIA *World Factbook* through WAIS.) We were lucky, WWW will only let you see up to 39 listings—if it finds more, it just ignores from number 40 on.

## Save the Info You Find

The Web is not always very helpful when you want to save something. If you are using your own WWW browsers, or one set up by your service provider, you can use the **print** command to print a document, or the > ***filename*** command (on a UNIX system) to save the document in a file (use >> ***filename*** to append it to the end of an existing file). Unfortunately, WWW doesn't currently provide a way to mail documents back to you (as, for instance, WAIS can do).

# Using Gopher et al

Sometimes you'll find yourself using other "resources" from the WWW. You may select a topic and notice something like this, for instance:

```
gopher://orion.lib.virginia.edu:70/11/alpha/bmcr
```

WWW has just hooked into Gopher, and taken you to a computer connected through the Gopher menu system. If you connect to the CIA *World Factbook* through WWW, you'll see this:

```
Connection Machine WAIS server.
WWW has connected through the WAIS system.
```

You can connect through WWW to WAIS, Gopher, FTP, X.500, Whois, and so on. And you can use Telnet from your own WWW browser (though not from a public one like nxoc01.cern.ch). But WWW probably won't always work well for you in these other systems. You may be able to view a document through WAIS and Gopher, but you won't be able to download a file. And if you try to view a binary file (through FTP, for instance), WWW may try to do it, but at best you'll see garbage on your screen—at worst it will crash your computer. Still, you can use WWW to find what you are looking for—to search directories on a distant computer, for instance, it can be easier to use WWW than FTP. Then you can use FTP to go back to that system to grab the files you need.

# Loading Your Own WWW Browser

If you are really brave and have time to spare, you can install your own WWW browser. There are currently about 18 different browser programs (also known as *clients*), for MS-DOS, Windows, X-Windows, NeXt, UNIX, Macintosh, and so on. These programs have a wide variety of options, and provide the ability to customize your WWW system. For instance, you can pick a particular document to set up as the one you see each time you start WWW, saving you from digging your way through the system each time. You could also print documents that you find in WWW. You could even set up your own notes, with links to the WWW-at-large, so you could view your notes and travel—*through links in your notes*—to sources of information on the other side of the world.

If you want to find out more about the software that's available, start WWW, type **m**, and press **Enter** to see the online manual. Select the **deeper details** topic, then the **Other WWW browsers** topic, and finally the **Client software** topic. You'll find a list of the different programs, with information about the status and availability of each one.

But be warned. Most of these are *"beta" versions*—that is, they are not regarded as finished, stable products. They are "in development." WWW browsers may have lots of bugs, may have minimal or no technical support, and are almost certainly *not* for computer novices. Only try to set up one of these browsers if you know exactly what you are doing—and have a permanent or dial-in direct connection.

## The Least You Need to Know

- The World Wide Web is a hypertext system that lets you follow cross-references between documents.
- You can telnet to **nxoc01.cern.ch** to use a WWW browser, or use one set up by your service provider.
- Follow references by typing the **number** and pressing **Enter**.
- To get back to the first page you saw, use the **ho** command.
- Travel around in a document with the **top**, **bottom**, and **up** commands. Press **Enter** to go down one page.
- Type **l** and press **Enter** to view a list of the document's topics.
- If you see **FIND <keywords>** below the document, you can type **f keyword** to search the document.

# Part V
# Wonderfully Useful Stuff

*These "un-chapters" provide a little extra information to help you get working on Internet as swiftly and easily as humanly possible. You'll find a list of service providers and Free-Nets, to help you find the best deal on Internet, and a list of WHOIS servers. There's also a glossary of the techno-babble used on Internet, to help you when you are first getting started (or when you run into an Internetie who can't speak English).*

*And you'll find information about the computer disk we've bundled with this book—several software goodies for DOS-based PCs, just waiting to be discovered.*

*Consider this section your "expedition outfitter."*

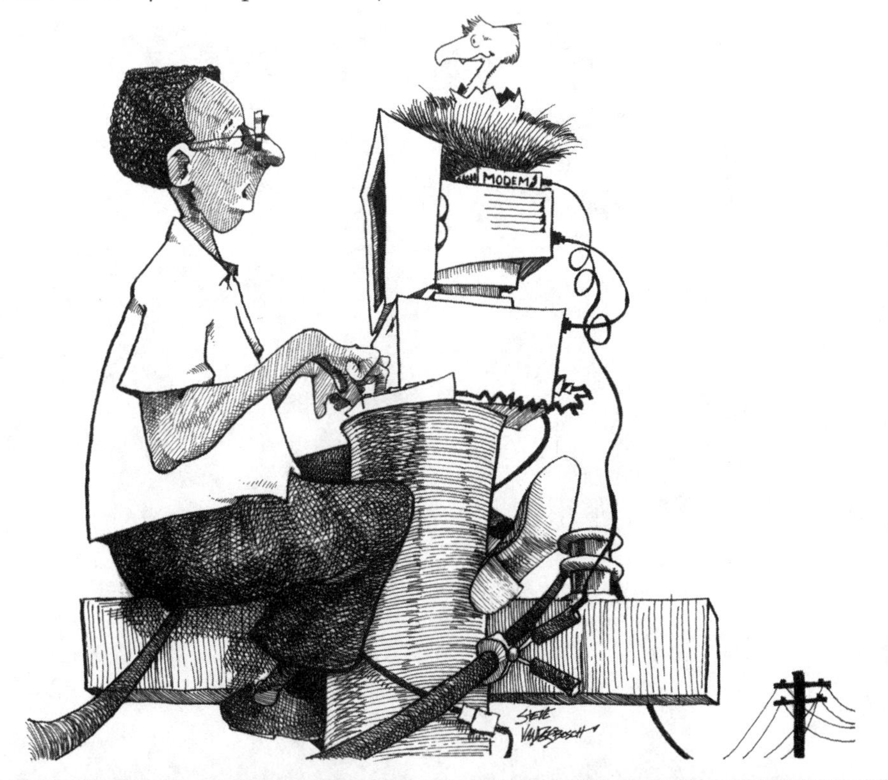

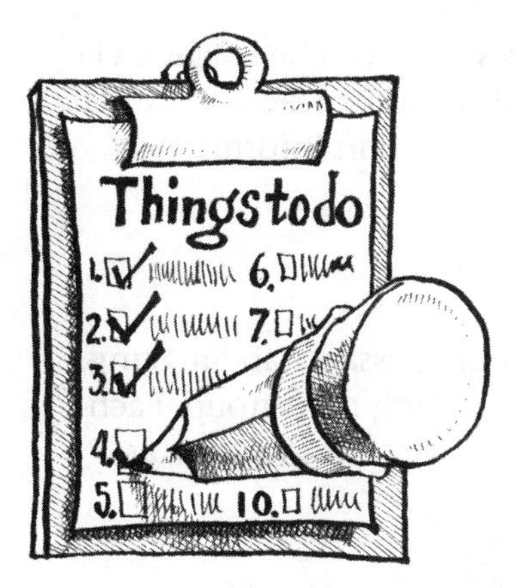


# Things to Do, Places to Visit

This "un-chapter" contains a few ideas for playing around on the Internet. Places to visit, things to do. This is *not* intended to be a comprehensive listing of what's available on the Internet—we could fill a book with that (and by the time you read it, it would be out of date). It's simply meant to give you a *taste* for what's out there. Spend some time with Gopher, HYTELNET, WAIS, and World Wide Web, and you'll find all sorts of amazing things.

You'll find literally *thousands* of other things to do in the files on the computer disk.

Under each entry, I've explained how to get to the resource. **Gopher:** means the resource can be reached from Gopher. Start the Gopher client, go to the menu that lists "all the gopher servers in the world," and then search for the first name (press /, type the name or part of the name, and press **Enter**). The names after the backslash are the menu options, though of course these may be changed by the time you get to them. For instance, **Internet Wiretap/ Electronic Books at Wiretap** means go to the **Internet Wiretap Gopher** server, then select the **Electronic Books at Wiretap** menu option. There are a lot of Gopher resources in this list, because Gopher's a great way to find your way around the Internet.

Remember that you will often find associated information. For instance, I've mentioned the Children, Youth, and Family Consortium Clearinghouse Gopher server, where you can find articles on raising children. Dig around a little at this site, and you'll also find statistics, as well as information about services and programs for families.

**Telnet:** means the resource can be reached via Telnet, and **FTP:** means it can be reached via FTP. In some cases I've included login information.

## Aging

A collection of newsgroup messages about aging, from the bionet.molbio.ageing newsgroup. Each message is a menu option. Recent messages are grouped by month.

Gopher: **BIOSCI/AGING**

## American Chemical Society

Descriptions of books sold by the American Chemical Society.

Gopher: **Inforonics' TitleBank Internet Catalog/American Chemical Society - Publications**

## American Demographics

The table of contents and article summaries of the latest issue of *American Demographics*. Online articles are also available.

Gopher: **American Demographics**

## Anesthesiology

Book reviews, lectures, and research abstracts related to anesthesiology.

Gopher: **Anesthesiology Gopher**

## Artificial Intelligence Lectures

Mostly in German (this is in Vienna).

Gopher: **Dept.Med.Cybernetics and Artif.Intelligence**

## Asia-Pacific Business and Marketing Resources

Find information about doing business in China, Japan, Korea, and other Asian countries. Articles such as "Taiwan Management Communication Practices."

Gopher: **Asian Institute of Technology (Thailand)**

## Astrophysics

Astrophysics databases maintained by the NASA/Goddard HEASARC (High Energy Astrophysics Science Archival Research Center).

Gopher: **High Energy Astrophysics Science Archive Research Center/HEASARC On-Line Data and Software**

## CD-ROM

Walnut Creek, a distributor of CD-ROMs, provides an area from which you can download information about authoring and working with CD-ROMs, a list of CD-ROM titles, utility programs for working with CD-ROM drives, and more.

FTP: **ftp.cdrom.com**

Directory: **pub/cdrom**

## Childrearing

Various articles and newsletters on parenting, from caring for babies to dealing with teens.

Gopher: **Children, Youth, and Family Consortium Clearing house/Brochures, Newsletters & Short Articles**

## Cola Machines

If you are interested in trivial interneting, check out the stock in a distant drinks machine:

**finger graph@drink.csh.rit.edu**

## Colorado Alliance of Research Libraries (CARL)

CARL is a great way to do library research at home. Search for books or magazine articles. About 40 city, community college, university, and hospital libraries are connected.

Telnet: **pac.carl.org or 192.54.81.128**

Login: PAC

## Computer Science Technical Reports from Australia

Read papers such as "An Overview of Secure Electronic Mail" and "Techniques for Implementing the RSA Public Key Cryptosystem."

Gopher: **Australian Defense Force Academy/Research Activities/Computer Science Technical Reports**

## Computer World Magazine

A few articles, and the current table of contents, from *ComputerWorld.*

Gopher: **Computer World Magazine**

## Consumer Information

Buying cheap air travel, computers, cars, and so on. How to protect yourself when buying and selling.

Gopher: **AMI - A Friendly Public Interface/Consumer**

## Diary of the August '91 Soviet Coup

One person's experiences during the coup in Russia.

Gopher: **Internet Wiretap/Various ETEXT Resources/Historical Texts Archive @ MS State FTP/diaries/diary.soviet**

## Disabilities

A community resource for people looking for information about disabilities—government documents, computing for the disabled, legal issues, and so on.

Gopher: **Cornucopia of Disability Information**

## Disaster Information

Reports about disaster management and current disasters all over the world—earthquakes, floods, tropical storms, and more.

Gopher: **Volunteers in Technical Assistance (VITA)/Disaster Situation and Status Reports**

## Discographies

Find out about albums from musicians such as Frank Zappa, Alien Sex Fiends, and Genesis. Over 50 bands.

Gopher: **Internet Wiretap/Wiretap Online Library/Music/ Discographies**

## Discovery Channel Magazine

Television program listings for the Discovery Channel. Articles and the table of contents from the latest *Discovery Channel Magazine.*

Gopher: **Destination Discovery - Discovery Channel Magazine**

## DragonMud

An online, text-based adventure game.

Telnet: **eve.assumption.edu 5000**

## Earthquake Information

Recent earthquakes, a "calendar of events" (conferences about earthquakes, not predictions!), the Emergency Preparedness Information eXchange, and more.

Gopher: **Earthquake Information Gopher**

## Economic Democracy Information Network

Information on labor issues, human rights, the environment, the economy, and more.

Gopher: **Economic Democracy Information Network**

## Economics and Business

Loads of info for economists and business people.

Gopher: **AMI - A Friendly Public Interface/Business Resources and Services**

## (The) Economist Magazine

Read articles, check the table of contents, and subscribe to the magazine.

Gopher: **Economist, The (Magazine)**

## Einstein Online Service, Smithsonian Astrophysical Observatory

Everything you ever wanted to know about astrophysics.

Telnet: **cfa204.harvard.edu or 128.103.40.204**

login: **einline**

## Electronic Books

Over 150 books, such as the CIA's *Psychological Operations in Guerrilla Warfare*, Sir Thomas More's *Utopia*, and Darwin's *The Voyage of the Beagle*.

Gopher: **Internet Wiretap/Electronic Books at Wiretap**

## Electronic Frontier Foundation

An organization fighting to "ensure that the principles embodied in the Constitution and the Bill of Rights are protected as new communications technologies emerge."

Gopher: **Electronic Frontier Foundation**

## Electronic Periodic Table of the Elements

A periodic table of the elements through which you can navigate and view information about each element.

Telnet: **131.174.82.239 2034**

No login required.

## Erotica

Articles and subscription information from this journal of erotica.

Gopher: **Yellow Silk, Journal of Erotica (Magazine)**

## The Flora of Costa Rica

Search for information about plants found in Costa Rica.

Gopher: **Missouri Botanical Garden/Manual of the Plants of Costa Rica**

## Flying

Information about recreational flight, including articles, stories, and pictures.

Gopher: **rec.aviation gopher**

## Food

Dozens of recipes for Oriental and Italian food, appetizers, breads, casseroles, etc.

Gopher: **University of Minnesota/Fun & Games/Recipes**

## The Future of Computer Networking

Information about how computer communications may be able to enhance communications with the objective of reducing conflict to secure a more promising future.

Gopher: **Communications for a Sustainable Future**

## Germplasm

Search for information about "working" collections of bacteria, bacteria, viruses, fungi, nematodes, and so on. Find the phone number and address of the researchers working with the germplasm.

Gopher: **Microbial Germplasm Database**

## Global Land Information System

GLIS is a source of information for use in earth science research and global-change studies.

Telnet: **glis.cr.usgs.gov or 152.61.192.54**

## History of Science

"Classes" in the form of ASCII documents that teach about the history of science.

Gopher: **Scientists on Disk - JHU History of Science and Medicine**

## Human Genome Project

Databases of genes, genetic markers and map locations.

Gopher: **Human Genome Mapping Project Gopher Service (UK)**

## The Internet Hunt

A game that builds your research skills. The Hunt provides ten questions. You then use the Internet resources to find the answers.

Gopher: **CICNET gopher server/The Internet Hunt**

## Islam

Information about Muslim projects—a Muslim computer network, Muslim TV, an Islamic bank, and Cybermuslim, resources on the Internet for Muslims. You can also find an ASCII copy of the Quran (in English).

Gopher: **ISLAMIC Resources**

## Job Openings in Academe

Find a job in the academic world.

Gopher: **ACADEME THIS WEEK/JOB OPENINGS in Academe**

## Journals

Electronic journals, including *Gov-Line, Disabilities Newsletter, Advanced Squad Leader Digest, Bangkok Post,* and dozens more.

Gopher: **CICNET gopher server/Electronic Serials**

## Lawyer Jokes

A few dozen pages of lawyer jokes.

Gopher: **University of Minnesota/Fun & Games/Humor/ Lawyer Jokes**

## Learning About Chance

A database containing information for teaching about chance and statistics, based on current "chance" events reported in newspapers.

Gopher: **CHANCE database**

## Long-Term Ecological Research

Articles about long-term ecological research.

Gopher: **Long-Term Ecological Research Network/LTER Core Dataset Catalog/Files in ASCII text**

## Macintosh Freeware and Shareware

Download software for the Macintosh.

Gopher: **Apple Computer Higher Education/Macintosh Freeware and Shareware**

## Magazine Articles

Articles from magazines such as *Worth, The New Republic, ComputerWorld, Financial World, Inc., Yellow Silk (the Journal of Erotic Arts)* and about 40 others, along with current tables of contents, book reviews, and entertainment reviews.

Gopher: **Electronic Newstand**

## Movies

Select from hundreds of movie reviews, from "Buffy the Vampire Slayer" to "Throw Momma From the Train."

Gopher: **University of Minnesota/Fun & Games/Movies**

## National Center for Atmospheric Research

Search NCARs libraries for papers and books related to the atmosphere.

Telnet: **library.ucar.edu**

## National Institutes of Health Library

Search for health-related publications.

Telnet: **nih-library.nih.gov or 137.187.166.250**

## New Age Magazine

Read articles and the table of contents from, and subscribe to, *New Age Magazine*.

Gopher: **New Age Magazine**

## Notre Dame Fighting Irish Football Team

Articles from the *Blue & Gold Illustrated* magazine.

Gopher: **Blue & Gold Illustrated Magazine**

## OS/2 Software

Thousands of files for IBM's OS/2 operating system.

FTP: **ftp-os2.cdrom.com or ftp-os2.nmsu.edu**

Directory: **pub/os2**

## OSHA Regulations

Read the Occupational Safety and Health regulations.

Gopher: **Occupational Safety & Health Gopher (OSHA regulations)/OSHA Occupational Safety & Health Regulations**

## Papyrus

Research information about papyri held in university papyrus collections.

Gopher: **Classics and Mediterranean Archaeology/Papyrology**

## Poultry

Information about raising poultry, and pictures of domestic fowl.

Gopher: **Poultry Science Gopher**

## Presidential News

Contains documents from the *Federal Register*, public statements by White House aides, speeches by Bill Clinton, and so on.

Gopher: **Internet Wiretap/Clinton Press Releases**

## Primates

Information about primate research.

Gopher: **Primate Info Net**

## Progressive Club Music

Play music directly from the Internet. Unfortunately, you'll need special software to play these "tribal, trance and house beats."

Gopher: **N-Fusion**

## Project Gutenberg

Hundreds of books, articles, and speeches in ASCII format, from President Clinton's speeches to *The War of the Worlds*.

FTP: **mrcnext.cso.uiuc.edu**

Directory: **/pub/gutenberg/**

## Raves

Information about who's holding "raves" and where, about the media perception of the rave "scene," and about techno music.

Gopher: **Techno/Rave gopher**

## "Real Programmer" Jokes

Such as: "Real programmers don't eat quiche. Real programmers don't even know how to spell quiche. They eat Twinkies, Coke and palate-scorching Szechwan food."

Gopher: **University of Minnesota/Fun & Games/Humor/Real Programmers**

## Scandinavian Studies

Everything you could possibly need to know about Scandinavian studies.

Gopher: **The Society for the Advancement of Scandinavian Study**

## SchoolNet

A Canadian network of schools. Information about scholarships and grants, Globe and Mail articles, and so on.

Gopher: **SchoolNet Gopher**

## School Networking

Information about getting a school onto the Internet.

Gopher: **Coalition of School Networking**

## Software

Thousands of shareware and public domain programs for a variety of computers, including MS-DOS, the Macintosh, and NeXT. One of the most popular ftp sites on the Internet.

FTP: **garbo.uwasa.fi**

See also the Microcomputer Software archive at the University of Lancaster in England. It features software for the Amiga, Apple, PC, Atari,

BBC, and others.

Gopher: **HENSA micros/The HENSA/micros archive at Lancaster University/Microcomputer Software**

## Song Lyrics

Find the lyrics from hundreds of different songs, modern and folk.

FTP: **ftp.uwp.edu**

Directory: **/pub/music/lyrics**

## Space Program Graphics

Pictures in a variety of formats from NASA.

FTP: **toybox.gsfc.nasa.gov**

Login: **anonymous**

Directory: **/pub/images**

## Space Shuttle

Information about the Space Shuttle's Small Payloads project, including GIF graphics, newsletters, and information on conferences.

Gopher: **NASA Shuttle Small Payloads Info**

## Supreme Court Rulings

The "Project Hermes" electronic copies of the U.S. Supreme Court's opinions in various formats (ASCII, WordPerfect, and so on).

FTP: **ftp.cwru.edu**

Directory: **U.S.Supreme.Court**

## Teach Yourself Law

The Center for Computer-Assisted Legal Instruction produces software for learning about the law.

Gopher: **CALI - The Center for Computer-Assisted Legal Instruction/Gopher**

## Texas

Information about Texan history for the middle school.

Gopher: **Armadillo, the Texas Studies Gopher**

## The Tropics

A database and electronic publications—a "biodiversity/biotechnology information resource."

Gopher: **Base de Dados Tropical (Tropical Data Base), Campinas, Brasil**

## Turkey

Find out about Internet services in Turkey.

Gopher: **Bilkent University, Ankara, (TR)**

## UFOs

I couldn't get through to this Gopher site, but it looks fun, so I'm listing it anyway. (Maybe it will be back online by the time you read this.)

Gopher: **UFONet - UFO and Alien information**

## United Nations

Keep up to date with what the United Nations does.

Gopher: **United Nations**

## Weather Forecasts

Find satellite maps, information about storms and earthquakes, and weather forecasts for anywhere in the United States.

Gopher: **National Center for Atmospheric Research (NCAR)/ National Weather Service Forecasts**

## World Health Organization

Information about the programs of the World Health Organization.

Gopher: **World Health Organisation (WHO)**

## World Peace

A foundation dedicated to "facilitating positive global change by establishing communications and information systems that inventory and integrate the resources and needs of people, projects and organizations in service to humanity and the Earth.

Gopher: **Together Foundation for Global Unity**

# Service Providers and Free-Nets

Use this listing when you are looking for a way to get an Internet account. If you can't get one free from your company, school, university, or employing government department, find out if there's a Free-Net near you. If not, check the list of service providers.

## Free-Nets

Free-Nets provide free Internet access to local communities—there might be one near you. I've included the modem number of each Free-Net, so all you need to do is install a modem in your computer, find some simple communications software, then dial up the Free-Net. Follow instructions to "register with" or "join" the Free-Net. (There may be a $10 registration fee, but after that, it *will* be free.) I've also included the Internet host addresses, so you can "telnet" onto these systems if you want to visit the Free-Net using your existing Internet account (see Chapter 17). You will usually log into the Free-Nets as a *guest*—I've indicated the login name you should use (some require *visitor* or *bbguest*). To log into a new Free-Net when you are not sure of the required login name, try these three options.

Not all Free-Nets will provide full access to the Internet. For security reasons, some may limit certain services (for instance, they may not want you to use FTP to bring possibly virus-laden files into their system).

The list of Free-Nets is growing rapidly. By the time you read this, there will be more. For information, contact the National Public Telecomputing Network.

National Public Telecomputing Network
Box 1987
Cleveland, OH 44106
Internet e-mail: tmg@nptn.org
Voice: 216-247-5800
FAX: 216-247-3328

## Free-Nets

Big Sky Telegraph—Dillon, MT
Modem: 406-683-7680
Telnet: bigsky.bigsky.dillon.mt.us

Buffalo Free-Net—Buffalo, NY
Modem: 716-645-6128
Telnet: freenet.buffalo.edu

CapAccess
National Capital Area Public Access Network
Washington, D.C.
Modem: 202 785-1523
Telnet: cap.gwu.edu
Log in as visitor
Password: guest

Cleveland Free-Net—Cleveland, OH
Modem: 216-368-3888
Telnet: freenet-in-a.cwru.edu
or hela.ins.cwru.edu
or 129.22.8.38
Log in as: guest

COIN (Columbia Online Information Network)—Columbia, MO
Modem: 303-884-7000
Telnet: bigcat.missouri.edu
Log in as: guest

Dayton Free-Net
Modem: 513 229-4373
e-mail: sysadm@dayton.wright.edu
Telnet: dayton.wright.edu or 130.108.128.174
Log in as: visitor

Denver Free-Net—Denver, CO
Modem: 303-270-4865
Telnet: freenet.hsc.colorado.edu
Log in as: guest, visitor, or bbguest

Freenet Finland
Modem: 358-2923 (TeleSampo users only)
Telnet: freenet.hut.fi or 130.233.208.40
Log in as: visitor
Password: Press Enter
(in English, Finnish, or Swedish)

Heartland Free-Net—Peoria, IL
Modem: 309-674-1100
Telnet: heartland.bradley.edu
Log in as: bbguest

Lorain County Free-Net—Elyria, OH
Modem: 216-366-9721
Telnet: freenet.lorain.oberlin.edu
Log in as: guest

Medina County Free-Net—Medina, OH
Modem: 216-723-6732
Telnet: Not connected to Internet at the time of writing

Milwaukee Free-Net—Milwaukee, WI
Modem:
Telnet: freenet.uwm.edu or 129.89.70.58
Log in as: visitor

National Capital Free-Net—Ottawa, British Columbia, Canada
Modem: 613-780-3733
Telnet: freenet.carleton.ca

Prairienet, the East-Central Illinois Freenet
Modem: 217 255-9000
Voice: 217 244-7365

Fax: 217 244-3302
Telnet: firefly.prairienet.org or 192.17.3.3
e-mail: gbnewby@uiuc.edu or gnewby@ncsa.uiuc.edu
Log in as: visitor

RioGrande Free-Net
Modem: 915-755-5600
Voice: 915 775-6077
e-mail: aa100@rgfn.epcc.edu
Telnet: rgfn.epcc.edu or 192.94.29.9
Log in as: visitor

Tallahassee Free-Net—Tallahassee, FL
Modem: 904-576-6330 or 904-488-5056
Telnet: freenet.fsu.edu
Log in as: visitor

Toledo Free-Net—Toledo, OH
Telnet: 131.183.4.100 (not responding at time of writing)
Log in as: visitor

Traverse City Free-Net
Modem: 616-922-1096
e-mail: connie@nmc.edu
Telnet: leo.nmc.edu or 192.88.242.239
Log in as: visitor

Tri-State Online—Cincinnati, OH
Modem: 513-579-1990
Telnet: 129.137.100.1
Log in as: guest

Vaasa FreePort Bulletin Board (BBS)—Finland
Modem: (Finland—358) 61 3170 972 and 61 3170 974
Telnet: garbo.uwasa.fi or 128.214.87.1
Log in as: guest

Victoria Free-Net—Victoria, British Columbia, Canada
Modem: 604-595-2300
Telnet: freenet.victoria.bc.ca

Wellington Citynet—Wellington, New Zealand
Modem: (New Zealand—64) 4 8013060
e-mail: brockie@wcc.govt.nz or hardy@wcc.govt.nz

Telnet: lx.wcc.govt.nz or jethro.wcc.govt.nz
(Currently doesn't allow guests.)

Youngstown Free-Net—Youngstown OH
Modem: 216-742-3072
Telnet: yfn.ysu.edu
Log in as: visitor

## A Free Account in Washington

If you live in or near Washington, or a long way from a service provider's telephone number, you may want to follow up on the International Internet Association's offer of a free Internet account.

The International Internet Association
Suite 852
2020 Pennsylvania Ave. N.W.
Washington, D.C. 20006.
Voice: (202) 387-5445
Fax: (202) 387-5446

## A List of Service Providers

The rest of this chapter contains a list of service providers. Compare the rates of all the ones that have service in your area (not just the ones headquartered near you). See Chapter 4 for information on comparing services. If you can't find a service provider with a local number in your area, you should look for one with a 1-800 number that you can dial into, or a one that is connected to a network such as the CompuServe Packet Network or PC-Pursuit; you can dial a local number in your city, and the network will let you connect to the service provider's computer.

**By the Way . . .**

Not all these service providers have all types of service. If you call an organization that *doesn't* have the service you are looking for, ask them if they know of one that does. Also, there are other organizations who asked *not* to be listed—these organizations don't provide service to individuals and small businesses, only to large organizations.

If you can't find a service provider in your area, or would like a more recent listing of service providers, contact one of the organizations listed at the end of this chapter under "Internet Information." And here, without further ado, is the list of service providers.

### By the Way . . .

I've complicated comparing service providers for you—I've convinced a number of them to provide a special discount to the readers of *The Complete Idiot's Guide to the Internet.* I'm not endorsing any service providers—you should still compare rates (and take the discounts into consideration) when buying an Internet account. The discount is simply a little extra, a gift from us to you (sweet, huh?). To see who's providing a discount, take a look at the coupons at the back of this book.

Notice that some of these service providers have an **info@** e-mail address. In most cases, sending a message to one of these will elicit an automatic response. If you already have an Internet account, you can send a message—without any subject or message text—and will receive a response describing the organization's services.

## a2i Communications

Area: Local numbers in San Jose and Redwood City, CA, but subscribers from all over the U.S. and international.

1211 Park Avenue #202
San Jose, CA 95132

Voice: 408-293-8078
Modem: 408-293-9010 (Interactive 'guest' login)
Internet: info@rahul.net

## AARNet

Area: Australia

AARNet Support
GPO Box 1142
Canberra ACT 2601 Australia

Voice: (Aust.) 6 249 3385
Fax: (Aust.) 6 249 1369
Internet: aarnet@aarnet.edu.au

## AccessNB

Area: New Brunswick

Computer Science Department
University of New Brunswick
Fredericton, NB Canada E3B5A4

## America Online, Inc.

Area: United States. America Online startup kit available at bookstores and software retailers.

8619 Westwood Center Drive
Vienna, VA 22182-2285

Voice: 800 827-6364
Voice: 703 448-8700

## ANS (Advanced Network and Services)

ANS CO+RE Systems, Inc. Area: USA, Canada, Germany, Mexico, Switzerland, United Kingdom.

1875 Campus Commons Drive
Suite 220
Reston, VA 22091

Voice: 800 456-8267
Voice: 703 758-7700
Fax: 703 758-7717
Internet: info@nis.ans.net

## ARnet

Area: Alberta

Ralph Penno
Alberta Research Council
P.O. Box 8330
Edmonton, Alberta, Canada
T6H 5X2

Voice: 403 450-5188
Fax: 403 461-2651
Internet: penno@arc.ab.ca

## BARRNet

Area: CA, NV, OR, some international (particularly Pacific Rim).

Pine Hall Rm. 115
Stanford, CA 94305-4122

Voice: 415-725-1790
Voice: 415-725-7003
Fax: 415-723-0908
Internet: info@barrnet.net

## BCnet

Area: British Columbia

515 West Hastings Street
Vancouver, BC Canada
V6B 5K3

Voice: 604 291-5029
Internet: Mike@BC.net

## CERFnet—General Atomics/CERFnet

Area: W. U.S., plus nationally via 800 line.

P.O. Box 85608
San Diego, CA 92186-9784

Voice: 800-876-2373
Voice: 619-455-3900
Fax: 619 455 3990
Internet: roblesc@cerf.net
help@cerf.net

## CICNet, Inc.

Area: Midwest (MN, WI, IA, IN, IL, MI, OH).

Kimberly Shaffer
Marketing and Sales Coordinator
ITI Building
2901 Hubbard Drive
Ann Arbor, MI 48105

Voice: 313 998 6104
Voice: 313 998 6103
Fax: 313 998 6105
e-mail: info@cic.net
shaffer@cic.net

## Colorado Supernet

Area: Colorado.

CSM Computing Center
Colorado School of Mines
1500 Illinois
Golden, CO 80401

Voice: 303 273 3471
Fax: 303 273 3475
Internet: info@csn.org

## CompuServe

Area: Worldwide. At the time of writing, CompuServe was planning to introduce Internet access. They expect to have some kind of Internet access toward the end of 1994. (CompuServe already has a message service to and from Internet.) Call 1-800-848-8199 for more details.

## CONCERT (Communications for NC Education, Research, and Technology)

Area: North Carolina.

P.O. Box 12889
3021 Cornwallis Road
Research Triangle Park, NC 27709

Voice: 919 248-1999
Fax: 919 248 1405
Internet: info@concert.net

## CSUnet

Area: California (education K-12, Community Colleges, Universities, public libraries, government).

California State University
Office of the Chancellor
Information Resources and Technology
P.O. Box 3842
Seal Beach, CA 90740-7842

Voice: 310-985-9661
Fax: 310-985-9400
Internet: chris@calstate.edu
nethelp@csu.net

## Delphi

Area: National. If you have a current Internet account you can Telnet to delphi.com to check out their services.

1030 Massachusetts Avenue
Cambridge, MA 02138

Voice: 800-695-4005
Voice: 617-491 3393

Modem: 800-365-4636
Internet: info@delphi.com

***Discount***: At the time of writing, Delphi offers a 5-hour free trial to anyone (not just *Idiot* readers). The free time must be used during evenings and weekends—you'll get full details when you log on. Dial Delphi's modem number; press **Enter** once or twice when you connect; when prompted for the username type **JOINDELPHI** and press **Enter**; when prompted for the password type **PMCGA93** and press **Enter**.

## Demon Internet Limited

Area: United Kingdom.

Demon System Ltd.
42 Hendon Lane
London N3 1TT
England

Voice: (UK) 081 349 0063
internet@demon.co.uk

## EUnet

Area: Europe, CIS-region, and Northern Africa.

Voice: (Netherlands—31) 20 592 51 09
Internet: info@eu.net

## EUnet

Area: Germany.

EUnet Deutschland GmbH
Emil Figge Strasse 80
44227 Dortmund
Germany

Voice: (Germany) 231 972 00
Internet: info@Germany.EU.net
FTP info: ftp.Germany.EU.net

## EUnet GB

Area: Great Britain and Northern Ireland.

Kent R&D Business Centre
Giles Lane
Canterbury
CT2 7PB, Kent, UK

Voice: (UK—44) 227-475497
Fax: (UK—44) 227 475478
Internet: sales@britain.eu.net

## ICNet

Area: Michigan.

2662 Valley Drive
Ann Arbor, MI 48103

Voice: 313 998-0090
Internet: interconnect@ic.net
connect@ic.net

## JVNCnet

Area: U.S. and International.

Global Enterprise Services, Inc.
Sergio Heker
3 Independence Way
Princeton, NJ 08540

Voice: 800 358-4437
Fax: 609 897-7310
Internet: info@jvnc.net
market@jvnc.net
Internet FTP: ftp.jvnc.net directory: pub/jvncnet-info
Internet Gopher: telnet to gopher.jvnc.net,
log in as: gopher, /jvncnet/marketing information

## MBnet

Area: Manitoba, Canada.

Gerry Miller
Director Computer Services
University of Manitoba
603 Engineering Building
Winnipeg MB
Canada

R3T 2N2
Voice: 204 474-8230
Fax: 204 275-5420
Internet: Gerry_Miller@MBnet.MB.CA
Bill_Reid@MBnet.MB.CA

## MichNet

Area: Michigan. Merit Network Inc.

2200 Bonisteel Blvd.
Ann Arbor, MI 48109-2099

Voice: 313-764-9430
Fax: 313 747-3185
Internet: info@merit.edu

## MIDnet

Area: Mid U.S. (NE, OK, AR, MO, IA, KS, SD)

Network Information Center
208 N 8th Street, Suite 421
Lincoln, NE 68508

Voice: 402 472 7600
Internet: nic@mid.net

## MRNET (Minnesota Regional Network)

Area: MN and nearby.

511 11th Avenue South, Box 212
Minneapolis, Minnesota 55415

Voice: 612 342 2570
Fax: 612 344 1716
Internet: info@mr.net
dfazio@mr.net

## MSEN, Incorporated

Area: Michigan.

Attn: Owen S. Medd
628 Brooks Street
Ann Arbor, MI 48103

Voice: 313-998-4562
FAX: 313 998-4563
Internet: info@msen.com

## MV Communications

Area: Southern New Hampshire and northern Maine.

MV Communications, Inc.
POB 4963
Manchester, NH 03108

Voice: 603 429-2223
Modem: 603 429-1735 (login as "info" or "rates")
Internet: mv_admin@mv.mv.com

## NAIC (Network Applications and Information Center)

Area: Worldwide for users of the NASA Science Internet Information Desk. (Note: this service is for use by people involved in NASA-related research only.)

NASA Ames Research Center
MS 204-14
Moffett Field, CA 94035-1000

Voice: 800 858 9947
Voice: 415 604 0600
Fax: 415 604 0978
Internet: naic@nasa.gov

## NB*net

Area: New Brunswick

Voice: 506-453-4573

## NETCOM

Area: CA, CO, DC, GA, MA, TX.

Desirree Madison-Biggs
Netcom On-line Communications Services
4000 Moorepark Ave. #200
San Jose, CA 95117

Voice: 800 501-8649
Voice: 408 554-8649
Voice list of local numbers: 800 488-2558
Fax: 408 241-9145
Internet: des@netcom.com

## NetILLINOIS

Peter Roll, Executive Director
1840 Oak Ave.
Evanston, IL 60201

Voice: 708 866-1825
Internet: p_roll@nwu.edu

Joel Hartman, President
Bradley University
1501 W. Bradley Ave.
Peoria, IL 61625

Voice: 309 677-3100
Fax: 309 677-3092
Internet: joel@bradley.edu

## NevadaNet

Area: Nevada.

University and Community College System of Nevada
4505 Maryland Pkwy
Las Vegas, NV 89154

Voice: 702-895-4580
Voice: 702-784-6133
Fax: 702 895 3791
Internet: info@nevada.edu
Internet: mitch@nevada.edu
Internet: zitter@nevada.edu

## NLnet

Area: Newfoundland and Labrador.

Voice: 709-737-8329
Internet: wilf@kean.ucs.mun.ca

## NovX

Area: U.S. through an 800 number.

316 Occidental Ave.
Seattle, WA 98104

Voice: 206-447-0800
Fax: 206 447-9008
Internet: mgoodman@novx.com

## NSTN Inc.

Area: Nova Scotia (9 POPs); Ottawa, Ontario.

900 Windmill Road, Suite 107
Dartmouth, NS Canada B3B 137

Voice: 902-468-6786
Internet: martinea@hawk.nstn.ns.ca
dow@hawk.nstn.ns.ca

## NYSERnet

Area: New York.

200 Elwood Davis Road
Suite 103
Liverpool, NY 13088-6147

Voice: 315-453-2912
Fax: 315-453-3052
Internet: info@nysernet.org

## OARnet

Area: U.S.A.

OARnet
1224 Kinnear Road
Columbus, Ohio 43212

Voice: 614 292-8100
Fax: 614 292 7168
Internet: info@oar.net

## ONet

Membership Co-ordinator: Dr. Warren Jackson
4 Bancroft Ave., Rm. 118
University of Toronto
Toronto Ontario Canada M5S 1A1

Voice: 416 978-8948
Fax: 416 978 6620
Internet: Warren_Jackson@poczta.utcc.UToronto.CA

Chairman: Dr. John Drake
Voice: 905-525-9140x4000
Fax: 905-528-3773
Internet: Drake@offsv2.CIS.McMaster.CA

## Panix

Area: NY, NJ, U.S. via PC-Pursuit.

Modem: 212 787-3100
Voice: 212 787-6160
Internet: info@panix.com
info-person@panix.com

## PEINet

Area: Prince Edward Island.

P.O.Box 3126
Charlottetown, PEI C1A 7N9

Voice: 902-892-7346
Internet: admin@peinet.ca
cabgardi@upei.ca

## Pipex

Area: United Kingdom, Europe.

D J Mooring
PIPEX Limited
216 The Science Park
Cambridge CB4 4WA England

Voice: (UK—44) 223 250100
Fax: (UK—44) 223 250101
Internet: sales@pipex.net

## Portal Communications

Area: San Franscisco, worldwide through Sprintnet.

Portal Communications Company
20863 Stevens Creek Blvd.
Suite #200
Cupertino, CA 95014

Voice: 408 973-9111
Fax: 408 725-1580
Internet: info@portal.com
CS@portal.com

## PREPnet

Area: Pennsylvania.

305 S. Craig, 2nd floor
Pittsburgh, PA 15213

Voice: 412 268 7870
Fax: 412 268 7875
Internet: twb+@andrew.cmu.edu

## PSINet

Area: North America, Pacific Rim, Europe.

Performance Systems International
Suite 1100
1800 Sunrise Valley Drive
Reston, VA 22091

Voice: 800-827-7482
Voice: 703 620 6651
Fax: 703 620 4586
Internet: wls@psi.com
info@psi.com

## RISQ

Area : Quebec.

RISQ
1801 Avenue McGill College
Bureau 800
Montreal (Quebec)
Canada H3A 2N4

Voice : (514) 398-1234
Internet : cirisq@crim.ca
cirisq@crim.ca

## SASK#net

Area: Saskatchewan.

Dean Jones
Computing Services
56 Physics Building
University of Saskatchewan
Saskatoon, SK S7N 0W0
Canada

Voice: 306 966-4860
Fax: 306 966-4938
Internet: dean.jones@usask.ca

William Maes
Libraries and Information Services
University of Regina
Regina, SK S4S 0A2
Canada

Voice: 306 585-4132
Fax: 306 585-4878
Internet: wmaes@max.cc.uregina.ca

## SESQUINET

Area: Texas.

Office of Networking and Computing Systems
Rice University
Houston, TX 77251-1892

Voice: 713 527-6038
Fax: 713 527-6099
Internet: info@sesqui.net

## SURAnet (Southeastern Universities Research Association Network)

Area: Southeastern U.S. (WV, VA, SC, NC, TN, KY, LA, MS, AL, GA, FL), Washington D.C. area (Washington DC, MD, DE), Caribbean, and South America.

8400 Baltimore Boulevard
College Park, MD 20740-2498

Voice: 800 SURANET
Voice: 301 982-4600
Fax: 301 982-4605
Internet: info@sura.net
marketing@sura.net

## SwipNet

Olle F. Wallner
SwipNet AB
P.O.Box 62
S-164 94 KISTA
Sweden

Tel: +46 8-6324040 (switch board)
Tel: +46 8-6324058 (direct)
Fax: +46 8-6324200
e-mail wallner@swip.net

## THEnet

Area: Texas. (No private-individual accounts; only accepts businesses if involved in research, education, and government.)

The University of Texas System
Office of Telecommunication Services
Service Building, Room 319
Austin, TX 78712-1024

Voice: (512) 471-2400
Fax: (512) 471-2449
Internet: info@nic.the.net

## The Well

Area: United States, Europe, Latin America, Pacific Rim.

1750 Bridgeway
Sausalito, CA 94965

Voice: 415-332-4335
Modem: 415-332-6106 (register online)
Internet: email info@well.sf.ca.us
or telnet and log in as *guest* to see sample files

## The World

Area: U.S.

Software Tool & Die
1330 Beacon Street
Brookline, MA 02146

Voice: 617 739 0202
Internet: info@world.std.com

## TIPnet

Area: Sweden

Technical Sales Support
MegaCom AB
121 80 Johanneshov
Stockholm Sweden

Voice: (Sweden) 8 780 5616
Fax: (Sweden) 8 686 0213
Internet: "Anders Halldin" <atg@rd.r.tvt.se>

## UUNET

Area: Worldwide.

3110 Fairview Park Drive, Suite 570
Falls Church, Va 22042

Voice: 800 488 6384
Voice: 703 204 8000
Fax: 703 204 8001
Internet: info@uunet.uu.net
uunet-request@uunet.uu.net
e-mail (uucp): uunet!uunet-request

## World dot Net

Area: Pacific Northwest (OR, WA, ID).

Internetworks, Inc.
Voice: 206-576-7147
Internet: info@world.net

## WVNET

Area: West Virginia.

Voice: 304-293-5192
Internet: cc011041@wvnvms.wvnet.edu

# Internet Information

These organizations can help you find a service provider.

## FARNET

Ms. Laura Breeden, Executive Director
FARNET, Inc.
100 5th Avenue, 4th Floor
Waltham, MA 02154

Voice: 617-890-5117
Voice: 800-723-2763
Fax: 617-890-5117
Internet: breeden@farnet.org

## InterNIC Information Services Referral Desk

General Atomics/CERFnet
P.O. Box 85608
San Diego, CA 92186-9784

Voice: 619-455-4600
Voice: 800-444-4345
Fax: 619-455-3990
Internet: info@internic.net

## Network Information Services Center

Ms. Vivian Neou, Manager, Information Services
SRI International, NISC, Room EJ294
333 Ravenswood Avenue
Menlo Park, CA 94025

Voice:415-859-5318
Fax: 415-859-6028
Internet: vivian@nisc.sri.com

# Whois Servers

In Chapter 14, you learned about using **whois** to track down a user. There are quite a few servers on which you can search for a user; here's a list of some of them.

| United States | |
|---|---|
| Auburn University | ducserv.duc.auburn.edu |
| Bates College | whois.bates.edu |
| Baylor College of Medicine | whois.bcm.tmc.edu |
| California Institute of Technology | caltech.edu |
| California Institute of Technology | horton.caltech.edu |
| California State University, Fresno | csufres.csufresno.edu |
| California State University, Hayward | csuhayward.edu |
| California State University, Sacramento | csus.edu |
| Cambridge Computer Associates | camb.com |
| Case Western Reserve University | whois.cwru.edu |
| Corporation for National Research Initiatives, Knowbot interface | info.cnri.reston.va.us |
| Dana-Farber Cancer Institute | whois.dfci.harvard.edu |

*continues*

| | |
|---|---|
| DDN Network Information Center | whois.nic.ddn.mil |
| Energy Sciences Network | wp.es.net |
| Florida State University | cc.fsu.edu |
| George Mason University | gmu.edu |
| Gettysburg College | gettysburg.edu |
| GTE Laboratories | gte.com |
| Indiana University | indiana.edu |
| Kean College | kean.edu |
| Kutztown University | acad.csv.kutztown.edu |
| Lawrence Livermore National Laboratory | llnl.gov |
| Massachusetts Institute of Technology | mit.edu |
| Minnesota State University, Winona | vax2.winona.msus.edu |
| Mississippi State University | whois.msstate.edu |
| NASA Ames Research Center | x500.arc.nasa.gov |
| NASA Goddard Space Flight Center | x500.gsfc.nasa.gov |
| NASA Langley Research Center | larc.nasa.gov |
| National Energy Research Supercomputer Center | wp.nersc.gov |
| Naval Research Laboratory | whois.nrl.navy.mil |
| Network Solutions, Inc. | whois.internic.net |
| Network Solutions, Inc. (non-MILNET/non-POC) | ds.internic.net |
| New Jersey Institute of Technology | earth.njit.edu |
| New Jersey Intercampus Network | pilot.njin.net |
| New York University, Courant Institute | acfcluster.nyu.edu |
| North Carolina State University | whois.ncsu.edu |
| Northern Arizona University | nau.edu |
| Occidental College | whois.oxy.edu |
| Ohio Northern University | austin.onu.edu |
| Ohio State University | osu.edu |
| Oregon State University | ph.orst.edu |

| | |
|---|---|
| Pacific Bell | whois.pacbell.com |
| Pennsylvania State University | info.psu.edu |
| Performance Systems International | wp.psi.com |
| Rochester Institute of Technology | cs.rit.edu |
| Rutgers University | whitepages.rutgers.edu |
| San Diego State University | whois.sdsu.edu |
| Sandia National Laboratories | seda.sandia.gov |
| Sonoma State University | sonoma.edu |
| St. John's University | stjohns.edu |
| Stanford University | stanford.edu |
| Stanford University | camis.stanford.edu |
| Stanford University | hpp.stanford.edu |
| State University of New York at Binghamton | bingsuns.cc.binghamton.edu |
| State University of New York at Stony Brook | sunysb.edu |
| Sunquest Information Systems | whois.sunquest.com |
| Syracuse University | syr.edu |
| Texas State Technical College | tstc.edu |
| U.S. Department of Energy | dirsvc.xosi.doe.gov |
| University of Akron | directory.uakron.edu |
| University of Arizona | ns.arizona.edu |
| University of Baltimore | ub.umd.edu |
| University of California at Berkeley | whois.berkeley.edu |
| University of California at Davis | directory.ucdavis.edu |
| University of California at Los Angeles | oac.ucla.edu |
| University of California at San Diego | ucsd.edu |
| University of California at San Diego, Division of Social Sciences | weber.ucsd.edu |

*continues*

| | |
|---|---|
| University of California at San Francisco, School of Pharmacy | cgl.ucsf.edu |
| University of California at Santa Barbara | whois.ucsb.edu |
| University of Chicago | uchicago.edu |
| University of Cincinnati | uc.edu |
| University of Cincinnati | thor.ece.uc.edu |
| University of Florida | whois.eng.ufl.edu |
| University of Houston | whois.uh.edu |
| University of Maryland | umd5.umd.edu |
| University of Maryland, Baltimore County | umbc.edu |
| University of Miami, Rosentiel School of Marine and Atmospheric Sciences | whois.rsmas.miami.edu |
| University of Minnesota | umn.edu |
| University of Mississippi | sun1.mcsr.olemiss.edu |
| University of Nebraska at Lincoln | ns.unl.edu |
| University of Notre Dame | nd.edu |
| University of Oregon | whois.uoregon.edu |
| University of Pennsylvania | whois.upenn.edu |
| University of Rochester | whois.cc.rochester.edu |
| University of San Diego | teetot.acusd.edu |
| University of Texas at Austin | x500.utexas.edu |
| University of Virginia | whois.virginia.edu |
| University of Wisconsin | wisc.edu |
| Virginia Institute of Marine Science | whois.vims.edu |
| Wake Forest University | whois.wfu.edu |
| Wladyslaw Poniecki Charitable Foundation | poniecki.berkeley.edu |
| Worcester Polytechnic Institute | wpi.wpi.edu |

| Austria | |
|---|---|
| Wirtschaftsuniversitaet Wien | whois.wu-wien.ac.at |

| Australia | |
|---|---|
| Australian Academic and Research Network | archie.au |
| Deakin University | deakin.edu.au |
| Monash University | whois.monash.edu.au |
| University College, Australian Defense Force Academy | sserve.cc.adfa.oz.au |
| University of Adelaide | whois.adelaide.edu.au |
| University of Adelaide | wp.adelaide.edu.au |
| University of Sydney | jethro.ucc.su.oz.au |
| University of Western Australia | uwa.edu.au |
| University of Western Australia, University Computer Club | whois.gu.uwa.edu.au |

| Belguim | |
|---|---|
| Inter-university Institute for High Energies | elem4.vub.ac.be |

| Canada | |
|---|---|
| Communications Canada (The Federal Department of Communications) | whois.doc.ca |
| Queen's University, Kingston, Canada | whois.queensu.ca |
| University of New Brunswick | whois.unb.ca |
| University of Ottawa | panda1.uottawa.ca |
| University of Saskatchewan | whois.usask.ca |
| University of Saskatchewan, Engineering | dvinci.usask.ca |

*continues*

| | |
|---|---|
| University of Victoria, Physics & Astronomy | phys.uvic.ca |
| University of Western Ontario | whois.uwo.ca |
| York University | horton.yorku.ca |

| Switzerland | |
|---|---|
| SWITCH Teleinformatics Services | nic.switch.ch |

| Germany | |
|---|---|
| Darmstadt University of Technology | whois.th-darmstadt.de |
| Gesellschaft fuer Mathematik und Datenverarbeitung | dfnnoc.gmd.de |
| Technische Universitaet Chemnitz | whois.tu-chemnitz.de |
| University of Dortmund | deins.informatik.uni-dortmund.de |

| Denmark | |
|---|---|
| Danish Computing Centre for Research and Education | whois.uni-c.dk |

| Finland | |
|---|---|
| Helsinki University of Technology | cs.hut.fi |
| Jyvaskyla University | cc.jyu.fi |
| Oulu University | oulu.fi |
| Technical Research Centre of Finland | vtt.fi |

| France | |
|---|---|
| CITI Lille - France | whois.citilille.fr |
| Universite Claude Bernard Lyon I | whois.univ-lyon1.fr |

| Greece | |
|---|---|
| FORTHnet (Foundation of Research and Technology Hellas) | whois.forthnet.gr |
| FORTHnet (Foundation of Research and Technology Hellas) | wp.forthnet.gr |

| India | |
|---|---|
| National Centre for Software Technology | sangam.ncst.ernet.in |

| Iceland | |
|---|---|
| Association of Research Networks in Iceland | isgate.is |

| Italy | |
|---|---|
| GARR-NIS c/o CNR-CNUCE | dsa.nis.garr.it |
| GARR-NIS c/o CNR-CNUCE | whois.nis.garr.it |

| Japan | |
|---|---|
| Keio University | whois.cc.keio.ac.jp |
| Japan Network Information Center | whois.nic.ad.jp |

| Korea | |
|---|---|
| Korea Network Information Center | whois.nic.nm.kr |

| Netherlands | |
|---|---|
| Eindhoven University of Technology | whois.tue.nl |

*continues*

| | |
|---|---|
| Reseaux IP Europeens | whois.ripe.net |

| New Zealand | |
|---|---|
| University of Canterbury | cantsc.canterbury.ac.nz |
| Victoria University, Wellington | directory.vuw.ac.nz |
| Waikato University | waikato.ac.nz |

| Poland | |
|---|---|
| Faculty of Electronic Engineering, | |
| Warsaw University of Technology | whois.elka.pw.edu.pl |
| Institute of Automatic Control, Warsaw University of Technology | whois.ia.pw.edu.pl |

| Portugal | |
|---|---|
| Instituto de Engenharia de Sistemas e Computadores | archie.inesc.pt |

| Sweden | |
|---|---|
| Chalmers University of Technology | chalmers.se |
| Gothenburg Universities' Computing Centre | whois.gd.chalmers.se |
| Royal Institute of Technology | kth.se |
| Royal Institute of Technology | othello.admin.kth.se |
| SUNET (Swedish University Network) | whois.sunet.se |
| Swedish Institute of Computer Science | sics.se |

| Slovakia | |
|---|---|
| SANET (WAN of Slovak academic institutions) | whois.uakom.sk |

| United Kingdom | |
|---|---|
| Imperial College | src.doc.ic.ac.uk |
| Loughborough University | whois.lut.ac.uk |

| South Africa | |
|---|---|
| Rhodes University, Grahamstown | hippo.ru.ac.za |
| University of Natal (Durban) | whois.und.ac.za |

**Okay, people, move along,**
**nothing to see here.**

# About the Software

The disk at the back of this book is in MS-DOS format. If you have an IBM-compatible PC, you can use the programs and text files on this disk. If you *don't*, you may still be able to use the text files—some other computers (such as newer Macintoshes and some workstations) can read DOS-format disks. Or you might ask a friend or colleague who has a computer that *can* read the disk to convert into a format your machine can read (or have them put it on a BBS or e-mail it to you, so you can download the text to your computer).

Almost everything on this disk is, of course, available on the Internet somewhere. But there are some advantages to having these files on disk. First, it will save you the time and hassle of searching for them, should you need them. If you are a new user who knows little more than how to send e-mail, and for instance are trying to subscribe to a newsgroup, the last thing you want to be told to do is use FTP to search for a list of groups, or to join a particular group and download a list. And even where I've given instructions on where to find information, those instructions may no longer be correct—things get moved, and while a file may have been stored one place when I wrote this book, it may be somewhere totally different by the time you *read* the book. I'm afraid that's just life in the Information Age.

The files on the disk provide you with a useful utility, and an enormous amount of information about the Internet resources. Spend a little time reading through the text files to learn more of what is available on the Internet.

These text files were created by several Internet users. You'll find there are many Internet users out there compiling information and making it available to everyone. That seems to be the spirit of the Internet: a voluntary system in which a lot seems to get done purely through the goodwill of many users.

## The Files

These are the files that you'll find on the disk.

| | |
|---|---|
| UUCODE.EXE | Contains UUENCODE and UUDECODE, programs for converting any computer file to and from ASCII, so you can send it across the Internet in e-mail. |
| MAILGUID.EXE | Contains a text file explaining how to address e-mail to various networks connected to the Internet. Use this if you think your e-mail is not reaching its destination because of addressing problems. |
| NWSGROUP.EXE | Contains a text file with over 60 pages of newsgroups. Use this for tracking down newsgroups in which you may be interested. |
| LISTSERV.EXE | Contains a text file listing over 4,000 LISTSERV groups. Use this for finding more news-group-type discussion groups. |
| MAILLIST.EXE | Contains a text file listing almost 700 mailing-list discussion groups. |
| MAILTIPS.TXT | Contains a description of how to track down a mailing list in which you are interested. |
| BIGFUN.EXE | Contains a list of a variety of different resources spread around the Internet, some serious, some just plain fun. |
| SERVICES.EXE | Contains yet another list of things to do, places to go, on the Internet. |
| FTP-COMP.EXE | A list of FTP sites with information related to computer science. |

| | |
|---|---|
| **LIBRARY.EXE** | Contains seven text files with information about accessing hundreds of libraries in the Americas, Europe, and Asia. |
| **FILEFMT.TXT** | A small text file explaining the different types of file formats you may run across while you work in the Internet. |
| **COUNTRY.EXE** | Describes the Internet's country code system, and lists the current codes. |
| **SIE.EXE** | Contains two newsletters with information about doing business on the Internet, and an article about the Internet "culture." |

# Using the Files

Most of the files I have just mentioned are "archive files." That is, they contain one or more compressed files. (Some are simple ASCII text files.) For instance, MAILGUID.EXE is less than 10 KB. It contains a file called MAILGUID.TXT, an ASCII text file, that is about 27 KB. These files are also "self-extracting" files; when you "execute" the files, they will extract the compressed file (or files) they contain, automatically.

You can copy any of these files into any directory you want, and then "execute" or "run" the file to extract the compressed file(s) it contains. For instance, if you copy MAILGUID.EXE into a directory called **MAIL** in disk C:, you can execute the file by typing **c:\mail\mailguid.exe** at the DOS prompt. (Once you've extracted the files, you can then delete the archive files, if you wish.) See your DOS documentation for more information about copying and executing.

If you are using Microsoft Windows, you can use File Manager to copy the archive in which you are interested from the disk to your hard drive. Then double-click on the archive file—or move the highlight onto it, and press **Enter**. The file will self-extract—you may see a black DOS screen for a few moments, then you'll be back at File Manager. The directory won't automatically update, so you won't see the files at first; just click on another directory, then back to the archive directory, and you'll see the files.

It's a good idea to keep the UUENCODE files in their own directory, and the text files in a separate directory.

## UUCODE.EXE

This file contains UUENCODE.EXE and UUDECODE.EXE, created by Richard Marks. These are used to convert a computer file—a sound, spreadsheet, picture, or whatever—into ASCII so it can be transmitted over the Internet, and then convert it back to its original format at the other end. I explained how to use these files in Chapter 12. It also contains UUDECODE.DOC, and ASCII text file that contains full information about how to use the programs.

Richard Marks released version 5.25 to coincide with this book. Earlier versions sometimes had problems dealing with files that were transmitted over network "gateways"—for instance, UUENCODED files sent from the Internet to CompuServe were sometimes modified by the gateway in such a way that they could not be decoded properly. The new version fixes this problem.

UUENCODE and UUDECODE are *freeware*. That is, you don't have to register them if you use them, though the source code is not in the public domain. (If you want to include the programs in a product, contact Richard Marks—see the documentation file for more information.)

The new version of UUDECODE now ignores the 0x7f and 0x00 pad characters which are inserted by some communication systems, such as when e-mail is transferred from Internet to CompuServe.

## MAILGUID.EXE

MAILGUID.EXE contains a file called MAILGUID.TXT, created by Scott Yanoff. This is an ASCII text file—you can open it in virtually any word processor or text editor. It contains detailed instructions for addressing mail to dozens of different networks connected to the Internet.

You can find the latest MAILGUID.TXT file via anonymous ftp at **csd4.csd.uwm.edu** (change to the **pub** directory, then get the file named **internetwork-mail-guide**).

## NWSGROUP.EXE

This contains an ASCII file called NWSGROUP.TXT which lists thousands of newsgroups. It is compiled, with a few minor modifications, from four files published by David Lawrence, two that list the USENET newsgroups, and two listing "alternative" or non-USENET newsgroups. Use this file to track down newsgroups related to subjects in which you are interested. You can use your word proccessor's "find" function to search for keywords.

You can get the latest lists, or find a list if you don't have a DOS computer, by copying the appropriate postings from the news.announce.newusers newsgroup. (You should find four files in this newsgroup that list newsgroups, two for USENET groups and two for "alternative" groups.)

## LISTSERV.EXE

This file contains an ASCII text file called LISTERV.TXT. This contains a list of over 4,000 LISTSERV discussion groups, with a short description of each one. Again, use your word processor's "find" function to search for areas of interest.

You can get the latest list by sending an e-mail message to **listserv@bitnic.educom.edu**. In the body of the message, type **list global**.

## MAILLIST.EXE

This file contains MAILLIST.TXT, a file compiled by Stephanie da Silva. It contains almost 700 mailing list discussion groups. You've seen (in Chapter 16) how LISTSERV mailing lists work as discussion groups, and a number of these mailing lists are LISTSERV groups. But there are many more that are not (so they're not in the LISTSERV.TXT list).

You can find this list by ftping to **pit-manager.mit.edu**, and changing to the **pub/usenet/news.announce.newusers** directory. The information is stored in several files currently called **Publicly_Accessible_Mailing_Lists,_Part_*n*_6**.

## MAILTIPS.TXT

This file contains a description, by Arno Wouters, of "How to Find an Interesting Mailinglist." You can get a copy of this file by sending e-mail to **LISTSERV@vm1.nodak.edu** with the command **GET NEW-LIST WOUTERS** in the body of the message. Or FTP to vm1.nodak.edu change to the new-list directory, and get the **new-list.wouters** file.

## BIGFUN.EXE

This file contains BIGFUN.TXT, compiled by Jeremy Smith. It's a compilation of *stuff* that you can find on the Internet—Coke machines and fortune cookies, U.S. Geological Survey Maps, Harris Polls, information on solar flares, the exact time, book reviews—almost 20 pages of it.

You can find this file by ftping to **ftp.csos.orst.edu**. Login as anonymous and change to the **/Pub/networking/bigfun** directory and get **bigfun.txt**.

## SERVICES.EXE

This file contains SERVICES.TXT, Scott Yanoff's "Special Internet Connections" file (sometimes known as the Internet Services file). This contains everything from archaological databases to White House press releases.

You can find this file in a variety of places. It's published in the **alt.internet.services** newsgroup, you can get it by ftping or gophering to **csd4.csd.uwm.edu (get /pub/inet.services.txt)**, and you can send an e-mail message to **bbslist@aug3.augsburg.edu** (the recipient autoreplies with the list).

## FTP-COMP.EXE

This contains FTP-COMP.TXT, a text file containing Mac Su-Cheong's "List of servers for CS-related resources." It lists FTP sites that contain information related to computer science. You can get the latest version of the list using the **finger** command: **finger msc@eembox.ncku.edu.tw >ftp-comp.txt** will put the list into a text file called **ftp-comp.txt**.

## LIBRARY.EXE

This file contains several text files. Created by Billy Barron and Marie-Christine Mahe, these files contain Accessing On-Line Bibliographic Databases, a report with lots of information about libraries throughout the Americas, Europe, Africa, and Asia.

You can find a copy of these files by anonymous ftp to **ftp.utdallas.edu**. Change to the **/pub/staff/billy/libgui** directory and get the **libraries** files. You can also Gopher to **yaleinfo.yale.edu 7000**, and select the Libraries directory. (Or select **Yale University** from a gopher directory, and then select /Research and library services/More research & library services at Yale and beyond/Catalogs Listed by Location.) The real advantage to this system is that you can read about a particular library online, and then telnet directly to it from the Gopher. In fact, the authors of the ASCII catalog recommend using the gopher rather than reading the catalog, due to its ease of use.

## FILEFMT.TXT

This is small text file (I haven't bothered compressing it) created by Jim Wright; it describes the various types of file format that you might run across—ARJ, BinHex, LHWarp, LU, tar, compress, and so on. It's only about six pages, and you can scan through quickly—take a look to get an idea of what sorts of files you will want to avoid, and which ones may be useful to you.

You can find this file posted to the **comp.virus** newsgroup once a month.

## COUNTRY.EXE

This contains COUNTRY.TXT, a file compiled by Olivier M.J. Crepin-Leblond; it explains the country domain-name system and lists the Internet's country codes. You can find this file from the **news.answers** newsgroup.

### SIE.EXE

This file contains three text files from Michael Strangelove of Strangelove Internet Enterprises. ESSNTIAL.TXT, an article about the "culture" of the Internet, is a reprint from *Online Access* magazine. ADVERT.TXT is issue 1.1 of the Internet Advertising Review, an electronic newsletter about advertising on the Internet. And BUSJOURN.TXT is an issue of the Internet Business Journal. You can find more information about these publications from Michael Strangelove at mstrange@fonorola.net.

## Viewing the Files in DOS

If you have DOS version 5.0 or higher, you have a program called EDIT which enables you to view, edit, and print text files such as the ones that came on the disk. Using EDIT is a no-frills way of looking at the files—the font they appear and print in is a dreary, difficult to read system font (usually Courier on most printers).

To use edit:

1. Change to the directory where your text files are kept. (Use the CD command—for example, CD\TEXTDIR if your text files are in the TEXTDIR directory.
2. At the DOS prompt, type EDIT *filename*.txt and press Enter, where *filename* is the name of the file. For example, if you wanted to view MAILGUID.TXT, you would type EDIT MAILGUID.TXT.
3. To view pages of the file that are not onscreen, press the PageDown key.
4. To print the file, press Alt+F (hold down the Alt key and press F) to open the File menu, and then press P to select the Print command.
5. To Exit from EDIT program, press Alt+F to open the File menu, and then press X to select the Exit command.

## Viewing the Files in Windows

There are two common ways you can view these text files from Windows' Program Manager: with Notepad or with Write. The procedure for opening a file is the same with both programs.

1. Start Windows by typing WIN at the DOS prompt and pressing Enter.
2. Open the Accessories group by double-clicking on the Accessories icon, then find the Notepad or Write icon and double-click on it.
3. When the Notepad or Write screen opens, click on the word File in the menu bar, the click on Open. The Open dialog box will appear, allowing you to specify which file you want to open.
4. If you're using Write, change the entry in the List Files of Type list box to **Text Files (*.TXT)**. (Click the down arrow next to the text box to drop down the list, then click on **Text Files**.)
5. Use the Directories list box to navigate to the directory on your hard drive that you copied the file to. Then, double-click on the text file you want to see.
6. If you're using Write, a dialog box will pop up asking if you want to convert the file to Write format. Click on **Convert** to change the file to Write format (it looks prettier in Write format than in text format).

After a few seconds, the file will appear on-screen. You can scroll through the file and read it if you want (press the PageDown key), or you can print it out:

1. Click on **File** to open the File menu.
2. Click on Print.
3. If you're using Write, a dialog box appears. Press Enter to continue.

To exit from Write or Notepad, select the Exit command from the File menu, then answer Yes or No when asked if you want to save the changes you've made.

## Deciphering What You See

The file might look a little strange at first, as if it wasn't actually written in English. Don't worry; it's in English. Those are addresses and descriptions. Most of what you see on the Internet is plain text because not everyone has the same word processor.

Sometimes tabs get messed up during conversion, and sometimes paragraphs get split in strange places and columns turn out weird. If it really bothers you, you can zip through the file and fix all the tabs so it's easier to read.

With Write, you can also change the way the text looks by changing the font. You can use the Character menu to change the font, style, and size of the words you see. If you choose Fonts from the Character menu, you'll see a dialog box. From there, you can choose a different font for the text you have selected.

# Speak Like a Geek: The Complete Archive

**AFS** A system (not yet widely used) that allows you to work with files on a remote host as if you were working on your own host. For instance, FTP would not be required to get a file, you could simply copy it to your home directory.

**alias** A name that is substituted for a more complicated name. For instance, a simple alias may be used instead of a more complicated mailing address or for a mailing list.

**America Online** An online information system.

**anonymous ftp** A system by which members of the Internet "public" can access files at certain *FTP* sites without needing a login name—they simply login as *anonymous*.

**Archie** An index system that helps you find files in over 1,000 FTP sites.

**archive file** A file that contains other files, generally *compressed files*. Used to store files that are not used often, or files that may be *downloaded* by Internet users.

**ARPAnet** Where it all began—the Advanced Research Projects Agency (of the U.S. Department of Defense) computer network that was the forerunner of Internet.

**article** A message in an Internet *newsgroup*.

**ASCII** The American Standard Code for Information Interchange, a standard way for computers to use bits and bytes to represent characters. An ASCII file contains simple text without any special formatting codes.

**backbone** A network through which other networks are connected.

**baud rate** A measurement of how quickly a *modem* transfers data. Although, strictly speaking, this is not the same as *bps* (bits per second), the two terms are often used interchangeably.

**BBS** See *bulletin board system.*

**BIND** Berkeley Internet Name Domain, a UNIX implementation of the *DNS* standard.

**BITNET** The "Because It's Time" network (really!). A large network connected to Internet. Before the Internet became affordable to learning institutions, BITNET was the network of choice for communicating.

**bits per second** A measure of the speed of data transmission—the number of bits of data that can be transmitted each second.

**bps** See *bits per second.*

**bulletin board system** A computer system to which other computers can connect so their users can read and leave messages, or retrieve and leave files.

**chat** A system by which two users can "talk" with each other by typing; what you see the other person sees almost instantly and vice versa. (This is unlike e-mail, in which you send your words, and wait for the recipient to read and respond.)

**CIX** The Commercial Internet Exchange, an organization of commercial Internet service providers.

**client** A program or computer that is "serviced" by another program or computer (the *server*). For instance, a *Gopher* client program requests information from the indexes of a Gopher server program.

**compressed files** Computer files that have been reduced in size by a compression program. Such programs are available for all computer systems. For instance, PKZIP in DOS, tar and compress in UNIX, and StuffIt for the Macintosh.

**CompuServe** A computer information service owned by H&R Block. CompuServe is part of the Internet network (though few CompuServe users realize this).

**CSLIP** Compressed SLIP. See *SLIP*.

**Cyberspace** The "area" in which computer users travel when "navigating" around on a network.

**daemon** A UNIX *server*, a program running all the time in the "background" (that is, unseen by users), providing special services when required.

**DARPANET** The Defense Advanced Research Projects Agency network, created by combining ARPANET and MILNET. The forerunner of the Internet.

**DDN** The Defense Data Network, a U.S. military network that is part of the Internet. *MILNET* is part of the DDN.

**dedicated line** A telephone line that is *leased* from the telephone company, and used for one purpose only. In Internetland, dedicated lines connect organizations to service providers' computers, providing dedicated service.

**dedicated service** See *permanent connection*.

**DFS** A variation of *AFS*.

**dial-in direct connection** An Internet connection that is accessed by dialing into a computer through a telephone line. Once connected your computer acts as if it were an Internet host. You can run client software (such as *Gopher* and *WWW* clients), and can copy files directly to your computer. This type of service is often called *SLIP*, *CSLIP*, or *PPP*. See also *dial-in terminal*.

**dial-in service** A networking service that is used by dialing into a computer through a telephone line.

**dial-in terminal connection** An Internet connection that is accessed by dialing into a computer through a telephone line. Once connected, your computer acts as if it were a terminal connected to the service provider's computer. This type of service is often called *Interactive* or *dial-up*. See also *dial-in direct.*

**dial-up service** A common Internet term for a *dial-in terminal connection.*

**direct connection** See *permanent connection.*

**DNS** See *Domain Name System.*

**domain name** A name given to a host computer on the Internet.

**Domain Name System** A system by which one Internet host can find another so it can send *e-mail*, connect *FTP* sessions, and so on. The hierarchical system of Internet host names (***hostname.hostname.hostname***) uses the Domain Name System. The DNS, in effect, translates words into numbers that can be understood by the Internet's computers. For instance, if you use the domain name *firefly.prairienet.org*, DNS translates it into 192.17.3.3.

**download** The process of transferring information from one computer to another. You *download* a file from another computer to yours. See also *upload.*

**EARN** The European network associated with *Bitnet.*

**Elm** An *e-mail* program.

**e-mail or email** Short for *electronic mail*, this is a system that lets people send and receive messages with their computers. The system might be on a large network (such as Internet), on a bulletin board, (such as CompuServe), or over a company's own office network.

**emoticon** The techie name for a *smiley.*

**etext** Electronic text; a book or other document in electronic form, usually simple ASCII text.

**Ethernet** A system by which computers may be connected to one another, and exchange information and messages.

**FAQ** Frequently-Asked Questions. A menu option named FAQ or Frequently Asked Questions will lead you to a document that answers common questions. You may also find text files named FAQ.

**Fidonet** A network connected to the Internet.

**File Transfer Protocol** See *FTP*.

**finger** A UNIX program used to find information about a user on a host computer.

**flame** An abusive newsgroup message.

**flamer** Someone who wrote a *flame*.

**forum** The term used by CompuServe for its individual bulletin boards. In Internet-speak, the term is *newsgroups*.

**Free-Net** A community computer network, often based on the local library, which provides Internet access to citizens, from the library or sometimes from their home computers. Free-Nets also have many local services, such as information about local events, local message areas, connections to local government departments, and so on.

**freeware** Software provided free by its originator. Not the same as *public domain software*, as the author retains copyright. See also *shareware*.

**FTP** File Transfer Protocol. A *protocol* defining how files are transferred from one computer to another. FTP is also the name of a program used to move files. And FTP can be used as a verb (often in lowercase) to describe the procedure of using FTP. As in, "ftp to **ftp.demon.co.uk**," or "I ftp'ed to their system and grabbed the file."

**FTPmail** A system maintained by Digital Equipment Corporation (DEC) that lets people use e-mail to carry out FTP sessions.

**gateway** A system by which two incompatible networks or applications can communicate with each other.

**GEnie** A computer information service owned by General Electric.

**Gopher** A system using Gopher *clients* and *servers* to provide a menu system used for navigating around the Internet.

**Gopherspace** Anywhere and everywhere you can get to using Gopher is known as *gopherspace*.

**Gore, Al** A vice president who believes the "information highway" is critical to the U.S.'s future. Reportedly wants all the United States' high schools connected to the Internet in the next few years.

**host** A computer connected directly to the Internet. A service provider's computer is a host, as are computers with *permanent connections*. Computers with *dial-in terminal* connections are not—they are terminals connected to the service provider's host. Computers with *dial-in direct* connections can be thought of as "sort of" hosts. They act like a host while connected.

**hypertext** A system in which documents contain links that allow readers to move between areas of the document, following subjects of interest in a variety of different paths. The *World Wide Web* is a hypertext system.

**HYTELNET** A directory of *Telnet* sites. A great way to find out what you can do on hundreds of computers around the world.

**IAB** See *Internet Architecture Board*.

**IETF** See *Internet Engineering Task Force*.

**Interactive service** See *dial-in terminal connection*.

**internet** The term *internet* spelled with a small i refers to networks connected to one another. "The Internet" is not the only internet.

**Internet Architecture Board** The "council of elders," elected by *ISOC*, who get together and figure out how the different components of Internet will all connect together.

**Internet Engineering Task Force** A group of engineers that makes technical recommendations concerning the Internet to the *IAB*.

**Internet Protocol** The standard protocol used by systems communicating across the Internet. Other protocols are used, but the Internet Protocol is the most important one.

**Internet Society** The society that runs Internet. It elects the Internet Architecture Board, which decides on technical issues related to how Internet works.

**InterNIC** The Internet Network Information Center. This *NIC*, run by the National Science Foundation, provides various administrative services for the Internet.

**IP** See *Internet Protocol.*

**ISO/OSI Protocols** The International Organization for Standardization Open Systems Interconnect Protocols, a system of protocols that may someday replace the *Internet Protocol.*

**ISOC** See *Internet Society.*

**KIS** See the *Knowbot Information Service.*

**Knowbot** A program that can search the Internet for requested information. Knowbots are in an experimental stage.

**Knowbot Information Service** An experimental system that helps you search various directories for a person's information (such as an e-mail address).

**leased line** See *dedicated line.*

**LISTSERV lists** Mailing lists—using *mail reflectors*—that act as *newsgroups.* Messages sent to a LISTSERV address are sent to everyone who has subscribed to the list. Responses are sent back to the LISTSERV address.

**logging on** Computer jargon for getting permission from a computer to use its services. A "logon" procedure usually involves typing in a username (also known as an account name or userID) and a password. This procedure makes sure that only authorized people can use the computer. Also known as *logging in.*

**logging off** The opposite of logging on, telling the computer that you've finished work and no longer need to use its services. The procedure usually involves typing a simple command, such **exit** or **bye**.

**login** The procedure of *logging on.*

**lurker** Someone involved in *lurking.*

**lurking** Reading *newsgroup* or *LISTSERV* messages without responding to them. Nobody knows you are there.

**mail reflector** A mail address that accepts e-mail messages and then sends them on to a predefined list of other e-mail addresses. Such systems are a convenient way to distribute messages to a group of people.

**MB** Abbreviation for *megabyte.*

**MCIMail** An *e-mail* system owned by MCI.

**megabyte** A measure of the quantity of data. A megabyte is a lot when you are talking about files containing simple text messages, not much when you are talking about files containing color photographs.

**MILNET** A U.S. Department of Defense network connected to the Internet.

**MIME** Multipurpose Internet Mail Extensions, a system that lets you send computer files as e-mail.

**modem** A device that converts digital signals from your computer into analog signals for transmission through a phone line (**mod**ulation), and converts the phone line's analog signals into digital signals your computer can use (**dem**odulation).

**navigator** A program that helps you "navigate" your way around a complicated BBS. Several navigator programs are available for CompuServe, for instance. Navigators can save you money by letting you prepare for many operations—such as writing mail—offline, then go online quickly to perform the operations automatically. Internet navigators are currently in a developmental stage, and not in wide use.

**netiquette** Internet etiquette, the correct form of behavior to be used while working on the Internet and Usenet. Can be summed up as "Don't waste computer resources, and don't be rude."

**Network Information Center** A system providing support and information for a network.

**newsgroup** The Internet equivalent of a BBS or discussion group (or "forum" in CompuServe-speak) in which people leave messages for others to read. See also *LISTSERV*.

**newsreader** A program that helps you find your way through a *newsgroup's* messages.

**news server** A computer that collects *newsgroup* data and makes it available to *newsreaders*.

**NFS** The Network File System, a system that allows you to work with files on a remote host as if you were working on your own host.

**NIC** See *Network Information Center.*

**NOC** Network Operations Center, a group that administers a network.

**NREN** The National Research and Education Network.

**NSF** National Science Foundation, a U.S. government agency. The NSF runs the *NSFNET*.

**NSFNET** The "National Science Foundation" network, a large network connected to the Internet.

**online** Connected. You are online if you are working on your computer while it is connected to another computer. Your printer is online if it is connected to your computer and ready to accept data. (Online is often written *on-line*, though the non-hyphenated version seems to be gaining acceptance these days.)

**packet** A collection of data. See *packet switching*.

**Packet InterNet Groper** A program that tests whether a particular host computer is accessible to you.

**packet switching** A system that breaks transmitted data into small *packets* and transmits each packet (or package) independently. Each packet is individually addressed, and may even travel over a route different from that of other packets. The packets are combined by the receiving computer.

**permanent connection** A connection to the Internet using a leased line. The computer with a permanent connection acts as a *host* on the Internet. This type of service is often called *direct*, *permanent direct*, or *dedicated service*, and is very expensive to set up and run.

**permanent direct** See *permanent connection.*

**Pine** An e-mail program.

**PING** See *Packet InterNet Groper.*

**point of presence** Jargon meaning a method of connecting to a service locally (without dialing long-distance). If a service provider has a POP in, say, Podunk, Ohio, people in that city can connect to the service provider by making a local call.

**Point-to-Point Protocol** A method for connecting computers to Internet via telephone lines, similar to SLIP (though, at present, less common).

**POP** See *point of presence.*

**port** Generally, "port" refers to the hardware through which computer data is transmitted—the plugs on the back of your computer are ports. On the Internet, "port" often refers to a particular application. For instance, you might telnet to a particular port on a particular host. The port is actually an application.

**posting** A message (*article*) sent to a *newsgroup* or the act of sending such a message.

**postmaster** The person at a *host* who is responsible for managing the mail system. If you need information about a user at a particular host, you can send e-mail to **postmaster@*hostname***.

**PPP** See *Point-to-Point Protocol.*

**PRODIGY** A computer information service.

**protocol** A set of rules that defines how computers transmit information to each other, allowing different types of computer and software to communicate with each other.

**public domain software** Software which is not owned by anyone. You can freely use and distribute such software. See also *freeware* and *shareware.*

**reflector, mail** A kind of public mailing list. Messages sent to a mail reflector's address are sent on automatically to a list of other addresses.

**remote login** Another term for *telnet.*

**rot13** Rotation 13, a method used to "encrypt" messages in newsgroups, so you can't stumble across an offensive message. If you want to read an offensive message, you'll have to decide to do so.

**router** A system used to transmit data between two computer systems or networks using the same protocol. For instance, a company that has a permanent connection to the Internet will use a router to connect its computer to a *leased line.* At the other end of the leased line, a router is used to connect it to the service provider's network.

**Serial Line Internet Protocol (SLIP)** A method for connecting a computer to Internet using a telephone line and modem. (See *dial-in direct.*) Once connected, the user has the same services provided to the user of a *permanent connection.*

**server** A program or computer that "services" another program or computer (the *client*). For instance, a *Gopher* server program sends information from its indexes to a Gopher client program.

**service provider** A company that provides a connection to Internet. Service providers sell access to the network, for greatly varying prices. Shop around for the best deal.

**shareware** Software that is freely distributed, but for which the author expects payment from people who decide to keep and use it. See also *freeware* and *public domain software.*

**shell** In UNIX, a shell is a program that accepts commands that you type and "translates" them for the operating system. In DOS, a shell is a program that "insulates" you from the command line, providing a simpler way to carry out DOS commands.

**signature** A short piece of text transmitted with an *e-mail* or *newsgroup* message. Some systems can attach text from a file to the end of a message automatically. Signature files typically contain detailed information on how to contact someone—name and address, telephone numbers, Internet address, CompuServe ID, and so on.

**SLIP** See *Serial Line Internet Protocol.*

**smiley** A symbol created by typing various keyboard characters, used in *e-mail* and *newsgroup* messages to convey emotion, or simply for amusement. For instance, :-( means sadness. Smileys are usually sideways—turn your head to view the smiley.

**Sprintmail** An *e-mail* system used on Sprintnet. Back when Sprintnet was called Telenet, the mail portion used once was called Telemail.

**Sprintnet** A network owned by SPRINT. It used to be called Telenet (not to be confused with Telnet.)

**tar files** Files compressed using the UNIX Tape ARchiver program. Such files usually have filenames ending in **.tar**.

**TCP/IP** Transmission Control Protocol/Internet Protocol. A set of *protocols* (communications rules) that control how data is transferred between computers on the Internet.

**Telnet** A program that lets Internet users log into computers other than their own host computers, often on the other side of the world. Telnet is also used as a verb, as in "telnet to **debra.doc.ca**."

**telneting** Internet-speak for using *Telnet* to access a computer on the network.

**tn3270** A *Telnet*-like program used for remote logins to IBM mainframes.

**Token Ring** A system used for creating small local area networks. Such networks may be connected to the Internet.

**UDP** The User Datagram Protocol, a *protocol* used in Internet communications.

**UNIX** A computer operating system. Most *hosts* connected to the Internet run UNIX.

**upload** The process of transferring information from one computer to another. You *upload* a file from your computer to another. See also *download.*

**USENET** The "User's Network," a large network connected to the Internet.

**UUCP** UNIX to UNIX copy Program, a system by which files can be transferred between UNIX computers. The Internet uses UUCP to provide a form of e-mail, in which the mail is placed in files and transferred to other computers.

**UUCP network** A network of UNIX computers, connected to the Internet.

**uudecode** If you use *uuencode*, you'll use uudecode to convert the *ASCII file* back to its original format.

**uuencode** A program used to convert a computer file of any kind—sound, spreadsheet, word processing, or whatever—into an *ASCII file* so that it can be transmitted as a text message.

**UUNET** A service provider connected to the Internet.

**Veronica** The Very Easy Rodent-Oriented Net-wide Index to Computerized Archives, a very useful program for finding things in *Gopherspace.*

**virus** A program that uses various techniques for duplicating itself and traveling between computers. Viruses vary from simply nuisances to serious problems that can cause millions of dollars' worth of damage.

**VT100** The product name of a Digital Electronics Corporation computer terminal. This terminal is a standard that is "emulated" (duplicated) by many other manufacturer's terminals.

**W3** See *World Wide Web.*

**WAIS** See *Wide Area Information Server.*

**The Web** See *World Wide Web.*

**White Pages** Lists of Internet users.

**whois** A program used for searching for information about Internet users.

**Wide Area Information Server** A system that can search databases on the Internet for information in which you are interested.

**World Wide Web** A *hypertext* system that allows users to "travel through" linked documents, following any chosen route. World Wide Web documents contain topics that, when selected, lead to other documents.

**WWW** See *World Wide Web.*

**XRemote** A rarely-used type of *dial-in direct* connection.

# Index

## Symbols


$ (UNIX prompt), 78
% (UNIX prompt), 78
.mailrc file, 124
:-) (smiley) e-mail messages, 98
<g> (grin) e-mail messages, 98
> (DOS prompt), 78
@ (at) e-mail addresses, 101
^7M wrong terminal type message, 69
__p/÷_´#£ä__ garbage message, 69
~~xx~xxx~xx baud rate set incorrectly message, 69


## A


access
  buying, 18
  free, 24–25
  limited, 35
  options, 66
accessing
  archie, 236-238
  ftp (World Wide Web), 285
  fred server, 158
  Gopher
    UNIX, 250-252
    World Wide Web, 285
  UNIX
    mail system, 110
    shell, 78
  WAIS, 268
    telnet, 268
    World Wide Web, 285
  whois (World Wide Web), 285
  World Wide Web, 278–279
    telnet, 279
  X.500 (World Wide Web), 285
accounts, 4
  dial-in direct, 4
  dial-in terminal, 4
  Free-Net, 307–311
  mail, 4

permanent, 4
*see also* connections
addresses (e-mail), 143
aliases, 123–124
automatic mail responses, 125–126
host computers, 53
LISTSERV groups, 183
locating, 144–153
finger command (UNIX mail), 145–146
KIS (Knowbot Information Service), 148–150
Netfind, 150–153
newgroups, 147
postmaster, 145
mailing lists (UNIX mail), 124
problems, 143
addressing
e-mail messages, 101–102
UNIX mail messages, 116–117
AFS system, 347
aliases, 123–124, 347
alternative newsgroups hierarchies, 165
America Online, 347
sending e-mail, 103
American Standard Code for Information Interchange, *see* ASCII
anonymous ftp, 202, 206, 347
placing files, 215
anti-virus programs, 233
archie, 5, 235–247, 347
accessing, 236
by telnet, 237–238
commands, 243–246
finding files, 239–241
Help, 246–247
mail, 241, 245–247
searches, 238–239
exact, 238
regex, 238
subcase, 239
search results
mailing, 241
saving, 244
servers, 236
denying access, 238
viewing ftp sites, 242
whatis search, 242
archive files, 343, 347
ARPANET (Advanced Research Projects Agenceny network), 12, 347
arrow keys, 62
articles (newsgroups), 348
ASCII (American Standard Code for Information Interchange), 348
converting files, 127, 344
transferring files, 211–213
assigning
domain names, 55
function keys, 64–65
attaching
signature to UNIX mail messages, 117–118
text files (newsgroup messages), 179
automated ftp (file transfer protocol), 76, 228-229
automatic mail responses, 125–126

## B

backbone (network), 348
baud rate (modems), 348

set incorrectly, 69
Terminal, 63
BBS's (bulletin board systems), 7-8, 161, 348
communications software, 8
connecting, 8
messages, 8
modem, 8
online games, 8
Berkeley Internet Name Domain, *see* BIND
BIGFUN.EXE file, 340, 344
binary transfers, 44
Binary Transfers command
Settings Menu (Terminal), 225
files (transferring), 211–212
BIND (Berkeley Internet Name Domain), 348
BITNET, 348
sending e-mail, 103–104
bits per second, *see* bps
blank lines in text (troubleshooting), 69
blind carbon copies, 136
bookmarks (Gopher), 250, 260
entering, 261
viewing, 261
boot sector viruses, 232
bps (bits per second), 348
browser (World Wide Web), 278
installing, 286
browsers, 11
*see also* navigators
buffer lines, 62
bugs, 232–233
modems, 42
bulletin board systems, *see* BBS's
buying
access, 18
modems, 42
byte size (UNIX directory files), 84

## C

canceling
commands (UNIX), 91
subscriptions
LISTSERV groups, 184–185
newsgroups, 173
can't send error, 142
CARL, 14
carriage returns, 61
carrier detect (Terminal), 63
case-sensitivity
file naming (UNIX), 87
grep command (UNIX), 90–91
logon names, 45
UNIX, 87
changing passwords, 47, 70–71
characters
file names (UNIX), 87
strain (UNIX directory files), 84
chat, 348
checking passwords, 71
CIX (Commercial Internet Exchange), 348
clients, 249, 348
closing
telnet, 191-192
UNIX Mail, 114, 121
vi text editor (UNIX), 121
columns, 62
com (domain name), 54
command line (UNIX shell), 73

command mode (vi text editor), 119-120
  moving cursor, 120
  typing text, 120
command prompt, 73
commands
  archie, 243–246
  File menu (Terminal)
    Save, 66
  finger (UNIX mail), 145–146
  ftp (file transfer protocol), 206-208
    get, 211, 214–215
    grep, 209–210
    open, 205
  Gopher, 254–255
    bookmark commands, 260–262
  LISTSERV, 185–186
  newsreaders, 181
  Phone menu (Terminal)
    Dial, 66
  Pine mail program, 131–136
  rn newsreader, 169
  Settings menu (Terminal)
    Binary Transfers, 225
    Communications, 63
    Function Keys, 64
    Modem Commands, 64
    Phone Number, 59
  telnet, 191–197
    close, 191-192
    open, 192
    quit, 193
  Transfers menu (Terminal)
    Receive Binary Files, 226
  UNIX, 85
    canceling, 91
    Help, 91
    mail, 110
    repeating, 91
    typing, 87
    shell, 78
    xmodem, 225
  whois, 155
  World Wide Web, 280–281
  xmodem, 226
  zmodem, 227
Commercial Internet Exchange, *see* CIX
commercial services, 76
Communications command (Settings menu), 63
Communications dialog box, 63
  Baud Rate, 63
  Carrier Detect, 63
  Data Bits, 63
  Flow Control, 63
  Parity, 63
  Parity Check option, 63
  Stop Bits, 63
communications programs, 43
communications software, 8
community computing systems, 25–26
  *see also* Free-Nets
compressed files, 343, 349
  sending, 217
  tar files (UNIX), 358
  transferring, 213, 216–217
  uncompressing, 216–217
CompuServe, 162, 349
  sending e-mail, 102–103
computer addresses, 53
computer science, 346

connecting, 41–43
BBSes, 8
login names, 45
newsgroups, 77
passwords, 46
connections
fees, 17, 32
evening rates, 35
hourly rates, 35
night rates, 35
setup fees, 32
toll-free number rates, 30
weekend rates, 35
data networks, 30–31
determining user needs, 33–38
discounts, 38
free access, 24–25
Free-Net, 45
hardware requirements, 40–41
dumb terminal, 40
modems, 40-43
host computer, 19
International Internet Association, 26
leased line, 19
routers, 19
software requirements, 40
types, 18–22
dial-in direct, 18–20, 51–56, 351
dial-in terminal, 18, 20–21, 23–24, 51, 352
mail, 18, 21–22
permanent, 18–19
TCP/IP, 19
UUCP, 22
connectors (Terminal), 63
converting files, 344
copying (UNIX)
files, 88–89
mail messages, 113–114
costs, 17
data network connections, 31
dial-in direct connections, 23, 32
dial-in terminal connections, 24, 33
mail connections, 33
permanent connections, 22, 32
countries (domain names), 55
country codes, 347
COUNTRY.EXE file, 343, 347
creating
menu (Gopher), 250
newsreader file home directory, 169
UNIX directories, 86
creation date (UNIX directory files), 84
creation time (UNIX directory files), 84
CSLIP (compressed serial line Internet protocol), *see* SLIP
Ctrl keys, 62
current directory, 86
Curses Gopher, 253
cursor, 62
Cyberspace, 349

## D

daemon (UNIX server), 349
DARPANET (Defense Advanced Research Projects Agency Network), 349
data bits

modems, 59
Terminal, 63
data communications protocols, 59
data networks connections, 30–31
data transfers (modems)
xmodem, 44
zmodem, 44
databases
menu systems, 76
searching (WAIS), 271–274
transferring files, 212
DDN (Defense Data Network), 349
DEC VMS systems (ftp), 229
decoding files, 128–129
dedicated connections,
*see* permanent connections
dedicated
lines, 349
service, 349
defaults (modems), 64
Defense Advanced Research Projects Agency Network, *see* DARPANET
Defense Data Network, *see* DDN
deleting
files (UNIX), 88
text (vi text editor), 120
UNIX mail, 114
DFS system, 349
Dial command (Phone menu), 66
Dial text box (Phone Number dialog box), 60
dial-in direct accounts, 4, 51–56
domain names, 53
host numbers, 52
logging on, 58
registering, 52
setup (WAIS client), 275
dial-in direct connections, 19–20, 32, 51–56, 349
advantages, 23–24
costs, 19, 23–24, 32
running multiple sessions, 20
software, 23
costs, 35
setup, 23
software requirements, 43
TCP/IP software, 51
dial-in service, 349
dial-in terminal accounts, 4, 59
dial-in terminal connections, 18, 20–24, 33, 51, 352
costs, 24, 33
file transfers, 24
modems, 23
service providers, 21
software requirements, 43
dial-up connections, *see* dial-in terminal connections
dial-up service, 350
dialing in
header line, 68
Terminal, 66–68
signaling when connected, 60
timeout, 60
dialog boxes
Communications, 63
Modem Commands, 64
Phone Number, 59–60
Terminal Preferences, 61–62
direct connection, 352
directories, 81–84, 144–153
creating, 86
current directory, 86
e-mail, 4

ftp, 208
home directory, 77, 82
KIS (Knowbot Information Service), 148–150
path, 82
removing, 86
RIPE, 148
searching (archie), 235
subdirectories, 82
telnet (HYTELNET directory), 194–195
tree, 82
UNIX, 84
Whois, 155–160
working directory, 86
directory name (UNIX directory files), 84
directory-of-servers (WAIS), 271–272
discussion groups (newsgroups), 180-181, 345
domains, 54, 350
BIND, 350
names, 37, 53, 350
assigning, 55
com (commercial domain), 54
countries, 55
edu (educational domain), 54
e-mail addresses, 101
geographical, 55
mil (military domain), 54
selecting, 55-56
states, 55
service, 37
subdomains, 54
DOS
prompt (>), 78
systems (ftp), 230
double typing, 69
download, 350
dumb terminal, 40

## E

e-mail (electronic mail), 4, 95–108, 350
accessing Whois, 157
addresses, 101-102
@ symbol, 101
domain name, 101
finding, 4
Internet, 21
login name, 101
looking up, 4, 155-160
saving, 106
archie, 241, 245–247
directories, 4
FTPmail, 230–231
interfaces, *see* programs
legal issues, 107
limitations, 97
LISTSERV
groups, 4, 182-183
servers, 231–232
mail reflectors, 182, 354
mailing groups, 96
MCIMail, 356
menu systems, 77
messages
:-) (smiley), 98
<g> (grin), 98
editing, 107
length of lines, 107
limitations, 97

shorthand, 100
smileys, 98–99
ways to stress words, 100
programs, 106
sending, 101
America Online users, 103
archie sites, 236
Bitnet users, 103–104
CompuServe users, 102–103
Fidonet users, 104
GEnie users, 103
MCImail users, 104
other network users, 103–106
Prodigy users, 103
Sprintmail users, 104
UUNET users, 105
White House, 96
signatures, 358
smileys, 99, 358
Sprintmail, 358
tone of messages, 107
transferring files, 129, 213
WAIS search results, 274
*see also* UNIX mail
EARN, 350
editing
e-mail messages, 107
UNIX mail messages, 113
editors (UNIX), 112-113
edu (domain name), 54
educational menu systems, 76
electronic mail, *see* e-mail
Elm mail, 350
emoticons, 98–99, 350
encoding files, 128–129
encrypted messages (newsgroups), *see* rot 13
ending sessions, 71
fred server, 160
ftp, 218
UNIX, 91
errors
can't send, 142
host unknown, 142
service unavailable, 142
user unknown, 142
etext (electronic text), 350
Ethernet, 351
etiquette (e-mail), 106–108
editing messages, 107
length of message lines, 107
tone of messages, 107
events & entertainment menu systems, 76
exiting, 71
external modems, 41


## F


FAQs (frequently asked questions), 351
Fidonet, 351
sending e-mail, 104
file carbon copies, 136
File menu commands (Terminal)
Save, 66
file size (UNIX directory files), 84
File Transfer Protocol, *see* ftp
FILEFMT.TXT file, 345
filename (UNIX directory files), 84
files, 342–343
archive, 343
archive files, 347
ASCII, 211, 344

transferring, 211
BIGFUN.EXE, 342, 346
compressed, 349
tar files, 358
converting, 344
COUNTRY.EXE, 343, 347
decoding, 128–129
determining transfer type, 212–215
encoding, 128–129
extracting compressed files, 343
FILEFMT.TXT, 345
finding
archie, 239–241
ftp, 207
formats, 347
ftp
ASCII, 211
binary files, 211–212
reading, 208
FTP-COMP.EXE, 340, 344
LIBRARY.EXE, 341, 345
LISTSERV.EXE, 340, 343
MAILGUID.EXE, 340, 342
MAILLIST.EXE, 340, 343
.mailrc, 124
MAILTIPS.TXT, 344
MILSTIPS.TXT, 340
NWSGROUP.EXE, 340, 343
receiving transferred files, 225–228
saving Gopher files, 258–259
searching (archie), 235–247
SERVICES.EXE, 340, 344
SIE.EXE, 341, 346
signature files, 137
transferring, 77, 88
binary files, 211-212
determining transfer type, 212–214
dial-in terminal connections, 24
e-mail, 129
using get command, 211
transmitting, 127–129
UNIX, 84
copying, 88–89
deleting, 88
finding, 89
home directory, 83
moving, 88
naming, 86–87
opening directory files, 83
renaming, 88
searching for file names, 90–91
viewing, 89
UUCODE.EXE, 340, 342
viruses, 232
finding
e-mail addresses, 4
files
archie, 239–241
ftp, 207
UNIX, 89
finger (UNIX program), 351
finger command, 145–146
firmware (modems), 42
fixed fees, 35
flamer (newsgroups), 351
flames (newsgroups), 351
Flow Control
Communications dialog box, 63
flow control (modems), 59

fonts, 62
forums, 351
forwarding UNIX mail messages, 115
fred server (X.500) 157-160
  accessing, 158
  ending sessions, 160
  Help, 158
  searching for e-mail addresses, 158–160
  Telnet, 157
Free-Net, 25-26, 76, 306-311, 351
  connecting by Telnet, 76
  connections, 45
  logging on, 57
  menus, 26
  The International Internet Association, 311
  National Public Telecomputing Network, 308
freeware, 342, 351
Frequently Asked Questions, *see* FAQs
ftp (file transfer protocol), 5, 201–234, 351
  accessing (World Wide Web), 285
  anonymous ftp, 202, 347
  automating
    login procedure, 228–229
    system, 76
  changing directory, 210
  commands, 206–208
    get, 211, 214-215
    grep, 209–210
    open, 205
  directories, 208
  ending session, 218
  files
    finding, 207
    reading, 208
  FTPmail, 230–231, 351
  getting files, 214–215
  logging on
    anonymous, 206
    login name, 206
  menu systems, 202–204
  passwords, 206
  receiving files, 225-228
    FTPmail, 231
    xmodem, 225–226
    zmodem, 226–227
  sites, 203–204
    hostnames, 205
    navigating, 210
    searching with archie, 235
    viewing in archie, 242
  systems
    DEC VMS, 229
    differences, 229–230
    DOS, 230
    IBM/VM, 230
    Macintosh, 230
  transferring files
    ASCII, 211
    binary files, 211-212
    compressed files, 213
    database files, 212
    e-mail files, 213
    PostScript files, 213
    program files, 213
    spreadsheet files, 212
    UNIX tar files, 213
    UUENCODed files, 213
    word processing files, 213

using get command, 211
FTP-COMP.EXE file, 340, 344
FTPmail, 351
function keys, 64–65
asssigning, 64–65
terminal preferences, 62
Function Keys command (Settings menu), 64


## G


games (BBS's), 8
gateway, 351
GEnie, 352
sending e-mail, 103
geographical domain names, 55
get command (ftp), 211, 214–215
GIF viewer, 257
Gopher, 5, 249–265, 352
accessing
UNIX, 252
WAIS, 268, 275
World Wide Web, 285
bookmarks, 250, 260-262
clients, 249
setup, 251
viewers, 257
commands, 254–255, 260-262
Curses Gopher, 253
menus
creating, 250
options, 254
symbols, 255
systems, 76
saving files, 258–259
servers, 249, 254
sites (telnetting), 250
software, 249, 251, 264-265
telnet, 252–253
transferring files, 259
gopherspace, 352
Gore, Al, 96
grep command
ftp, 209–210
UNIX, 90–91
case-sensitivity, 90–91
group name (UNIX directory files), 84


## H


handles (e-mail addresses), 156
Hangup (Phone menu command)
Terminal, 71
Hayes compatibility, 64
header line (dial-in), 68
Help
archie, 246–247
fred server, 158
menu systems, 76
UNIX commands, 91
home directory, 77, 82, 86
creating newsreader file, 169
opening files, 83
path, 82
UNIX files, 83
host computers, 19, 53, 352
host numbers (dial-in direct accounts), 52
host unknown error, 142
hostnames (ftp sites), 205
hypertext, 352
hypertext system, 277

HYTELNET, 4, 352
  directory, 194–195
  logging on, 196

## I

IBM mainframes (telnet sites), 193–194
IBM/VM systems (ftp), 230
Inbound CR/LF
  turning "off", 69
  turning "on", 69
indexing systems
  archie (ftp sites), 235
  veronica (gopher), 262-264, 359
information systems, *see* online services
input mode (vi text editor), 119
inserting signature in mail messages, 118
installing
  UNIX text editors, 113
  World Wide Web
    browser, 286
    client, 278
interactive service, 352
interactive services (dial-in terminal connections), 20
interfaces (e-mail), 106
internal modems, 41
International Internet Association, 26–27
Internet, 9-10
  accounts, 40
  advertising, 346
  country codes, 345
  culture, 346
  directories, 144–153
    KIS (Knowbot Information Service), 148–150
    RIPE, 148
  *see also* connections
internet, 352
Internet Architecture Board, 352
Internet Engineering Task Force, 352
Internet Protocol, 353
Internet Services file, 344
Internet Society, 353
Internetiquette, 106–108
InterNIC, 353
invisible typing, 69
IP, *see* Internet Protocol

## J–K

jumbled menu system, 69
keyword searches
  stop words, 273
  WAIS, 272–274
  World Wide Web, 283–284
KIS (Knowbot Information Service), 148–150, 353
knowbots, 353

## L

leased line (dedicated telephone line), 19, 355
leaving running UNIX programs, 91
legal issues (e-mail), 107

libraries (menu systems), 77, 347
LIBRARY.EXE file, 345
limited access, 35
line wrap, 61
line-mode browser (World Wide Web), 279
linefeed, 61
link count (UNIX files), 84
list commands (UNIX), 85
LISTSERV
  commands, 185–186
  groups, 4, 177, 182–183
  lists, 355
  mail servers, 231–232
  subscription, 183–184
*see also* newsgroups
LISTSERV.EXE file, 340, 343
Local Echo, 61
  turning "off", 69
  turning "on", 69
local service providers, 30
locating addresses, 144–153
  finger command (UNIX mail), 145–146
  KIS (Knowbot Information Service), 148–150
  Netfind, 150–153
  newgroups, 147
  postmaster, 145
lockups (UNIX), 91
logging on, 44, 57, 353-354
  costs, 19–22
  dial-in direct accounts, 58
  dial-in terminal accounts, 59
  Free-Net, 57
  HYTELNET directory, 196
  permanent connection accounts, 58
logging out, 71, 353
  menu system, 71
  Terminal, 71
  UNIX shell, 71
login names, 45
  case-sensitivity, 45
  e-mail addresses, 101
lurker, 354
lurking, 354

## M

Macintosh (ftp), 230
mail, *see* e-mail, UNIX mail
mail accounts, 4
mail commands (UNIX commands)
  deleting mail, 114
  exiting mail system, 114
  forward message, 115
  include original message in reply, 115
  mbox, 112
  reply, 114
  send, 116–119
  undeleting message, 11
mail connections, 18, 21–22, 33
  costs, 33
  software requirements, 48
mail programs
  features, 137–138
  MCIMail, 150
  Pine, 130–137
mail reflectors, 124–125, 182, 354

mail software, 48
  newsgroup/mail readers, 48
  shareware versions, 48
MAILGUID.EXE file, 340, 342
mailing groups, 96
mailing lists, 343
  mail reflectors, 124–125
  UNIX mail, 124
MAILLIST.EXE file, 340, 343
MAILreading (Pine mail program), 134
MAILTIPS.TXT file, 340, 344
marking newsgroups messages, 174
MB, *see* megabytes
mbox file (UNIX mail), 114
MCIMail, 150, 354
  sending e-mail, 104
megabytes, 354
menu options, 76
menu systems, 73–77
  commercial services, 76
  databases, 76
  educational, 76
  events & entertainment, 76
  Free-Net, 76
  ftp, 202–204
  Gopher, 76, 249–265
  help, 76
  jumbled, 69
  libraries, 77
  logging out, 71
  mail, 77
  navigating, 75
  news and weather, 77
  phone books, 77
  searching tools, 77
  telnet, 195–197
message forums (newsgroups), 168
messages
  addresses, 143
  BBS's (bulletin board systems), 8
  blind carbon copies, 136
  domains, 143
  file carbon copies, 136
  newsgroups
    marking, 174
    posting, 179-181
    reading, 172–176
    replying, 178
    rot 13, 175
    saving, 178
    viewing, 174
  problems, 144
    can't send error, 142
    host unknown error, 142
    returned, 142–144
    sending, 143–144
    service unavailable error, 142
    user unknown error, 142
  UNIX mail
    copying, 113–114
    headers, 110–111
    reading, 112
    receiving, 110
    saving, 112
  writing (Pine mail program), 134–137
Microsoft Terminal, *see* Terminal
mil (domain name), 54
MILNET, 354
MILSTIPS.TXT file, 342
MIME (Multipurpose Internet Mail Extensions) attachments (Pine mail program), 135
Modem Commands command

(Settings menu), 64
Modem Commands dialog box, 64
modems, 40, 354
baud rate, 348
BBS's (bulletin board systems), 8
bugs, 42
buying, 42
data bits, 59
data transfers
xmodems, 44
zmodems, 44
defaults, 64
dial-in direct connections, 23
dial-in terminal accounts, 59
dial-in terminal connections, 23
external, 41
firmware, 42
flow control, 59
Hayes compatibility, 64
internal, 41
parity, 59
service providers' support, 37
setup (Terminal), 63
software (built-in), 43
speed, 63
stop bits, 59
modifying UNIX directory files, 84
moving files (UNIX), 88
moving between directories (UNIX), 86

## N

names (newsgroups), 165–167
naming files (UNIX), 86–87
National Public Telecommuting Network, *see* NPTN
National Research and Education Network, *see* NREN
National Science Foundation, *see* NSF
navigating
ftp sites, 210
menu systems, 75
newsreader subscription list, 170
search lists (World Wide Web), 281–282
search results
WAIS, 270–271
WAIS (keyword searches), 274
topic lists (World Wide Web), 282–283
navigators, 11, 354
Netfind, 150–153
netiquette, 355
Network File System, *see* NFS
network gateway systems, *see* mail connections
Network Information Center, *see* NIC
Network Operations Center, *see* NOC
networks, 9–10
ARPAnet, 347
backbone, 348
BITNET, 348
DARPANET (Defense Advanced Research Projects Agency Network), 349
data network, 30–31
DDN (Defense Data Network), 349
EARN, 350
Ethernet, 351
Fidonet, 351
Free-Net, 351

Internet, 9–10
MILNET, 354
NREN, 355
NSFNET, 355
routers, 357
Sprintnet, 358
token ring, 358
USENET, 164, 359
UUCP, 359
news and weather menu systems, 77
news servers, 355
newsgroup/mail readers (mail software), 48
newsgroups, 4, 14, 77, 162–186, 343, 355
alternative newsgroups hierarchies, 165
articles, 348
canceling subscription, 173
flames, 351
flamers, 351
locating user addresses, 147
lurker, 353
lurking, 353
message forums, 168
messages
attaching text files, 179
marking, 174
posting, 179-181
reading, 172-176
rejecting, 118
replying, 178
rot 13, 175, 357
saving, 178
viewing, 174
names, 165–167
news servers, 355
newsreaders, 167–168, 355
nn, 168
rn newsreader, 168
posters, 178
smileys, 358
subscribing, 164, 170-171
subscription list, 169
starting discussions, 180–181
USENET, 164
newsreaders (newsgroups), 167-168, 355
commands, 181
navigating subscription list, 170
nn newsreader, 168
opening newsreader file (vi text editor), 169
rn newsreader, 168
NFS (Network File System), 355
NIC (Network Information Center), 355
nn newsreader, 168
NOC (Network Operations Center), 355
nodes (registering), 52
non-text files (Pine mail program), 135
NPTN (National Public Telecommuting Network), 26
NREN (National Research and Education Network), 355
NSF (National Science Foundation), 13, 355
NSFNET (National Science Foundation network), 355
NWSGROUP.EXE file, 340, 343

## O


online, 355
  games (BBS's), 8
  services, 8, 31
  systems (America Online), 347
open command
  ftp, 205
  telnet, 192
opening
  home directory files, 83
  newsreader files (vi text editor), 169
Originate text box (Modem Commands dialog box), 64
Outbound CR/LF, 69
owner name (UNIX directory files), 84


## P


packet, 355
Packet InterNet Grouper, 356
packet switching, 356
parity
  modems, 59
  Terminal, 63
passwords, 46, 68
  case-sensitivity, 46
  changing, 47, 70–71
  checking, 71
  ftp, 206
  selecting, 46–47
path (home directory), 82
periods (UNIX file names), 87
permanent accounts, 4, 58
permanent connections, 18–19, 356
  advantages, 22–24
  costs, 19, 22–24, 32
  logging on, 19
phone books (menu systems), 77
Phone menu commands (Terminal)
  Dial, 66
Phone Number command (Settings Menu), 59
Phone Number dialog box, 59–60
  Dial text box, 60
Pine mail program (UNIX mail), 130–137, 356
  commands, 131–134, 136
  mail list, 131–134
  non-text files, 135
  reading mail, 134
  signature files, 137
  writing messages, 134–137
PING, *see* Packet InterNet Groper
placing
  anonymous ftp files, 215
  UNIX mail messages in editor, 113
planfile, 146
point of presence, 356
point-to-point protocol, 356
ports, 41, 356
posting (newsgroup articles), 179-181, 356
postmaster, 145, 356
PostScript files (transferring), 213
PPP (point-to-point protocol), *see* dial-in direct connections
Prodigy, 103, 357
program files (transferring), 213
programs

e-mail, 106
knowbots, 148
navigators, 11
Project Gutenberg, 14
Project Hermes, 14
protocols, 59, 357
TCP/IP, 358
UDP, 359
providers
selecting, 3
service charges, 3
systems, 4
*see also* service providers
public domain software, 357
pulse telephone lines, 64

## Q–R

quit command (telnet), 193
quitting (vi text editor), 170
reading
ftp files, 208
mail
Pine mail program, 134
UNIX mail, 112
newsgroups messages, 172–176
UNIX directories, 84
UNIX files, 84
Receive Binary File command (Transfers menu), 226
receiving
files
ftp, 225–228
FTPmail, 231
LISTSERV, 231–232
mail messages (UNIX), 110
reflectors, mail, 357
registering
dial-in direct accounts, 52
nodes, 52
remote login, 187, 357
*see also* telnet
removing UNIX directories, 86
renaming UNIX files, 88
repeating UNIX commands, 91
replying
newsgroups messages, 178
UNIX mail messages, 114
returned messages, 142–144
can't send error, 142
host unknown error, 142
service unavailable error, 142
user unknown error, 142
rn newsreader, 168
commands, 169, 181
reading messages, 173–174
starting, 169-170
root server (Gopher server), 254
rot 13 (Rotation 13), 175, 357
routers, 19, 53, 357
rules for naming UNIX files, 87
running multiple sessions, 20

## S

Save command (File menu), 66
saving
changes (vi text editor), 120
e-mail addresses, 106
files (Gopher), 258–259
messages
newsgroups, 178
UNIX mail, 112

search results
archie, 244
WAIS, 274
World Wide Web, 284
settings (Terminal), 66
scripts (logon procedure), 44
scroll bars, 62
search results
navigating
WAIS, 270–271
WAIS (keyword searches), 274
World Wide Web, 281-282
saving
WAIS, 274
World Wide Web, 284
searching
databases (WAIS), 271–274
e-mail addresses
fred server, 158–160
handles, 156
Telnet, 157
Whois, 155–160
X.500, 157
file names (UNIX), 90
files (archie), 5, 235–247
fred server, 158–160
tools
archie, 5, 235–247
fred, 158–160
Gopher, 5, 249–265
menu systems, 77
Telnet, 4
veronica, 262–264
WAIS, 5, 267–276
World Wide Web, 5, 277–287
users servers, 331–340
selecting
domain names, 55–56
passwords, 46–47
self-extracting archives, 217
sending
compressed files, 217
e-mail
archie sites, 236
messages, 101
America Online users, 103
Bitnet users, 103–104
CompuServe users, 102–103
Fidonet users, 104
GEnie users, 103
MCImail users, 104
other network users, 103–106
problems, 143–144
Prodigy users, 103
Sprintmail users, 104
UUNET users, 105
UNIX mail messages, 116–117
Serial Line Internet Protocol, *see* SLIP
serial ports, 41
servers, 357
archie, 236
computer science, 344
fred, 157–160
Gopher, 249
LISTSERV, 231–232
searching for users, 331–340
Veronica, 263
whois, 156
service charges, 3
service providers, 11, 18, 144, 311–329, 357

access options, 66
commercial organizations, 11
costs, 18, 30
dial-in terminal connections, 21
Gopher, 251
local, 30
newsgroups (subscription lists), 169
non-profit organizations, 11
permanent connections
host computer, 19
routers, 19
questions to ask, 34–38
technical support, 11
The World, 30
toll-free numbers, 30
service unavailable error, 142
SERVICES.EXE file, 340, 344
sessions (ending), 43, 71
setting up
modem (Terminal), 63
shareware programs, 48
Settings menu (Terminal), 60–66
Settings menu commands (Terminal)
Binary Transfers, 225
Communications, 63
Function Keys, 64
Modem Commands, 64
Phone Number, 59
setup
Gopher client, 251
WAIS client, 268
setup fees, 32
shareware programs, 357
mail software, 48
setup, 48
TCP/IP, 52
shell (UNIX), 358
SIE.EXE files, 346
signaling when connected (dial in), 60
signatures, 358
attaching to messages, 117–118
e-mail smileys, 99
files (Pine mail program), 137
inserting in mail messages, 118
SLIP (Serial Line Internet Protocol), 357
*see also* dial-in connections
smileys, 98-99, 358
*see also* emoticons
software
communications software, 8
freeware, 351
Gopher, 249, 251
gopher, 264–265
mail, 48
modems, 43
public domain software, 357
requirements
connections, 40
dial-in direct connections, 43
dial-in terminal connections, 43
mail connections, 48
TCP/IP, 51
shareware, 357
TCP/IP, 51
WAIS, 276
World Wide Web browser software, 286
setup (dial-in direct connections), 23
sound, 61
spaces (UNIX file names), 87
spreadsheet files (transferring), 212

Sprintmail, 358
  sending e-mail, 104
Sprintnet, 358
squeezed files, *see* compressed files
starting
  newsgroups discussions, 180–181
  rn newsreader, 169-170
states (domain names), 55
stop bits
  modems, 59
  Terminal, 63
stop words (WAIS keyword searches), 273
storing files (service providers' hard disk), 37
stressing words in e-mail messages, 100
subdirectories, 82
subdomains, 54
subscribing
  newsgroups, 164, 169-170
  LISTSERV groups, 183–184
symbols (Gopher menu items), 255
system administrators, 43

## T

tar files (UNIX), 213, 358
TCP/IP (transmission control protocol/ Internet protocol), 51, 358
  connections, 19
  commercial programs, 52
  shareware programs, 52
  software, 51
  technical support, 52
technical support
  service providers, 11
  TCP/IP software, 52
telephone lines
  dedicated lines, 349
  pulse lines, 64
telnet, 4, 187–188, 358
  accessing
    WAIS, 268–271
    World Wide Web, 279, 285
    World Wide Web browser, 278
  archie, 236-238
  clients, 187–188
  commands, 191–197
    close, 191-192
    open, 192
    quit, 193
  fred server, 157
  Gopher, 252–253
  Gopher sites, 250
  HYTELNET, 4, 352
  HYTELNET Directory, 194–195
  IBM mainframes, 193–194
  menu systems, 195–197
  searching (e-mail addresses), 157
  servers, 187–188
  terminal emulation, 191
  telneting, 188–191, 358
  tn3270, 358
Terminal, 59–66
  Binary Transfers (xmodem), 225
  connectors, 63
  dialing in, 66–68
    signaling when connected, 60
    timeout, 60
  logging out, 71

Phone menu (Hangup), 71
settings (saving), 66
Settings menu, 60–66
terminal emulation, 60
telnet, 191
troubleshooting, 69
TTY, 61
VT-52, 61
VT100, 61, 359
VT200, 61
terminal preferences
arrow keys, 62
buffer lines, 62
carriage returns, 61
columns, 62
Ctrl keys, 62
cursor, 62
font, 62
function keys, 62
linefeed, 61
local echo, 61
scroll bars, 62
sound, 61
text, 62
translations, 62
Terminal Preferences (Terminal), 61–62
Terminal Preferences dialog box, 61–62
terminals, 60
text
attaching
mail messages (UNIX), 117
newsgroups messages, 179
deleting (vi text editor), 120
displayed only on one line (troubleshooting), 69
e-mail limitations, 97
terminal preferences, 62
viewing (UNIX), 89
text editors (UNIX), 113, 118–121
The International Internet Association, 311
The Web, *see* World Wide Web
The World service provider, 30
timeout (dialing in), 60
tn3270 (telnet), 358
token ring, 358
toll-free numbers (service providers), 30
tone of e-mail messages, 107
topic lists (World Wide Web), 282–283
topic searches (World Wide Web), 277
transferring files, 77, 88, 201–218
ASCII, 211-213
binary, 211–212
compressed, 213, 216-217
database files, 212
determining transfer type, 212–215
e-mail, 129, 213
ftp, 5
Gopher, 259
PostScript files, 213
program files, 213
spreadsheet files, 212
UNIX tar files, 213
using get command, 211
UUENCODed files, 213
word processing files, 213

Transfers menu commands (Terminal)
Receive Binary Files, 226
translations, 62
transmission control protocol/Internet protocol, *see* TCP/IP
transmitting files, 127–129
transmitting non-text files (UNIX mail), 117
troubleshooting, 69
~~xx~xxx~xx (baud rate set incorrectly message), 69
blank lines in text, 69
double typing, 69
garbage messages, 69
invisible typing, 69
jumbled menu system, 69
text displayed only on one line, 69
wrong terminal type, 69
TTY (terminal emulation), 61
turning "off" Inbound CR/LF, 69
turning "off" Local Echo, 69
turning "off" Outbound CR/LF, 69
turning "on" Inbound CR/LF, 69
turning "on" Local Echo, 69
typing
double, 69
invisible, 69
vi text editor (UNIX), 120

## U

UDP (User Datagram Protocol), 359
uncompressing compressed files, 216–217
undeleting UNIX mail messages, 114
undo changes (vi text editor), 120
UNIX, 81–92, 359
accessing, 78
Gopher, 250, 252
World Wide Web, 278
case-sensitivity, 87
directory files, 84
byte size, 84
date created, 84
directory name, 84
file size, 84
filename, 84
modifying, 84
names, 84
time created, 84
changing password, 70
editors (mail messages), 113
MAILUNIX editor, 112
viewing mail, 112–113
ending sessions, 91
files
character strain, 84
copying, 88–89
deleting, 88
finding, 89
modifying, 84
moving, 88
naming, 86–87
renaming, 88
searching for names, 90–91
viewing, 89
home directory, 83
leaving running programs, 91
locking up, 91
logging on home directory, 83
logging out, 71
operating system, 78
programs (finger), 351

prompts
($), 78
(%), 78
shell, 77-78, 358
tar files, 213, 358
text editors
installing, 113
vi, 113, 118–121
UNIX commands, 78, 85
canceling, 91
case-sensitivity, 90–91
command line, 73
creating directories, 86
grep command, 90–91
Help, 91
list commands, 85
mail commands, 110
closing, 114, 121
copying messages, 113-114
deleting mail, 114
exiting mail system, 114
finger, 145–146
forward message, 115
include original message in reply, 115
mbox, 112
reply, 114
send mail command, 116
undeleting messages, 114
moving between directories, 86
open home directory, 83
removing directories, 86
repeating, 91
typing, 87
view commands, 85
xmodem command, 225
UNIX Mail, 109–122
.mailrc file, 124
accessing, 110
addresses, 116–117
attaching
signature to messages, 117–118
text to messages, 117
automatic mail responses, 125
commands, 110
*see also* UNIX commands: mail commands
converting files, 127–128
Elm, 352
mailing lists, 124
mbox file, 114
messages
forwarding, 115
headers, 110–111
including original message in reply, 115
reading, 112
receiving, 110
replying, 114
saving, 112
sending, 116–117
signature, 118
writing (vi text editor), 118–121
Pine mail program, 130–137, 356
transmitting non-text files, 117
UNIX to UNIX copy Program, *see* UUCP, 359
unwritable UNIX directory files, 84
upload (files), 359
USENET newsgroups, 164, 359
users
accounts, 4
fees

fixed, 35
maximum monthly, 36
minimum monthly, 36
interfaces, 10
searching for user servers, 331–340
User Datagram Protocol, *see* UDP
user unknown error, 142
username, 68
UUCODE.EXE file, 340, 342
UUCP (UNIX to UNIX copy Program), 359
connections, 22
network, 359
uuencode, 359
UUENCODEd files (transferring), 213
UUNET, 359
sending e-mail, 105

## V

veronica, 262–264, 359
searches
all titles searches, 263
directory title searches, 263
servers, 263
vi text editor (UNIX), 113, 118–121
closing, 121
command mode, 119-120
opening newsreader file, 169
quitting, 170
saving changes, 120
screen, 119
undo changes, 120
writing mail messages, 118–121
view commands (UNIX), 85
viewers (Gopher clients), 257
viewing
ftp sites (archie), 242
newsgroups messages, 174
text files (UNIX), 89
viruses, 232–233, 359
anti-virus programs, 233
boot sector viruses, 232
file viruses, 232
VT-52 (terminal emulation), 61
VT100 (terminal emulation), 61, 359
VT200 (terminal emulation), 61

## W

W3, *see* World Wide Web
WAIS (Wide Area Information Server), 5, 267-276, 360
accessing, 268
Gopher, 268, 275
telnet, 268–271
World Wide Web, 285
clients setup, 268, 275
directory-of-servers, 271–272
keyword searches, 271–274
search results
mailing, 274
navigating, 270-271, 274
saving, 274
searching databases, 267, 271–274
software, 276
whatis search, *see* archie
White Pages, 360
whois, 360
accessing
e-mail, 157
World Wide Web, 285

command, 155
directory, 155-160
Wide Area Information Server, *see* WAIS
Windows Terminal, *see* Terminal
word processing files (transferring), 213
working directory, 86
World Wide Web, 5, 277–287, 360
accessing, 278–279
ftp, 285
Gopher, 285
telnet, 278- 279
UNIX shell, 278
WAIS, 285
whois, 285
X.500, 285
browsers, 278
installing, 286
line-mode browser, 279
software, 286
client (installing), 278
commands, 280–281
keyword searches, 283–284
navigating
search lists, 281–282
topic lists, 282–283
saving (search results), 284
topic searches, 277
worms, 232–233
writing messages (Pine mail program), 134–137

## X–Y–Z

X.500
accessing (World Wide Web), 285
fred server, 157–160
searching (e-mail addresses), 157
xmodem, 44
commands, 226
receiving files (ftp), 225–226
xmodem command (UNIX), 225
xremote, 19, 360

ymodem (receiving files), 226

zmodem, 44
commands, 227
receiving files (ftp), 226–227

# ANSREMOTE

**LOW COST DIAL-UP INTERNET ACCESS**

**FROM ANYWHERE IN THE UNITED STATES**

With this coupon and an order form, you get:

- $25 set-up fee waived
- two free hourse of connect time

CO+RE Systems, Inc.

**1-800-456-8267**

email: info@ans.net

Call or email for an order form, or to find out about other ANS CO+RE services. Offer expires 9/30/94.

EUnet is European region's largest Internet service provider. Operating in over 27 countries from Iceland to Vladivostok, and from Tunisia to the Arctic Circle.

**Contact EUnet to experience a new world of communication!**

EUnet service providers participating in this offer:

Austria, Belgium, Bulgaria, Czech Republic, Denmark, Finland, France, Germany, Great Britain, Hungary, Ireland, Luxembourg, The Netherlands, Norway, Slovakia, Slovenia, Spain, Switzerland

Other EUnet providers in:

Algeria, Egypt, Greece, Iceland, Italy, Portugal, Romania, Russia (former Soviet Union), Tunisia

**For Business . . .**

**For the Professions . . .**

**For Everyone . . .**

**Contact:**

EUnet
Kruislaan 409
1098 SJ Amsterdam
The Netherlands

Tel: +31 20 592 5109
Fax: +31 20 592 5163
email: info@<country>.EU.net
or info@EU.net

**This coupon is redeemable for a discount on varying EUnet services at participating EUnet countries.**

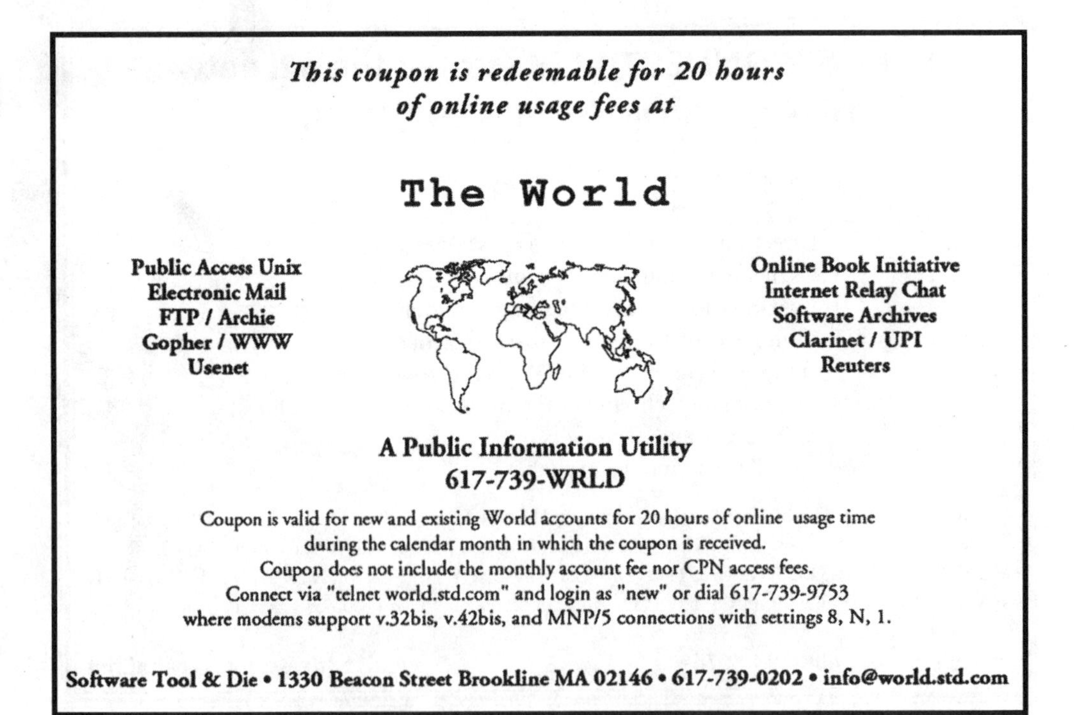
This coupon is redeemable for 20 hours
of online usage fees at
The World
Public Access Unix
Electronic Mail
FTP / Archie
Gopher / WWW
Usenet
Online Book Initiative
Internet Relay Chat
Software Archives
Clarinet / UPI
Reuters
A Public Information Utility
617-739-WRLD
Coupon is valid for new and existing World accounts for 20 hours of online usage time
during the calendar month in which the coupon is received.
Coupon does not include the monthly account fee nor CPN access fees.
Connect via "telnet world.std.com" and login as "new" or dial 617-739-9753
where modems support v.32bis, v.42bis, and MNP/5 connections with settings 8, N, 1.
Software Tool & Die • 1330 Beacon Street Brookline MA 02146 • 617-739-0202 • info@world.std.com